RESEARCHER'S GUIDE
HOW & WHY

DANIEL LLOYD SPENCER
PROFESSOR OF ECONOMICS

COLLEGE-HILL PRESS
SAN DIEGO, CALIFORNIA

College-Hill Press
4580-E Alvarado Canyon Road
San Diego, California 92120

Library of Congress Cataloging in Publication Data
Spencer, Daniel Lloyd
    Researchers guide.

    Includes bibliography and index.
    1. Economic research. I. Title.
HB74.5.S63   300' .72   81-2404
ISBN 0-933014-65-1   AACR2

Printed in the United States of America

PREFACE

Is there really anything permanent about science (i.e., "research"),
which does not change from time to time and the study of which will
give us an insight into the nature of science. I think there is and <u>it</u>
<u>is the method</u>. Theory may supersede theory and more accurate
analysis may demolish our apparent facts, but there is a unity and
continuity about the method that the mind should be able to grasp.[1]

Written a half-century ago, these words are timeless and tell us much when the
proponents of flux are all around. In a world of change, thinking persons
(researchers in particular) need something on which to rely--namely, a grasp of
sound research procedure and method; this guidebook attempts to provide such a
foundation.

The frontispiece of the Library of Congress Main Reading Room symbolizes
this idea of stability in the midst of change. For nearly a hundred years this
library has stood as a cathedral of learning in the United States, providing its
many resources to thousands of scholarly researchers in all fields of knowledge.
I conceived, wrote, and found the sources of this book on the shelves of this
great library. Following many researchers before me, I am greatly indebted to
the advice and guidance of its learned librarians, and I hope this book will pass
on some of this great research heritage to aspiring researchers.

The chief reason for writing this book has been my belief that a guide to
research would aid young men and women starting a research project. Years of
experience in working with students, both graduate and undergraduate, have
taught me that courses and term papers do not prepare most people to
appreciate how research projects should be planned and executed. As the
opening quotation suggests, the "why" of research also escapes the majority.
The idea that the research tradition has unity and continuity is seldom
understood; and the researcher, drowning in detail, sees little of the great
adventure of research.

More specifically, the objectives of this book are as follows: first, to
clarify for researchers and research students the methodology of scientific
research in the social sciences, an understanding of which will have permanent
value to their work; and secondly, to help the researcher design, carry out, and
report on a research project. Faculty members who select this textbook in
research courses will perceive quickly that its short length of eleven chapters is
conveniently adaptable to assignments, leaving enough time for students to

develop their research projects and report orally on their progress in class. Moreover, this book is suitable for all kinds of researchers interested in methods and procedures of modern research. In particular, there are many examples for economics and business. The main goal, however, is to address the unity of all scientific methods of research.

For many underlying ideas the author owes a long-standing dept of gratitude to his professors, among whom Howard Piquet, J.B. Condliffe, and the late scholars Ralph Linton and Fritz Karl Mann hold a special place. He also acknowledges the help of his colleagues, some of whom read chapters, used them in classes, made helpful comments, and showed much interest in the progress of this work. Among these, Howard Alford, Annan Amegbe, Joseph Houchins, Lien Fu Huang, Strephon Johnson, Mwangi Karangu, Joseph Kimani, Lawrence Padgett, Steve Gibson, Dinker Raval, Broadus Sawyer, Vidya Singh, Bala Subramanian, Gerald Turner, and Maw-Chen Yang must be named.

In a class by itself is my debt to the Library of Congress and its highly trained professional staff. In particular, the reference librarians of the Main Reading Room have been of vital help to me. Among others, James Gilreath taught me the SCORPIO system, embodied in chapter seven; Peter Petcoff helped me with the general references in chapter five; and Alan Solomon (with Margaret Hall of George Washington Univerisity Libraries) made available the Library of Congress Main Reading Room bibliography, which is published in the appendix. Evelyn Timberlake always found everything I asked for. The Library of Congress provided me with a special desk and other facilities with which I completed this and earlier books. The Library of Congress' Research Facilities staff went out of their way to assist me, and I wish to acknowledge particularly the help of Bruce Martin, Joseph Brooks, and William Sartain, their chief.

Last, but far from least, I am most grateful to my wife, Flora, for her patient encouragement and invaluable help over the years it has taken to write this book.

However, I must hasten to add that the responsibility for any errors of commission or omission is mine alone.

NOTES

1. A.D. Ritchie, Scientific Method: An Inquiry into the Character and Validity of Natural Laws (London: Kegan Paul, Trench, Trubner, 1923), p. 14.

CONTENTS

INTRODUCTION

In the late twentieth century the American economy has made this country a complex place to live and work. Business and government agencies, where most young people secure jobs, require a high order of problem-solving skills to meet this complexity. The role of research as a problem solver has become increasingly important to an ever-widening group of people. While only a few will find employment in research divisions, or "think tanks," most people today need a basic understanding of the methods and tools of modern research. It is a rare individual who will not be asked to read and review a research report in his or her professional or public life. More likely, this person will be put on a committee or task force required to look into some problem of concern to his or her organization or association. To function and discharge such obligations effectively, this individual needs a core of key ideas about modern research.

In particular, a compact and not-too-technical manual for research is needed in economics and business. Books in this field tend to be either philosophical essays on the nature of research or technical treatises on quantitative methods that are indistinguishable from statistics textbooks. The essays are too broad and the technical treatises too complex to be useful to the fledgling researcher. There is a need to strike a balance. Typically, neophytes are woefully ignorant of what research is all about, and usually they need some basic ideas to shape their independent projects. Beginners should be gradually led into the complexities of methodology, computer techniques, and interpretation. They need answers to such basic questions as what is the nature of research; what is research in the economics and business field; how to select and define a problem area; how to explore a field by reading, discussing, interviewing, and thinking critically; and how to isolate a topic for a project.

Once the topic is selected, the researcher needs to visualize how to proceed. He or she must understand how to state a problem, how to ask crucial questions, and how to formulate and test hypotheses. Along with such knowledge, how to develop a plan and crystalize it into a proposal, is also important information. Most importantly, questions on how to research literature by using library tools, how to work with data banks, and how to utilize computerized searches are novel questions that few books of this kind attempt to answer.

Procedural techniques of interviews, samples, survey questionaire construction, and types of surveys--their merits and drawbacks--are also important in a step-by-step guide. After such preparation, quantitative techniques are discussed, but the purpose is <u>not to duplicate the statistics textbook.</u> Instead, minimal concepts to whet the researchers appetite are given. It is well known that most people are afraid of statistics. Experience in teaching research to students shows that after receiving a lucid presentation of a few simple statistical concepts, the beginning researcher can be encouraged to work with quantitative data. Topics like probability sampling and statistical significance are, with some exceptions, left to standard works on statistics in the belief that the first duty is to interest the student researcher in quantitative methods. In addition a unique feature is a chapter on computer usage that stresses the availability of "canned" programs for handling data and urges the researcher to use SPSS (Statistical Package for the Social Sciences) even without a course in Fortran and/or Cobol, helpful as such information science training would be in research projects.

In the last phase of research work beginning researchers must know how to write about their findings. Though the student may consult style manuals and other excellent sources for an <u>in extenso</u> treatment of this subject, the final chapter in this book offers some standard guidelines for how to communicate research results. In addition, the oral report, or briefing, is given some space as an important part of research communications.

All in all, this book is a series of kaleidoscopic shots which set forth the process of research as exemplified by the economics and business fields. Yet taken together these kaleidoscopic shots provide an essential and suggestive sequence. From the core ideas the transition can be made from high-school and college term papers to thoughtful project planning and development in many technical fields. Perhaps even more importantly, the reader will learn to appreciate what research is all about. Whether or not called on to enter professional research, the reader will have grasped the basis for sophisticated research appreciation, application, and evaluation.

While this work is directed at undergraduate or graduate instruction in courses dealing with research methods and principles in economics and business, it is also intended for bewildered students and others who are confronted by some research effort. Essentially it is a guide of first principles for any researcher. It should likewise be useful to managers in both private and public sectors and others who seek a simple guide to research methods in order to do their work more effectively.

The table of contents shows the plan of this book. The first two chapters lay a foundation of what research and its variants in different fields are all about. Chapters three and four are concerned with focusing on research problems and methods, as well as developing strategic plans and proposals. Chapters five, six, and seven specify the procedure of finding literature, sources and data, both by conventional methods and computer methods. Chapters eight, nine, and ten deal with processing data and reaching conclusions. Chapter eleven is on reporting the research in either oral or written reports.

There is a short bibliography of books on economic and business research. The appendix contains a lengthier bibliography on basic information sources and research tools in the main reference collection of the Library of Congress. Even a glance at these bibliographies will show the huge literature of research. From this welter of materials, this book selects those sources, methods and principles that are basic for the researcher. Most research books give some kind of edifying experience; but for most people systematic, incisive guidelines are needed for launching and completing a research project. Though every experienced scholar develops his or her own idiosynchratic method of research, there are some commonly recognized rules of the road. If the beginning researcher knows many of these rules, he or she is likely to avoid wasteful effort, save time and money, and reach a successful result in his or her project.

1
NATURE OF RESEARCH APPROACH TO THE SUBJECT OF RESEARCH

APPROACH TO THE SUBJECT OF RESEARCH

Research is a complex subject, having many dimensions in many different fields of knowledge. It is often equated with science or, more precisely, scientific inquiry. Indeed, it may be broader than most people realize, being more equivalent to the German word Wissenschaften--embracing all knowledge (arts and humanities as well as science). Yet in spite of its dimensional diversity from one field to another, there is a certian unity in research methods. It is important that tyros of research in any field work with an awareness of this structural unity. Such awareness helps to guard against overspecialized and cultural ethnocentrism yet provides opportunities to transfer techniques. Moreover, it is a chastening experience to know that one is part of humanity's effort to achieve order and to live life rationally.

People have achieved a current "good life" (relatively high levels of personal income, longevity, ordered life styles, freedom of personal development) by the dint of the careful investigation that research implies. Even naysayers who hate science and technology often want to use them to "fix" conditions they dislike or to improve the lot of underdeveloped peoples. The history of research development, beginning with the cave man, parallels, for the most part, the history of human achievements. The novel Aton is suggestive of the methods by which early people solved their problems--a method of muddling through, of chancing on something that worked after many trials.[1]

True scientific inquiry, both deductive and inductive, developed with ancient civilization. It reached impressive heights in ancient Greece only to be lost after the collapse of the Roman Empire. People today have much more in common with the ancient world than with the intervening Dark Ages. Authority was the source of the post-Roman medieval world of the West, though the Arabic, Hindu, and Chinese cultures often flourished in brilliant cultural periods in which much research activity advanced the world's knowledge. The Renaissance gradually began to rebuild intellectual and technical progress. The slowness of this progress is realized when we read scholars who say that only by the eighteenth century did the level and richness of life compare to that in the Roman period. This reacquisition of knowledge and the progress made since Rome is a result of careful investigations in numerous fields of science. These careful investigations are called research. A classic authority has defined research as the "manipulation of things, concepts, or symbols for the purpose of generalizing, and to extend, correct, or verify knowledge, whether that

4

knowledge aids in the construction of a theory or in the practice of an art."[2]
Put simply, research is a technique resulting in knowledge accumulation, an
accumulation that has built the modern world.

MODERN MEANING OF RESEARCH

In the late twentieth century most of us have an intuitive feeling for the
scientific spirit that lies behind all kinds of research. The initial collection of
facts, or (put more technically) "securing data," is thought of as the first step.
These facts, supposedly free from interpretation or bias,   are obtained from
careful observation or from unimpeachable sources like the U.S. Bureau of the
Census.   In the hard sciences they are obtained by observation and
experimentation; in the social sciences, from publications of fact-gathering
agencies, often based on questionaires and interviews. (Of course, the latter
techniques are also employed by the scientific researcher.) However derived,
data are the basis of modern science; indeed, some would define research as
simply fact finding; however, most serious practitioners think it is much more.

The dictionary gives several definitions of research:

1. a careful or diligent search.

2. a studious inquiry or examination.

3. a critical and exhaustive investigation or experimentation having for its
   aim the discovery of new facts and their correct interpretation, the
   revision of accepted conclusions, theories, or laws.

4. a presentation incorporating the findings of a particular research.

All of these definitions tell us something of the subject. Perhaps research is
best thought of as a process, involving all of these definitions, though this
concept of research is still fuzzy.

Essentially it is a step-by-step investigation of some carefully selected
topic problem chosen from a larger ballpark arena. It is an objective, scientific
investigation of a subject that the researcher tries to understand by various
methods. On almost any topic the researcher first surveys the literature. For
some subjects this survey may be all that is needed. This inquiry may
rearrange existing studies, verify existing knowledge, and expand the frontiers of
knowledge by generalizing. But usually more is needed. In the physical
sciences experimentation is called for; in the social sciences data collection
from published sources or new data generated by carefully constructed and
applied questionaires are appropriate. Data are processed according to each
discipline's established methods.

Research is basically problem solving. On the simplest level everyone does
research to solve daily problems. If a student's car breaks down, he has a
problem to solve. He starts asking questions: Where to take it for repairs; is
the prospective garage reliable; is it reasonable or does it overcharge; how long
will it take? These questions are simple components of the problem. He goes
about solving the problem or answering these questions by various methods. He
may ask friends who he believes are knowledgeable about cars. This is one
method of beginning any research--interviewing knowledgeable persons for

suggestions.   Alternatively, he may bring the car to the service department of a dealer who specializes in that make.   Perhaps a better method would be to telephone a few garages for answers.

Most research problems are more difficult than where to repair a car.   In business or government agencies every manager needs to solve a multitude of operating problems.   For example, a student interning at a large naval base for summer work and experience was given a problem to solve by his supervisor. The supervisor wanted to know what copying machine among the many types offered was the best to buy for their organization.   The intern then made a research study, using a cost-benefit method of the various types of machines. He presented his findings in a formal report, setting forth the options, and recommending one that seemed the best buy.

In a modern, complex world the problems are much more complicated than these examples.   Scientific or scholarly research problems must be carefully defined and broken into subproblems or specific questions.   The latter are essential: questions refine our thinking.   If one working definition of research is problem solving, another is question posing.   The first important guide to becoming a researcher is to learn how to ask crucial questions about one's subject.

All types of research seek answers to some key question or questions. Much research uses a hypothesis against which to test the data.   An hypothesis is a tentative answer to the central question or questions posed.   It is tested be examining and manipulating the data by some orderly method until eventually a theory is born.   Thus in econometric studies, theory is developed by assuming some systematic relationship between or among variables, a relationship that statistical data can empirically test.   Based on the results of tests using statistical techniques such as regression or correlation, the first assumptions are modified to generate new hypotheses and modified again after further testing of the theories.

TYPES OF RESEARCH

Beginning researchers in the social sciences should recognize that they are part of a larger world of scientific research being carried on in many disciplines.   At minimum, a working knowledge of science groupings is required. One basic division is that of physical science, life science, and social science.   The first two are often called natural sciences.   Physical sciences--like physics and chemistry--or life sciences--like zoology, biology, and botany are termed hard sciences, in which the research is largely experimental.

Another related term is behavioral science--embracing psychology, sociology, and anthropology, some areas of which are heavily experimental. Social Science usually encompasses sociology, political science, economics, and sometimes geography and history.   The social sciences, of which economics is perhaps the most quantitative, are less experimental; but many agencies collect and publish data making possible a kind of experimentation at one level.   Much research is carried on in the arts and humanities, but these subjects are somewhat far afield for this book.

Economics is one of the social sciences.   Business administration is not a science like economics; it is an applied field depending on economics and other sciences for assistance. Some would claim business administration as an applied science, relating to economics and the social sciences in its application of concepts and theories. An analogy with engineering may be helpful. As engineering depends on physics and the hard sciences with feedback from the former to the latter, the relationship between business and economics is similarly one of dependency and interaction.

Pure and Applied Research

An important distinction for researchers to know at the outset is the difference between pure and applied research. Pure science, or pure (basic) research, is done with the objective of contributing to the store of knowledge; it is done for its own sake without regard for its use or application. In contrast, applied research is an addition to the store of knowledge; it is directed at some consumer of the research or, perhaps, sponsors of the project. Applied research is thought of as more problem oriented in that it aims to solve some pressing problems.

In practice the distinction between the two types of research is often blurred. Most pure scientists are aware that their research may have some practical applications. Conversely, applied research can often make a contribution to knowledge that is very theoretical. For example, when the transistor was developed, the original scientific investigations were university studies on the nature of conductivity of electricity in solid state matter. The applied research team with a problem to solve used this basic knowledge of the field. Further, this applied research did not result in a finished product but required a lengthy, expensive stage of development. Moreover, the transfer of this technology to many uses and places might be considered an additional stage in the sequence.

Research and Development Sequence

Researchers approaching their first project should be aware of the Research and Development or R & D sequence. The term R & D is often used as if everyone understood its meaning. It is popularly visualized as a kind of ham and eggs concoction in which basic researchers create new ideas, applied researchers improve that idea, and development people turn it into consumer products. In fact, the components in the R & D sequence are quite distinct entities. As noted, research is divided into pure or basic research and applied research. Pure research is typically done in university science departments; applied research is done in industrial or other applied laboratories. Development is a long, expensive process that carries a model or an innovation developed in the laboratory through pilot plants and market acceptance and use. The original ideas of the first stage of basic research usually are widely separated in time and place from the subsequent applied and development efforts. Sometimes the work of a lone inventor constitutes the applied stage.

The story of the transistor illustrates some of these disparities in the R & D sequence.[3] The transistor concept is credited to a team of research physicists led by William Shockley, who with two of his team was awarded a Nobel Prize in 1952 for this contribution. This team worked on the accumulated basic research of theoretical physicists that had existed as early as the nineteenth century and had stimulated other theories and experiments during the

1930's and 1940's. When Bell Laboratories launched the applied project shortly after World War II, a foundation of 50 years of theoretical (basic) research had already existed. Shockley's development of the transistor was a remarkable breakthrough, though it was predicted by the theoretical hypothesis already published in Shockley's book based on the 50-year accumulation. The subsequent development of the transistor for uses in military, space, and commerical activity is too lengthy to recite, but its applications are found everywhere in the modern world. The Japanese, for example, obtained patent rights and developed (miniature) commercial radios that invaded American markets in the post=war period.

Thus, this case of the R & D sequence shows a long gestation period of basic research in which published scientific results created a foundation for a laboratory breakthrough of a prototype invention for an applied innovation.[4] Its subsequent development and use in many fields have involved a long, costly investment in testing and engineering the product for market use. Many people with diverse backrounds contributed to the sequence over a long period . Figure 1-1 is a simple but deceptive way to understand the stages and feedbacks of what is inherently a complicated process varying in particular industries.

FIGURE 1-1

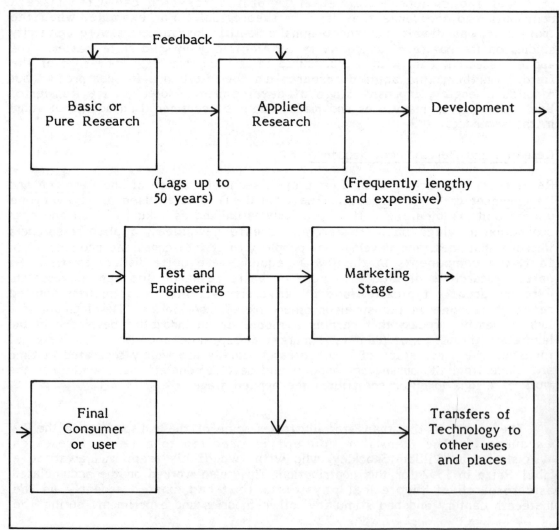

Deductive and Inductive Methods

Awareness of two fundamental procedural methods in research--deduction and induction--provides an essential foundation for the researcher. Deduction means reasoning from certain assumptions or fundamental premises from which consequences are inferred. Since the time of Aristotle the use of logic to derive consequences from a given set of assumptions has been a major scholarly method. Formal logic and mathematics are modes of inquiry relying primarily on the deductive method. Modern economics from its inception with Adam Smith and proceeding through classical, neoclassical, Keynesian, and current theoreticians has also been strongly deductive.

Thus, mainstream economics assumes that people are rational and in business they seek to maximize profits or minimize losses. Consequently, a firm can be predicted to move toward its optimum balance of revenues and costs. That such a rational move does not always happen in the real world is irrelevant, because other variables may prevent it from occurring. Logically, or in the abstract formal science, the consequences follow from the premises.

Scientifically, deduction is checked by verification of results. That is, reasoned conclusions are tested by observing reality to determine the degree of conformity to the deduced conclusion. The hard sciences conduct experiments in sufficient volume to verify the deduction, called the hypothesis. Adequate repetitions of these experiments either confirm or refute the hypothesis. In the social sciences, however, the verification test is much more difficult. Controlled experiments are often impossible; so surveys, historical cases, and statistical data serve the verification function.

In contrast to the deductive or abstract method the inductive method studies specific examples or cases to seek a generalization based on these facts. That is, the regularities or principles arise after examining the raw data for some common pattern. For example, one collects data from a survey, the facts may yield a pattern that can be explained. Individual cases or groups of cases are found to conform to the pattern, and a predictive capability is thus created. If a pattern is not forthcoming, that in itself is a conclusion.

This inductive procedure is the dominant form of most research projects in the social sciences and business. For example, in a study on technology transfer conducted at the Naval Post Graduate School, the concept of the linker, or transfer agent, was tested empirically in two types of people working for the Navy: officers and civilians.[5] The hypothesis to be tested was that civilians were better linkers than officers. The study involved collecting many cases to test the hypothesis, which in fact was not supported: no significant differences in linker ability were discovered between the two groups.

In practice the deductive and inductive methods are not as far apart as they seem. The research investigator uses both methods consciously or unconsciously in a complementary rather than competitive or alternative way. Some deduction is involved in setting up a hypothesis to examine empirical data. A researcher does not examine facts blindly but always with some guide as to what he or she may find. Thus, in business-cycle research deductive theory states that prices should rise in the upswing, less so in the initial phases and more so as the boom gathers momentum. During the upswing business picks up because of more spending by consumers, more business confidence for incurring debt, and more money in circulation. This deduction can be made from long=standing principles of the quantity of money theory and prices. The particular upswing to be studied is a particular case of the larger principle.

Thus, an educated guess or hypothesis is formed when data for an actual case of an upswing are examined. If the emergent pattern turns out to be the same as theorized, the hypothesis is supported. Both deduction and induction are necessary. Deduction without empirical work can fall into theorizing devoid of reality; induction alone can degenerate into meaningless fact collection.

Many seem prone to make this last error, collecting facts with the naive idea that facts alone will solve the problem. Although Francis Bacon gave this idea authority, the researcher must be warned to avoid it. In his autobiography the great researcher Charles Darwin tells us clearly why a blind fact=finding procedure does not work:

> I worked on true Baconian principles, and without any theory collected facts on a wholesale scale, more especially with respect to domesticated productions, by printed enquiries, by conversation with skillful breeders and gardeners, and by extensive reading....I soon perceived that selection was the keystone of man's success in making useful races of animals and plants. But how selection could be applied to organisms living in a state of nature remained for some time a mystery to me. In October 1838, that is fifteen months after I had begun my systematic enquiry, I happened to read for amusment "Malthus on Population," and being well prepared to appreciate the struggle for existence which everywhere goes on from long-continued observation of the habits of animals and plants, it at once struck me that under these circumstances favourable variations would tend to be preserved, and unfavourable ones to be destroyed. The result of this would be the formation of new species. Here then I had at last got a theory by which to work.[6]

Darwin says he developed his hypothesis (deduction) from Malthus, which he then proved by further collection of data (induction). The latter method alone was not adequate for him. Nor is it for modern researchers.

CHAPTER SUMMARY

Research--the systematic method of science, technology, and administration--is conceived as fundamental to the development of Western civilization. To it is ascribed the accumulation of knowledge that has been an essential factor in creating the civilized, and abundant life of modern Western countries.

Research is defined simply as problem solving, implying a careful investigation and analysis of data built on a rational method of a recognized discipline. Deductive and inductive methods are distinguished, as is pure and applied research. The R D sequence is outlined, and its components examined, using the famous case of transistor development as an example.

Research students should think of themselves as part of the larger entity of science with its remarkable unity of attitude, structure, and even method. Researchers, however inexperienced, should consider themselves inheritors of this mighty tradition and stand tall with pride in participating in this great venture. Their contributions as learners and doers, however humble, are increments to the knowledge-producing industry we call research.

The chapter concludes with a quotation from the great biologist Charles Darwin, emphasizing why research is not merely fact=finding.

DISCUSSION QUESTIONS

1. Define research.   Are you satisfied with the definition?

2. Is research the same as science or "doing" science?

3. Why is research in the social sciences less effective than in the hard sciences?

4. Why is there a unity of science in spirit and method?

5. Describe a researchable problem that you or a friend may have.

6. Compare and contrast deductive and inductive methods.

7. Why is it said that business research is chiefly inductive?

8. A small business you know is losing money. Suggest a planned research effort to aid it.

9. What criteria would you use to judge a written research report? Do these criteria apply to an oral report, or do they change?

NOTES

1. Irving A. Greenfield, Aton (New York: Avon Books, 1975).

2. Encyclopedia of the Social Sciences, XIII, pp. 330-34.

3. R.R. Nelson, "Case of Transistor" in National Bureau of Economic Research, Rate and Direction of Inventive Activity (Princeton, N.J.: Princeton Univ. Press, 1962), pp. 549-83.

4. Note the prototype transister is called invention as distinct from innovation, which is a new product or new process entering commercial use.

5. J.A. Jolly and W.J. Creighton, Technology Transfer and Utilization Methodology, technical report NPS-55JO74061 (Monterey, CA.: Naval Postgraduate School pp. 11-22.

6. Francis Darwin, ed., "Autobiography" in The Life and Letter of Charles Darwin. Vol.1, (New York: Appleton, 1888) p. 68.

2
ECONOMICS
AND BUSINESS RESEARCH

INTRODUCTION

In this chapter we seek to define, make some distinctions, and examine the spectrum of economic and business research. Essentially, the researcher should have a feeling for the substantive scope and the procedural methods that prevail in the disciplines and subdisciplines of this broad area. Undertaking a particular study without a larger perspective is to risk becoming the proverbial frog-in-the-well. Conversely, knowing what other specialists are doing can suggest, stimulate, and produce new ideas for the researcher.

This chapter has four parts. The first distinguishes economics and business research and discusses some characteristic methods and techniques of economic studies. The second defines the subjects of business and business administration, while the third examines typical types of economic and business research with examples from recent reports of research in the scientific journals. The last contains a brief survey of research in special sectors of business, such as management, marketing, business policy, and other business subdivisions. While highly selective, this summary should guide and stimulate beginning researchers to understand and appreciate the specialities and opportunities available to them. Perhaps after reading, they will identify clearly with some speciality or, at least, be stimulated to try something mentioned in this section in their own research.

ECONOMICS AND ECONOMIC RESEARCH

A clear distinction should be drawn between economics and business; yet like basic research and applied research, they overlap, influence, and penetrate each other in many ways. The academic world did not recognize the distinction until after World War I; prior to that time business administration was a part of economics departments in institutions of higher education. In Europe the distinction is still not emphasized, in spite of some recent European emulation of "B" schools. In America we have come full circle with departments of economics often located administratively in schools of business.

Economics has deep ties with liberal arts. It is one of the social sciences, taking its place near political science, history, geography, and sociology. It also is related to the behavioral sciences--psychology, social psychology, and anthropology--due to such new ideas as organization theory, for which Herbert Simon won a Nobel Prize in 1978.[1] Mathematics and statistics are tools for all economists and some knowledge of information science or the computer is important to carry on quantitative research in economics or business.

Economic theory is abstract and deductive, concerned with optimums or best position. Frequently, geometric configurations and algebraic formulations are used to develop analysis in pure theory. This method was developed before the computer made manipulation of much data possible. Even so, research still uses deductive theory extensively and often combines it with empirical analysis. Deductive theory is difficult for first research efforts; and unless one is particularly gifted in using abstract tools, it is better to wait until after numerous theory courses before attempting it in research. Yet beginners could try research problems that involve studying historical and comparative methods of exposition of theoretical ideas. For example, one could study the theory of comparative advantage by tracing its historical development from Ricardo and J.S. Mill. Or one might study modern textbooks in international trade theory to determine the best expostition of this famous economic theory.

Economics Defined

Economics has been defined in a number of ways. One simple definition calls it the science that deals with the production, distribution, and consumption of goods and services. The study of man in the "ordinary business of life" is a famous definition from Alfred Marshall, who first invented that trademark of economics--the crosstrees of supply and demand curves. A narrower definition limiting economics to efficiency in the use of resources has become popular in modern times. It states that economics is the study of the application of scarce resources to given ends. This definition suggests the idea that goals and methods to achieve goals must be considered in the light of efficiency criteria. That is, the economic problem is to find the optimum method of achieving some objective. In popular parlance it means to get the best yield for the least cost in whatever you seek to accomplish.[2] Much economic theory is concerned with achieving this optimizing idea.

Applied Economic Research

While much research in economics follows the spirit of this optimizing idea, another method seeks an array of solutions with alternative costs and benefits. For example, in adding converters to automobiles to control air pollution, the rising cost of modifications has to be weighed against the resultant clean=air benefits. Achieving 100 percent clean air might be too costly to be possible, whereas air quality less than 100 percent might be acceptable in terms of budgets and allocations. This is the method of cost=benefit or benefit=cost analysis. Cost effectiveness is another related term for this type of analysis, though it usually means merely minimizing cost without concern for the benefits. Benefit-cost analysis can be quite sophisticated, but particularly difficult is determining the benefits.[3]

The air polution example also brings up two big dimensions of economic inquiry: macroeconomics and microeconomics. Macroeconomics is concerned with the whole economy of a nation or even the world. Typically its elements are aggregates such as national income, consumption, saving, investment, or the foreign balance of payments. Microeconomics, in contrast, studies the unit elements of the economy: the individual, the household, the firm, and the industry. These studies are concerned typically with prices, output, costs, and profits.

Most broad economic subjects have aspects of both macro- and micro= economics. Thus, with a problem like air pollution, some macroeconomic considerations are the impact on the consumption and production of automobiles, the taxes required to support a bureaucracy to enforce national legal decisions, the international competitiveness of the automobile industry, and the effects on the international balance of payments. Equally varied, microeconomics would analyze impacts on cost, sales, prices, and product quality in the individual firms of the automobile industry. It would also consider the consumer's taste and budget.

Other methods of economic analysis include case-study, historical, institutional, and policy approaches. All of these methods are in use but are overshadowed by the rise of quantitative methods. Economic journals are filled with articles reporting studies involving quantitative models and methods. Student researchers should try to read these articles even at the beginning stage to appreciate quantitative methods, simple or sophisticated.

One of the most widely used quantitative models is the techinque of regression analysis. Quantitative data on a problem are found in source books or collected de novo by questionaire and are fitted to a mathematical relationship. In its simplest form the linear regression equation $y = a + bx$ is a device that estimates the value of one variable from another. Thus, we might want to estimate the quantities of, say, pork consumed in relation to its price. We would get the data for each year for the last ten or fifteen years from a government source. Each year we would have an observed price and an observed quantity consumed. By the least squares method, we would compute the linear regression equation as a kind of average relationship between the two variables. This equation could be used to predict the quantity of pork consumed in a future year if the price were known and other variables were equal or constant. As will be explained, the computer helps enormously in calculating relationships of this kind, especially those equations involving large data and more than two variables.

BUSINESS AND BUSINESS RESEARCH

Business, in contrast to economics, is a term for a vast system that produces and markets those goods and services needed by consumers. Perhaps a better word is business administration, for as economics studies the economy, so business administration studies business--its techniques and methods in "administering" or managing. Howard Bowen asserts that this study describes the technology of organizing and developing business activities.[4] The basic areas of the firm's existence--production, sales, finance, and support functions (like personnel)--are described and analyzed, and desirable practices are recommended. Improvement in the economic position of the firm is usually the key motive for business research.

The test of what constitutes "improvement" is mainly the profit position of the firm, but in recent years increasing recognition of the social dimensions of corporate activity have introduced other objectives. The courts have been increasingly recognizing social, moral, and environmental objectives, and this trend may be the wave of the future.[5] Yet the primary criterion of business success is still profit maximization and return to the stockholders. So, researchers in business examine business efficiency as evidenced by profit position improvements, profit maximization, or at least, profit satisfying.[6]

However we define the study of business efficiency, business in the real world is a system of producing and distributing goods and services, a system that depends on certain key foundations. The first foundation, the <u>private enterprise system</u> or <u>market system</u>, is the basis of private ownership of productive facilities.[7] The second main foundation is competition, or the market system of competing sellers providing alternative goods and services. Third, business efficiency depends on a high degree of specialization and exchange through a complex money and credit system. Fourth, it stresses profit or money incentive as the chief reward for "getting things done" and developing enterprising innovation (new products and processes). Last, business relies on government to establish rules of regulation and offer assistance.

Elementary textbooks in economics and business thoroughly discuss these foundations and other characteristics of the business system. it is important that researchers are fully aware of these underpinnings before launching into a research project. If such basic ideas are not clear, the business researcher should reexamine them before his or her research continues. For example, profit, a key but controversial motivation, has been the subject of numerous rationales. If a researcher contemplates research related to profits, he or she should have some feeling for these multiple views. The man in the street may think of profit as what remains from the sellers revenues when all the costs are covered. This view of profit as a residual is a basic accounting definition. Others see profit as the investor's reward for taking risks with his or her efforts and savings. It is also viewed as a measure of a firm's efficiency in accomplishing its objectives in a risk-filled world. Some emphasize its uncertainty. Since the future is unknown, profit depends on good luck and a shrewd estimation of the future. Others consider it a reward for innovation. People with new ideas should be given special incentives if they are successful in benefiting society. Profit, in this instance, is the reward to enterpreneurs and innovators.

TYPES OF ECONOMICS AND BUSINESS RESEARCH

As the previous profit discussion indicated, business research can have a broad scope; but more typically its scope is narrower, concerning itself with the study of just one firm or industry. Put another way, business studies tend to be more microeconomic than macroeconomic, more inductive than deductive.

However, there may be considerable fusion with economic and/or behavioral science research and other social science research. Other disciplines use inductive research to measure how consumers, employees, and management make decisions, and some of their discoveries are transferred, modified, and absorbed into business studies. Yet business research has identifiable concerns that are focused on the subdisciplines of business administration, such fundamental fields as management, marketing, and finance. Other fields are production, business law, insurance, real estate--to list a few.

Another characteristic of business research is it is mostly applied research. In a firm, research is decision oriented; it is aimed at helping managers make pressing decisions. In a university or research organization, studies lean toward the basic research side of the R & D sequence; but even here, the researcher seldom loses sight of how to use results as guides to decisions, strategies, and actions. The contrast of research results found in articles from the American Economic Review and the Harvard Business Review is revealing. Those in the AER are mostly basic research studies contributing to scientific knowledge; those in the HBR are strongly applied, decision-oriented studies, the results of which add to the technology of administration.

Examples of economic research taken from recent economic journals are:

Craven, J. "On the Marginal Product of Capital." Oxford Economic Papers, 29 (November 1977), 472-78.

Hu, S.C. "On A Two-Sector Model of Economic Growth with Exhaustible Natural Resources," Southern Economic Journal, 44 (April 1978), 725-39.

Schumacher, E.F. "Technology in Human Perspective." Nebraska Journal of Economics and Business, 17 (Winter 1978), 7-21.

The first two articles represent highly theoretical, sophisticated research. Beginning researchers would do well to become familiar with such research but recognize that emulating such efforts will require considerable graduate study in economics. The third article is much less technical, representing the policy-oriented research of a British economist who stressed the desirability of "intermediate technology" for development of less developed economies. While the theoretical articles will provide a heightened appreciation of more complex research methods--less technical or descriptive research is more appropriate for early research.

For business research there is the same division into advanced sophisticated research--often involving abstract mathematical models--and simpler descriptive, applied, or policy-oriented studies. The following is an example of the latter, the title of which makes clear its applied orientation--helping managers make an important decision:

White, George R., and Graham, Margaret B.W. "How to Spot a Technological Winner." Harvard Business Review, 56 (March-April 1978), 146-52.

Specifically, the researchers found four major considerations in assessment of managers technological innovations. Their report contained nothing more mathematical than charts and tables.

More theoretical and abstract examples of business research are as follows:

Boseman, F.G., and Schellenberger, R.E. "Business Gaming: An Empirical Appraisal." Simulation and Games, 5 (December 1974), 383-402.

This type of research might not be too difficult for beginning researchers, but the next article reports model-oriented quantitative research, which, like its economic counterparts, has inspirational rather than emulative value for a starting researcher:

> Dillon, W.R., et. al. "Appropriateness of Linear Discriminant and Multinomial Classification Analysis in Marketing Research." <u>Journal of Marketing Research</u>, 15 (February 1978), 103-12.

Another report of research in industrial organization and market structure is less sophisticated but requires considerable statistics:

> Friedland, T.S. "Advertising and Concentration." <u>Journal of Industrial Economics</u>, 26 (December 1977), 151-60.

Note the line between business and economics is often blurred. This last article illustrates how close some business research can be to economic research.

RESEARCH IN THE FIELDS OF BUSINESS

Management Research

Management deals with the problem of how to coordinate people in the production process. Essentially, it is the problem of organization, and courses on this subject are often called "organization and management theory." This subject not only covers management of business but also of government, the military, educational and non-profit organizations. Research on management may include such problems as guidelines for managers to perform their duties, to better their relationship with personnel, or to assess the nature of the organization. Such questions as what makes successful managers or what type of training is most beneficial for managers are also typical areas of study. "Management by Objective" or MBO is a relatively new and interesting area for broad research efforts.

Sub-Sectors

Personnel management is a sub=sector of the general field. Personnel management research deals with span of control, job requirements and specifications, and recruitment and selection of employees. Training, development, promotions, awards and fringe benefits are also part of this area. So, too, are morale, motivation, health, safety, drug and liquor problems, absenteeism, and a host of other people-related issues.

Production management is another important subset. Interesting, exciting research areas include such subdivisions and techniques as quality control, PERT (Program Evaluation and Review Technique), production and inventory control, quality control, and production planning.

Sales, office, financial, and R & D management--indeed management of any unit of the corporation--involve researchable topics. R & D and industrial project management have special appeal for researchers attracted to new products, technological innovations, or innovative tasks. This type of management can be a joy to study but can also be disheartening. This type of advanced technology manager must work with a high proportion of scientific or technical professionals, often "prima donnas," and he or she must also face the uncertain results of pioneer work.

Business Policy

For higher level management business policy is concerned with problems such as what products to adopt, continue, or discontinue; what pricing policies to use; and over a long run, what decisions to make on plant location, expansion, contraction, merger, and acquisitions. Research and development policy is another important area full of research topics and issues. Patent policy is one of its subsets. Other crucial areas are labor or union relations and collective bargaining. Tough, hostile unions may have very damaging effects on a company's profit and industry position. Indeed, some companies have even migrated to escape the effects of excessive unionism.[8]

The government's role also has a tremendous effect on management decisions; and many researchable problems in government regulation or laws affecting business decisions exist. For instance, anti-trust laws, enforcing competition and restricting monopolies are important areas open to study. Recently, environmental problems have become an increasing concern of the government, and environmental impact statement requires research by a team of experts. At this writing a great hostility to government regulation and strong political moves to eliminate it have surfaced.

Scenarios

Many larger business have research, statistics, and long run planning departments to help managers make decisions in the short and long run. In a changing world business has always been a dynamic institution, acting in what Joseph Schumpeter called the "process of creative destruction." Today the pressures seem to have intensified with changes coming so unexpectedly that managers need a spectrum of "scenarios" or plans that can deal with any conceivable situation. Research elaborating the details of such alternative plans now apparently becoming more fashionable.[9]

MARKETING RESEARCH

Marketing is a division of business that concerns itself with the distribution of products to consumers. It is broken into advertising, pricing, sales, market research, and other categories. Market research in particular has become established as central to the need to cater to "consumer sovereignty," that basic guide in a market economy. Though it is well recognized as the senior member of all classes of business research, it relies heavily on the basic social and behavioral sciences of economics, psychology, social psychology, and cultural anthropology. As noted earlier, in its more theoretical studies it is closely related to abstract economic research.

The public is perhaps more familiar with marketing research than any other kind. Few people have not heard of the TV industry's Nielson ratings, perhaps experiencing the loss of a favorite show. Many people have had some experience with a mail or telephone survey or have been accosted by an interviewer with a questionaire.

All of this activity is by no means as easy as it looks. As will be shown in a subsequent chapter, the design and planning of research in general, and the survey and questionaire in particular, are extremely important to the effort's success. Under professional circumstances it may take a long time to perfect the final questionaire prior to actually conducting the survey. When attempting a survey, beginners should be very careful in their objectives, length, question selections, phrasing, and other factors.

Though many good books discuss market research techniques,[10] a few main points should be noted. In general, market research deals with the process, structures, and techniques of how to convince a consumer to select a firm's goods from the competing myriad goods. In particular, market research deals with such specific matters as products, packaging, advertising, sales, and consumer evaluation.

Product research, concerned largely with innovations or new products, often starts with prototypes as they come from the firm's laboratory. Professional research houses such as Battelle Memorial Institute in Columbus, Ohio, have laboratories devoted to testing human reactions to these new products.

Packaging research, examining how to package products, closely relates to new product research and to advertising research. The latter examines the choice of media--TV, radio, newspapers, journals, or handbills. Moreover, it selects an advertising agency and allocates the amount of money used to advertise.

Evaluation of the yield or effectiveness of advertising is another subdivision of marketing research. A firm should determine the effectivness of its advertising decisions and expenditures. For example, if a million dollars is spent on TV advertising and the increase in sales is ten million dollars, the expenditure is justified. If, however, the expenditure evokes only a half-million of additional sales, it is unlikely to be judged effective. In this instance, the concept of elasticity is relevant. It refers to a percentage change of one variable with respect to another independent variable. In the example, the specific elasticity is a percentage change in increased sales or market share with respect to a percentage change in increased advertising expenditure.[11]

Still another area of marketing research is sales or sales effort, aimed at examining who buys and where and why they buy. It is also concerned with potential buyers and the mechanics of buying. The techniques of sales studies may be quite interesting and indirect. For example, to find out which physicians prescribe a new drug first, the researchers analyzed studies of physicians' prescriptions at drugstores rather than asking the physicians directly. In this study conclusions were also drawn not only on how quickly these physicians prescribed new drugs but also on their leadership attitudes--in other words, who would adopt a new pharmaceutical early. The Charles Pfizer Company, who financed the study, wanted to learn what need motivated physicians to purchase new products and how to design their sales effort accordingly.[12]

Forecasting market trends is another vital area in market research. Under uncertain conditions every business decision is based on some forecast, intuitive or carefully researched. Any businessperson is a forecaster. Formal forecasting is not a matter of merely projecting lines or curves but involves some complicated techniques. There are basically four recognized methods of forecasting: mechanical extrapolations, barometric techniques, econometric techniques, and opinion polling, including Delphi Method. These are not mutually exclusive methods. Mechanical extrapolations uses such techniques as moving averages and time series analysis of trends, cyclical and seasonal variations. Barometric techniques involve leading indicators that act as barometers of change. New orders for machinery and industrial equipment , for example, is a leading statistical series that signals changes in other series. Econometric techniques attempt to explain past economic or business activity by deriving mathematical equations used to predict future activity.[13]

In practice these methods are supplemented by sample surveys at expectations ranging from complicated government surveys like the "Survey of Consumer Finances," published by the Federal Reserve, to simple, minimum cost telephone surveys based on probabilistic calculations. A frequent survey used is executive polling for forecasting sales, a recent important development in this area being the Delphi technique. Other factors such as social structure of the consumers, the political climate, and technological change must be factored into the calculation. Technological change is so important that in recent years a new subject, technological forecasting, has developed.[14]

Research in Other Fields

In addition to management and marketing, other fields of business research are associated with divisions of a firm such as accounting, finance, and production; or with specialty areas like business law, real estate, and insurance. Research deals with specific topics found in these fields, each having special characteristics. For instance, financial research would include such areas as capital structure, capital budgets, ratio analysis, acquisitions, mergers, management of assets, portfolios, and corporate funds. Other fields would have similar breakdowns depending on the nature of the field.

CHAPTER SUMMARY

Economic and business research covers a wide field of scholarship, ranging from highly theoretical economic studies in basic (or pure) science to simpler applied research that examines everyday business. Any researcher should have some feeling for the kinds of research in adjacent areas.

In economics much traditional research is concerned with optimization such as the best operating position for the least cost. Other economic research is based on comparitive methods such as cost-benefit analysis. Though case studies, institutional and policy approaches are also used, quantitative methods using the computer have become the hallmark of sophisticated methods (so too, in business research).

Business research is divided into many subfields. Each has its own characteristics and journals devoted to its development. Researchers planning to work in subfields like accounting, finance, or real estate must become acquainted with some of the research reports in these fields.

DISCUSSION QUESTIONS

1. In research what do sophisticated methods mean?

2. How do we know when we are dealing with research in a special field, say accounting, or the economics of innovation?

3. Suggest some subfields of business or economics not mentioned
    in the text?

4. Read and jot down some article titles in the Harvard Business Review
    and the Quarterly Journal of Economics. How do they differ?

5. Take a new technological field that is about to develop (e.g., solar
    energy, hunter-killer satellites, gene splicing, technological
    forecasting). What are some researchable economic or business problems
    associated with these new developments?

6. Find some new areas of business not discussed in the text. Discuss its
    dimensions and likely research potentials in some detail.

7. What does cost-benefit analysis method mean? Give examples.

NOTES

1. Herbert Simon, Administrative Behavior 2nd ed. (New York: MacMillan,
1961); and New Science of Management Decisions (New York: Harper and
Row, 1960).

2. The Pentagon's research department in studying weapon systems,
popularized as its criteria, the catchy phrase "biggest bang for the least
buck."

3. Michael J. Frost, How to Use Cost-Benefit Analysis in Project
Appraisal (Hampshire, Eng.: Gower Press, 1975).

4. Howard R. Bowen, The Business Enterprise as a Subject for Research
(New York: Social Science Research Council, 1955), p. 19.

5. Phillip I. Blumberg, The Megacorporation in American Society: The
Scope of Corporate Power (Englewood Cliffs, N.J.: Prentice Hall, 1975) pp.
6-14; also "Ethics and Earnings," Wall Street Journal, 18 Nov. 1975, p. 1.

6. Profit satisficing comes from organization theory, see Simon,
Administrative Behavior. Maximization of sales, not profits, also has been
suggested by some economists as the goal actually being pursued by large,
oligopolistic companies.

7. The term capitalism or capitalist system is used but is best avoided
because its suggests a Marxist, socialist, or communist bias.

8. In recent years, management consultants have specialized in helping
management prevent unions getting started or unseat those unions already
established. See "Labor Nemesis," Wall Street Journal, 19 Nov. 1979, p. 1.

9. Business Week, 28 April 1975, pp 46-54.

10. See, for example, Chester R. Wasson, The Strategy of Market Research
(New York: Appleton, 1964).

11. For a good discussion of the concept and use of advertising elasticity,
see Milton Spencer, Managerial Economics, 3rd ed. (Homewood, Ill.: Irwin
1968), pp. 257-58.

12. Everett M. Rogers, _Diffusion of Innovations_ (New York: Free Press of Glencoe,   1962), pp. 46-48.

13. William P. Butler and Robert A. Kavish, eds., _How Business Economists Forecast_ (Englewood Cliffs, N.J.: Prentice Hall 1966).

14. See Robert Ayres, _Technological Forecasting and Long Range Planning_ (New York: McGraw-Hill, 1969); or Joseph P. Martino, _Technological Forecasting for Decision Making_ (New York: American Elsevier, 1972).

3
RESEARCH PROBLEMS: CHOICE AND METHOD

Research need not be dull routine. Research can arise from natural curiosity and be an instinctive function. Love and hunger, those two basic appetites, are not too much more acute than curiosity. Curiosity may be more or less the same whether we are alertly looking into our neighbors' business or writing a dissertation. The only real difference is whether or not we choose a topic that is worth investigating and recording. There are still such topics in multitudes. We have only to find those that interest and excite us. It is our own fault, if we choose topics in which we are not interested. But in research, as in creative writing, it need not always be clear just why we choose our particular topics. At best we choose topics because we fall in love with them. You can tell a young man that he ought to love a certain girl, and you can point out all the advantages of your plan; but it may not convince him. His choice must come from his own instincts and his own experience. If, however, he goes ahead and makes a dull marriage of convenience that is, chooses a dull topic because it is handed to him he deserves all the discomforts he gets.[1]

CONSIDERATIONS OF CHOICE

At the outset we must distinguish between research conducted to meet the needs of some business or government agency and research chosen by a student. Research dictated by the needs of a firm or agency must solve problems that the external environment or the internal structure and operations of the unit create. It is the manager's role to identify these problems and refer them to researchers for solution. The researchers, in turn, may discover and suggest study of other problems that emerge.

In the business firm or government agency management usually decides the research problem to be attacked. For the most part, the individual researcher has little to say in the decision except as a research staff member preparing a list of research problems needing attention. On a small staff crises confronting the organization may force the decision of what problem to select. In larger offices where a longer time horizon is possible, management generates agendas of possible research problems. It decides which studies to select by the pressures and priorities of the organization's internal condition and external environment. Moreover, the research design, methods, and time allocated to the effort are due to pressing needs. An answer may be due at the end of the week and the investigation done haphazardly, even though the topic merits a long, careful, well=designed effort.

In contrast, the student researcher is usually in a position to choose his or her topic. This freedom, properly used, allows the individual to select an area he or she likes or has some background in or to cultivate his or her expertise. For example, if one is interested in becoming a manager, one might choose a topic dealing with the qualifications and aptitudes of managers. In an actual case a student who was a Vietnam veteran chose to work in the Veteran's Administration's Home Loan Guarantee Program because he wanted to buy a home.

However, this freedom of choice can become a burden. Since a student may have had little experience even in writing term papers, the selection of a good topic may loom as a heavy responsibility. But some feeling of burden has its merits: It forces the student to make a wise decision about this topic--at least on the initial subject to choose. The student must do some serious thinking, and, once committed, he or she must live with that choice. The famed German poet Goethe warns us: "In the first step we are free; in the second, slaves."[2]

Guidelines

What are some guides to a wise choice? Do some initial thinking. What is it that interests you? It may be a broad subject you already know something about, which came out of a course you enjoyed or a TV program dealing with some current issue like the population problem, the energy crisis, or floating exchange rates. Similarly, it may come from a job you worked at last summer. One economics student who returned from Ghana where he had been a student intern with the AID mission selected that country's agriculture planning and performance as a topic. A registered nurse doing a degree in business administration chose to look into hospital administration costing.

Alternatively, the area may be one in which the prospective researcher knows little but has a strong desire to learn more about. An accounting student contemplating a career as a tax lawyer and an accountant chose to study conflict of interest between the two careers. Another person curious about solar energy visited an experimental house at the University of Deleware and was stimulated to work on the economics of solar installations in residential housing. Another looked into pleasure boats as a business to work in after graduation; still another examined the liquor industry, only later to become a sales representative in this area.

Familiarity with the ballpark subject may not be the best reason for its choice. The author has advised may foreign students against choosing topics concerning their home country. Data about their countries are often not available, and the benefit to the student may be greater if he or she explores a technical American topic since presumably he or she came to the United States to study American practices and gain some technical specialty. This advice may also apply to American student who have already special knowledge of a particular field. Students need mind=stretching experiences as well as safe topics.

Limitations on Choice

There are other limitations on choice of topic. The area of economics and business is itself a limitation. For example, a study of some aspect of prisons is in the field of sociology and should normally not be selected. However, business policies regarding the job opportunities and hiring of convicts is more of a business topic under the subdivision "social responsibilty of business." But even this subject is relatively marginal to the main thrust of economics and business. Moreover, it is an area so involved with social, cultural, and political variables that it is better for beginners to avoid. A general topic area that is typically business or economics--such as pricing, profits, wage determination--is preferable because of its relative simplicity. While it is true that in the social sciences everything depends on everything else, first research efforts should normally stay in more traditional disciplinary channels where there are some established paths or models to follow, imitate, or build on. As stated in the previous chapter, students are well advised to read some professional articles in their area of concentration for ideas and methods. For example, a management student should read some professional management articles to get some feeling of the the problems, the questions asked, and the methods of approach in the field. Similar advice goes for those specializing in economics, marketing, and accounting. Most fields have developed or are developing sophisticated methods, of which students at least be aware, if not try to emulate.

The equipment or tools available to the researcher also constrains selecting a general problem area. One constraint is the researcher's intellectual endowment, cultivated by years of training in some field or acquired practical experience. In particular, a big constraint would be poor knowledge of statistics, quantitative methods, and the computer being used for the chosen problem. Research design (covered in the next chapter) should reveal the character of the data needed and the necessary methods of handling it. If the student is not equipped or equipped poorly, he or she is advised to review statistics. If the student cannot regenerate his or her capabilities within the time available, this student better look for another problem area.

Time is clearly and important limitation for any research decision. It is essential to visualize the future and to establish a plan of procedure. Most people underestimate the time it takes to do anything. Estimating the time available to do research is certainly no exception. So, the choice of topic is automatically limited by this consideration. Students often write away for materials from a company, governement agency, trade association, or even another country and are chagrined when they received no reply, leaving them empty handed at the halfway mark of their time frame. Research requires a realistic time plan. The Gantt Chart for scheduling work, covered in chapter four is a good tool for insuring good time performance.

Obviously, money is another limitation. Choosing a topic that involves visits to companies other places often requires burdensome financial resources. But cost is also relative. If substantial benefit can occur from a visit for relatively little cost, monetary strain on one's finances might be worthwhile. In any case, even a simple research project plan should have a budget.

Availability of data is perhaps the biggest single limitation to the prospective researcher. If the research is largely library-based, developing from secondary materials, efforts invested in a preliminary search of sources should quickly indicate possible prospects. If the researcher must collect data directly from the company records or by interviews or surveys, the issue of feasibility must be faced. Often with company or agency documents the management may simply deny usage even to an insider. There was once a student who proposed to use her experience in an internship business position, but she was astonished to find that her former employer simply refused to release the necesary records. As noted earlier, business security or proprietary interest is an important limitation to business research. Offsetting this problem is the availability of published business reports, analytical articles, government data, and trade association statistics. The latter are less sensitive because they are aggregated and do not reveal data on the individual firm.

Other limitations or at least considerations in choice of topic are significance and timeliness. A beginning researcher has greater motivation if the area he or she chooses has some current interest or relevance. People who aid the project--advisors, interviewees, friends, or colleagues--all react to a significant, timely project with sustained interest. Also, results are usually more useful and likely to help the researcher in his or her career. Conversely, a dull, remote effort sparks little interest and appreciation.

PINPOINTING THE PROBLEM

After weighing the considerations and limitations noted and choosing a ballpark area, the next step is to isolate a meaningful problem. Problem solving is at the heart of the research process. Indeed, most scholars believe that all research aims to solve specific problems. This purpose is true for the result of research, but first, exploratory research is needed to discover what the problems are. After exploratory research a selection of a particular problem is made.

How to find a particular problem area? The first step is to explore the literature of the topic, or compile a preliminary bibiography. It means going to the library and finding some books, journal articles, newspaper accounts, and government documents, which relate to the topic area. Graduate students working on master's and doctoral degrees or seasoned researchers may spend much time in this exploratory phase. Not only do they need to know the dimensions and breakdown of the larger area in which they plan to work, but they must also skim through the published material to be sure that the problem they have in mind has not already been covered. If it has, they may drop the idea or further differentiate their proposed problem from the existing research studies.

Note the story, probably apocryphal, of a graduate student in history who narrowed his topic to the "Incunabula of the Fijian Islands." "Incunabula" means books published before the year 1500, which obviously narrowed his sources and data to a point at which they were almost non-existent. If you have decided on some specific problem and find it is so narrow that no source material is available, you may, of course, design your effort to generate your own data. But you might be concerned about the significance of such a specific problem. Alternatively, you might try to broaden your narrow formulation to something larger and more significant.

For most people there is always some initial oscillation between the general idea and the specific problem. Typically by trial and error the focus is sharpened to a manageable problem. Eventually the researcher will choose a research problem appropriate for the time and resources available.

Clearly the undergraduate effort cannot be delicately formulated because the time and resource constraints are too limiting to make possible a carefully selected problem. Often the first serious research effort is still a training experience designed for practice in principles of research. Nevertheless, the researcher must read exploratively, seek to limit his or her problem, and expand or contract it, if necessary, until some feasible problem is reached.

Another helpful method in narrowing the probem is discussion--kicking around the topic with friends, faculty, or knowledgeable persons in the field. In industry this is called brainstorming. In a research class or seminar, interactive class discussion may be a course requirement. Many good ideas can come from such sessions; others may see aspects of a subject that the prospective researcher does not. Further, people stimulate one another, and the total number of ideas will be greater than if individuals were thinking alone. Also, such sessions improve or refine ideas. Synergistic effect is the term often used to refer to this increased effectiveness resulting from interactive agents working together.

The researcher must be ready with a notebook for these ideas or they may be lost quickly. A separate, small notebook is excellent for jotting down ideas while the project is in progress. The notebook can also provide a running record or diary of dated entries showing how the work is progressing.

Reading current newspapers and journals in business and economics are other sources to help formulate a problem. The Wall Street Journal, The New York Times, Business Week, Barrons, Challenge, and even the local newspaper's financial and business pages help in topic selection and refinement. Current developments and trends may provide the cutting edge for a timely and significant problem. Reading the more scholarly research journals is more difficult, but it stimulates the beginning researcher's appreciation of theory and method being practiced currently in his discipline. Professional research in economics and business has become very sophisticated in its use of mathematical models and quantitative methods. While undergraduates cannot be expected to formulate studies that doctoral candidates work on over two or three years, some awareness and limited application of such methods may be desirable.

Those students with more training and aptitude for quantitative formulation should cultivate this propensity and introduce some element of it into their topic formulations. At minimum, all business and economics students should think in terms of analyzing their problem with tables, graphs, charts, and other fundamental tools of descriptive statistics. Of course, thinking about how quantitative the effort is to be interacts with how to decide what topic to pick. More of this quantitative aspect will be covered further in the chapter.

Example of Choice

Choosing a problem from the ballpark topic involves setting up a panorama or overview of the larger subject. Essentially two steps are involved; the first is to see what some problems in the field are; the second is to choose one for research concentration. The best way to find problems is to ask questions. Questions are keys to discovering what issues, gaps, and problems exist in a larger subject. Researchers are always asking questions, phrasing and rephrasing them, until they find what gap needs concentrated study. A quote from Kipling is a vivid reminder of the utility of asking questions:

> I keep six honest serving men
> They taught me all I knew
> Their names are What and Why and When
> And How and Where and Who[4]

An example on using questions may show how useful they can be. If the ballpark subject is "Minority Business Enterprise," we might proceed as follows:

BALLPARK SUBJECT: "MINORITY BUSINESS ENTERPRISE"

Broad Orientation Questions:

1. What is the meaning, rationale, and objective of a minority enterprise?

2. Where is it located? What is its size, composition, geographical distribution, length of life?

3. What problems does it encounter?

4. How is it financed?

5. What are its effects on minority people's developments?

6. Who are some typical business people who enterprise small minority businesses?

More Specific Questions:

1. What does minority enterprise mean?
    a. Definitions?
    b. History?
    c. What functions does it serve?
    d. What is its profit picture?

2. What are the characteristics?
    a. National? Regional?
    b. State and City?
    c. Rates of success, failure?
    d. Franchises?

3. What are the problems?
    a. Small=scale competition?
    b. Training of personnel?
    c. Trust of clientele?
    d. Location?
    e. Management problems?

4. How is it financed?
   a. Personal savings, or family loans?
   b. Credit Ratings?
   c. The SBA Program?
   d. Reverend Sullivan's case study?

5. What are its effects?
   a. Does is promote economic development in the
      community?
   b. Is it a training program?
   c. Does it promote integration or segregation?

Many other questions could be raised on this broad subject, but already the list is too large to be handled by a limited study. One of these questions should be isolated for concentration. Others may have some bearing; but if a key area is selected--say, finance--there is opportunity for concentrated, meaningful exploration. Within finance we may concentrate still further by choosing a subdivision--say, Reverend Leon Sullivan's efforts in Philadelphia to raise capital, finance enterprises, and shopping centers for minorities or his labor training program known as Opportunities Industrial Corporation (OIC), which now has branches in other cities. Clearly each of these subdivisions provide still further narrowing possibilities. The rule for beginners is don't try to do too much; if your topic is too narrow, it is easier to broaden than to do the reverse.

CHOICE OF METHOD

Equally important or perhaps more important for the researcher than choice of problem is choice of method. The general rule is that the method should be suitable to the problem; however, beyond this platitude it is not easy to specify procedure. More than one method may be appropriate, and the choice has much to do with the background, discipline, and training of the researcher. Also, it is a two way street, for the method of research may influence the choice of the problem. Methods or types of methods used in a discipline may influence, even dictate, the choice of topic or problem selected.

Because method or methodology is basic to the scientific, systematic approach to problem solving, many scholarly books and articles have been written about it.[3] Yet method is a complex concept and is indeed hard to set forth or condense for a working understanding. Perhaps a way to simplify its complexity is to realize that method is based on rationality; whatever method is followed, there is some systematic way of going about it, which other researchers can follow and indeed replicate.

In the previous chapters some elements of method have been discussed. The distinction between deductive and inductive method has been developed and how they interact as the research hypothesis is tested has been shown. Method has also been noted explicitly or implicitly in discussing the types of research found in each of the disciplines or subdisciplines of economics and business. In this chapter the discussion of method attempts to be more systematic and generic. We will attempt to set forth a more orderly classification of methods and procedures being used in modern research. Other attempts have been made to classify types of research, but none are widely accepted.

In economic and business research the most useful distinction of method is perhaps that between <u>quantitative</u> and <u>nonquantitative</u>. While no project is exclusively one or the other, usually the design of a particular project requires deciding on procedures or methods to which these terms have some application. Quantitative means having to do with quantities or amounts, hence being capable of measurement. Quantifiable meaning capable of being quantified, is an important related term because we frequently try to put the research problem in quantifiable terms, sometimes not succeeding. In contrast, nonquantitative methods or procedures (sometimes called <u>qualitative</u>, not to be confused with superiority) seek to find the inherent essential nature of what is being investigated.

In the past, economic and business research was primarily nonquantitative, but over the last twenty five years, with the advent of data availability and computers, the quantitative emphasis has increased and is very important for researchers. However, like the relationship between induction and deduction, both types of procedures are linked. It is really a question of what type of procedure is predominant in the design and planning of the research.

Perhaps the word "method" is not as good as "procedure" to characterize types of research efforts. The former is restrictive, while the latter permits a rough-and-ready description of what researchers do. Defining words in this way, we may visualize a spectrum of research procedural types ranging from a simple nonquantitative search for a bibliography to quite complex forms of quantitative methods. <u>Here are ten types of research procedures or methods that are useful to remember</u>:

1. Exploratory Research
   a. Surveys of the Literature

2. Descriptive Research

3. Historical Research

4. Case Studies

5. Comparative Research
   a. Ratios and Percentages
   b. Advantages and Disadvantages

6. Benefit-Cost Analysis

7. Experimental Method

8. Surveys and Statistical Analysis

9. Quantitative Models
   a. Econometrics
   b. Operations Research

10. Other Quantitative Types

A brief description of each of these methods may be helpful; more emphasis is accorded to benefit-cost analysis, a good method for researchers to acquire early because it is a workhorse method for many research projects.

Exploratory Research

Exploratory research, as its name indicates, is basically reviewing the literature of some field, but it may also include interviews with knowledgeable persons to diagnose problems in that field, or diagnostic interviews (a topic covered in chapter eight). During the exploration the researcher, uncertain of what he or she wants to do, finds a problem on which to concentrate. Alternatively, the researcher may find that the data are not adequate to solve that problem ot that the data cannot be obtained. Another reason for exploratory research is to comprehend the scope of the proposed effort. The researcher may find time and money costs too great to attempt the project. In some respects exploratory research may be compared to a pilot project in industry; it gives some experience, ideas, and opportunity to visualize a larger, more carefully planned effort. Depending on outcomes, it may be continued or abandoned.

Surveys of the Literature   Literature surveys may be viewed as first cousins of exploratory research, different only in the fact they result in expository reports that contribute to scholarship in the area. Some scholars regard these articles negatively because they consider them mere compilations and rehashes of what others have done, but such a judgment is unfair. If analytical, a literature survey may distill the essentials of a field or subfield of knowledge. Thus, it saves time for other researchers, allowing them to grasp salient developments quickly; moreover, such a survey may innovatively classsify types, make insightful interpretations, and suggest strategic agendas for future research. The Journal of Economic Literature publishes many surveys as one of its principal objectives.

Descriptive Research

Descriptive research refers to studies that simply describe the factual situation but do not attempt much analysis of its causes. If we are studying the treatment of woman in obtaining real estate mortgages, the tabular data of how many women got mortgages are descriptive if they break into certain categories--say, marital and family status, age, occupation, and size of the mortgage. When we try to explain why these data subdivide in this way, we are in an analytical mode, which is normally concerned with cause or correlation. This method is also called Descriptive Statistics.

Historical Research

The discipline of history is a proud possessor of a great research tradition beyond the purposes of this book.[5] In economics or business, historical research is employed in various ways; for instance, the statistical time series. Economic history is a well-established subdisicpline which in the last decade has had interesting quantitative developments; but by its nature, economic history is usually heavily descriptive. For any type of research project historical research is often useful as background, as setting or introductory materials and sometimes as case studies.

Case Studies

Case studies are a legitimate research approach found in the social sciences. This method is used extensively in social welfare, social anthropology, medicine, and psychiatry. In fact, case studies can be clinical situations. Legal research also relies very heavily on court cases for precedents.

In business and economic research case studies are in use as studies of a company or an industry and in special areas such as labor-management relations or anti-trust enforcement. Case books containing a selection of source case materials in business or, less frequently, economics are in wide use for instructional purposes.

Doing a case study means that one example is intensely studied or observed in order to make a generalization about that case. Its in-depth nature is both a strength and a weakness: unless the researcher uses careful criteria for inclusions, it can become lost in detail, degenerating into a little story about one case.[6] Thus many accuse it of being unrepresentative. Yet on the positive side case study research can generate powerful insights not obtainable by other methods.

Comparative Research

Comparative research compares and contrasts two or more things, persons, organizations, or policies. It is an examination of subjects in order to observe or discover similarities or differences. Holding a respected place as a method of analysis, used in many scholarly fields, as for example, comparative literature or comparative linguistics. In economics and business such fields of specialization as comparative economics systems, business policy, or investment analysis make great use of the comparative method. For example, if a business manager or investor has to decide among competing investments, he or she uses established criteria such as profit, yield, growth, or security, to decide the best alternative.

Ratios and Percentages   Probably the simplest type of scientific analysis is to employ ratios and percentages in analysis for comparative purposes. The term relative analysis is sometimes used for this procedure, which is contrasted to absolute data. Thus, if we say the firm made $100,000 profit, this figure is absolute. This profit is a fact, of course but does not help us very much unless it is compared to something else, like the firm's sales or net worth. A hundred thousand dollar profit compared to $1,000,000 sales would be a 10 percent profit rate, giving us something to compare to other firms in the industry. If the industry average is 5 percent our firm appears to do well; but if the average is 15 percent the opposite is true. This kind of relative or comparative analysis is essential for any researcher who has numerical data. Always he or she should ask: Is a meaningful ratio or percentage comparison possible? Financial or accounting research makes extensive use of such ratios.

Advantages and Disadvantages   Using the comparative method, we may also try the age=old method of listing the advantages and disadvantages, the positives and negatives of any phenomenon being researched. Obviously, this technique may include the weighing of one against the other and reaching some judgmental conclusion. Recommendations may then follow, it the research sponsor requires it.

BENEFIT-COST ANALYSIS

Benefit-cost or cost-benefit analysis is a type of comparative method widely used in business and government agencies. it is a quantitative or quasi-quantitative method that extends and quantifies the idea of comparing advantages and disadvantages in making a decision. It can be used in both private and public sector decisions, but because of the absence of profit as a measure of efficiency in the public sector, it is used more in the latter than in the private sector. Indeed it can be regarded as a proxy for the profit indicator.

The benefit-cost idea is easily grasped. If the benefits accruing from a decision to take an action exceed the costs, both calculated numerically, the action should be taken. If the opposite is true, the action should not be taken. Put numerically, a project should be undertaken if its benefits to cost ratio is greater than one:

$$\frac{\text{Benefit}}{\text{Cost}} > 1$$

Let us take a simple example from the household sector of economy. Suppose a consumer wants to buy a freezer. Do the benefits exceed the costs? Figure 3-1 illustrates how cost-benefit analysis works:

FIGURE 3-1

HYPOTHETICAL FREEZING LASTING FIVE YEARS

COST	BENEFITS
A. $500	A. $1,300
B. $250	B. $260
C. $100	
D. $150	
$1,000	$1,560

Cost-Benefit Ratio $\frac{1,560}{1,000}$ = 1.6.   Therefore, buy the freezer.

A. Original cost.

B. Electrical cost estimate at $50 per year for five years.

C. Estimated repairs.

D. Opportunity cost, means loss of interest @ 6 percent per year (500 x .06 x 5 = $150, ignoring compounding).

A. Freezer saves $5 per week on food purchasing every week for 52 weeks over five years ($5 x 52 x 5 = $1,300.)

B. By shopping less saves $1 gas and wear on cars every week ($1 x 52 x 5 = 260)

A more complicated but typical example of cost-benefit analysis is a public project comparison in road building in a South American country. The comparison was between two roads linking two cities, Caracas and Valencia. The old road, the Pan American Highway was an old, slow-moving mountian road that "beat up" vehicles traveling on it. The new road, a superhighway called Autopista, was a smooth run at high speed. The American economist, Charles Stokes, who did this cost-benefit analysis, calculated that the cost of a vehicle operation on the old highway was 19 centavos per kilometer against 55 centavos per kilometer on the superhighway. For each route he multiplied the length of the road by these unit costs per vehicle and other appropriate factors to determine the annual cost for direct users of each route.

The saving of the new highway over the old was 252 million bolivars, the number he took to be the benefit. Cost worked out to be 34 million bolivars: so the benefit-cost ratio for the new highway 254/30 or an 8:1 benefit-cost ratio. Figure 3-2 gives details of this calculation.

FIGURE 3-2
CALCULATION OF BENEFIT-COST RATIO--VALENCIA AUTOPISTA

Highway	Length (km)	Vehicle Operation Costs (Bs)	Vehicles Per Day	Days in Year	Total Cost of Vehicle Operation (Millions of Bs)
Panamerican	123	0.55	14,200	365	349
Autopista	99	0.19	14,200	365	97
					252

Cost of Autopista (Millions of BS)
Annualized construction cost (30 yrs.@ 8%)   Bs 29.0
Annual maintenance cost   5.1
                                                                         Bs 34.1

Less
Improvement cost of Panamerican
  Annualized construction costs (30 yrs.@ 8%) Bs 3.2
  Annual maintenance cost   0.8   4.0
Net additional cost of Autopista   Bs30.1

$$\text{Benefit-Cost Ratio} = \frac{\text{Annual Saving}}{\text{Annual Cost}} = \frac{252}{30.1} = 8.3$$

SOURCE: Adapted from C.J. Stokes, "The Tejerias-Valencia Autopista: A Case Study of the Development Impact of a Venezuelan Highway," Revista de Economia Latino-Americana, 15:15 (August 1965), 178. Reproduced in Stokes Managerial Economics op.cit:, p. 181.

However, it should be noted that indirect social costs and benefits were not included. For example, property values of land near the highway may have been reduced or increased by the new highway. More calculations would be needed to analyze such a problem. Still a survey of this cost-benefit analysis exists and gives details of the ways this type of analysis may be used, including planning large public projects, nationalized industries, roads, defense and social welfare services.[8]

The technique stems from the 1930's when TVA type projects in irrigation, flood control, and hydro-electric power were analyzed. Since World War II, military cost benefit analysis of operations and weapons systems has become usual.[9] Likewise, evaluations of electric power investments, transportation (road building, pipelines, etc.), and education and health care expenditures are other areas to which these ideas have been applied.

Experimental Method

Experiments done under laboratory controlled conditions are rare in economic-business research. A few examples can be found, as in marketing research on a new product. At Battelle Research Laboratories in Columbus, Ohio, may be observed human guinea pigs put in cubbyholes with no distraction but a questionaire on which to register responses. A plate of new food product was puched into each person, who recorded his or her sensations of taste, sight, and smell. Columbus, Ohio, where these experiments were taking place, is considered a city with tastes most representative of the U.S. as a whole.

Another type of experiment used in buiness is sometimes referred to as "before and after" experiments. In a selected region a label on a can of food or the packaging of any product may be changed. We observe the sales before the change and compare the sales after the change. If the sales increase, we ascribe it to the change of the label or packaging. Other variables such as tastes and income may have affected the outcome; so it is not a controlled experiment in a laboratory, but it is an experimental method.

Two large and famous socio-economic experiments are also valuable for researchers to know. One is the Hawthorne experiment (actually a series of experiments), which studied motivation and productivity in the Western Electric Company's Hawthorne Plant during the 1930's.[10] In recent years there has been considerable interest in experiments testing the effect of a negative income tax on low income individuals on reducing job seeking and work motivation.[11] Other such experiments have been tried, but it is difficult to design and carry out experiments in the social sciences.

Surveys and Statistical Analysis

The place of the experimental method in the research area under consideration is taken by surveys. Armed with questionaires, often called instruments, the researcher collects primary data on his subject with a survey sample. The researcher also uses the data collected by surveys made by government and private agencies even more extensively than that from his or her own surveys. Data are then processed by standard statistical methods, usually with a computer. Later chapters will discuss details of these procedures. This quantitative work is usually used to test hypotheses or models established by business or economic theory.

Quantative Models

Sophisticated researchers in economics and business build models that are representations of a problem in mathematical form. Essentially, an equation or set of equations is set up to represent the problem. These models take on many forms such as econometrics in economics and operations research in the business field.

Econometrics   Econometrics is a type of economic research that sets up a system of equations to formulate certain economic relations. The parameters of these equations are filled in by estimates from statistical data.[12]   The model so derived can be used for forecasting. For example, in macroeconomic models consumer demand can be forecast at various levels of income. These may be fairly simple models of two or three equations, or they may be much larger. One authority has distinguished medium scale models with 14 to 48 equations and large scale models with about 200 equations[13]   One thing they have in common is that they are represented by a lot of simultaneous equations that are solved with the use of computers. The general characteristics of these models including types of equations (definitional, stochastical, structural, etc.) are described conveniently by the same source which is readily available on most reference shelves.

These models are used for forecasting the state of the economy, but their success in comparison with subsequent actual happenings in the real world has not been as great as the model builders would like. Yet in spite of relatively poor performance with forecasts, these methods are being used by consulting firms, such as the Data Resources Inc. (DRI), Wharton Econometric Forecasting Associates of the University of Pennsylvania, and Chase Econometric Associates, a subsidiary of Chase Manhattan Bank.

Obviously, the researcher needs considerable training in this specialized field before attempting work in the field.

Operations Research   Quantitative techniques applied to solving operational problems was first used for military problems in World Wars I and II. Ships in convoy, for example, were analyzed by mathematical models for the best ways to avoid submarines on the Atlantic runs. After World War II operations research was widely adopted by decision makers in business trying to choose the optimum alternative. It is found in such areas as production, inventory, control, transportation scheduling, and traffic control.[14]   To describe briefly the types of operations research and their meanings is not easy, because such discussions are lengthy and technical; however, a well=known article by Robert Dorfman is a good referral point.[15]

Other Quantitative Types

There are other types of techniques, some of which are regarded as branches or close relatives of econometrics or operations research. Input-output technique is a type of econometrics pioneered by W.W. Leontief.[16]   Systems analysis can be considered an extension of operations research to an analysis of an economic unit as a total process.[17]   Simulation or computer simulation is a general term applying to models built of equations for a computer.[18] The latter often involves game theory, thus introducing several assumptions of what might happen under various conditions. More quantitative methods exist, but they are often related to other categories. Linear programming, for example, can be viewed as part of either econometrics or operations research. Without trying to touch all bases, we can leave the subject of quantitative methods with the thought that for the motivated and trained researcher there are many techniques to learn and use for varying problems.

Choice of Method

Looking over the spectrum of types of research previously set forth, the researcher must choose a problem and accompanying method for which he or she has the background and training. Clearly, to work with quantitative methods, the researcher must have had training in mathematics, statistics, and model building. However, much research is carried on with less quantitative methods; in fact, many problems may not be quantifiable. In any case, the nonquantitative side of the research spectrum is still widely used and a valid choice for researchers who have neither inclination nor training to work in more "sophisticated" and rare research problems. Indeed in the business field, less so in economics, the sponsor of the research, the supervisor, or the consumer of the final report may not understand a sophisticated method. Therefore, the researcher should try to design and to plan his or her research not only with an eye to his or her own qualifications and natural proclivities but also to the consumer of that research. Usually this consideration means that the final product must at least be readily understandable. Probably the vast majority of policy studies in business and government are written in straightforward English, minimizing mathematics or statistics in the text or consigning it to an appendix. For work with quantitative data and usage of the computer, the reader is referred to Chapters nine and ten of this book.

CHAPTER SUMMARY

The researcher who can choose his or her own topic is lucky and should make the most of this good fortune by a sound choice of topic. In a work situation, managers assign the topics for research according to the needs of the organization. They consider such factors as interest, knowledge, and motivation; and they examine such limitations as time, money, lack of training in some skill--for instance, statistics, accounting, or economic theory--lack of data available, and business proprietary secrets.

However, the researcher who can choose his or her own topic must realize that focusing on a specific problem from a broader field is part of the research process, a part that must be done effectively. One simple rule for beginners is to try not to select too large a problem.

In the selection of method or procedure to solve a problem, the big distinction is between quantitative methods and nonquantitative methods. A variety of research methods can be arranged on a rough spectrum of ten possibilities, ranging from nonquantitative to highly quantitative procedures. Cost-Benefit analysis, somewhere in the middle of the spectrum, is a useful method for researchers to consider.

DISCUSSION QUESTIONS

1. Select a topic from the current Wall Street Journal and discuss whether it is researchable in terms of guidelines and limitations. Defend your answer carefully with criteria selected by you.

2. Imagine you had a $10,000 budget to accomplish a chosen research task. Would your approach differ from an unfunded research project. How?

3. Compare typical topics chosen by students and those likely to be assigned a researcher in the work place. How do they differ?

4. Think tanks is a term applied to a certain type of organization. Identify and discuss this organization at some length.

5. When should you select quantitative methods to accomplish your research objective?

6. Discuss each of the following methods of analysis in terms of their advantages and disadvantages: a. historical method, b. comparative method, c. cost-benefit analysis, d. case studies.

7. If you select an exclusively quantitative topic, where do you get the data? Government data? Trade association data? Develop your own data? How about reliability of your choice? Other pros and cons?

NOTES

1. Carl Van Doren, "Choosing a Topic for Research," English Institute Annual, 1939 (New York: Columbia Univ. Press, 1940), pp. 29-30.

2. Das erste steht uns frei, beim zweiten sind wir knechte, Faust, 11. 1412.

3. Rudyard Kipling, "Just So Stories," in Collected Works, Vol. 12 (New York: AMS Press, 1975), p.77.

4. See for example, Howard W. Odum and K. Jocher, Introduction to Social Research (New York: Holt, 1929); Paul H. Rigby, Conceptual Foundations of Business Research (New York: John Wiley, 1965); Spiro J. Latsis, Method and Appraisal in Economics (London: Cambridge Univ. Press, 1976).

5. For an excellent introduction to historical method, see Jacques Barzun and Henry F. Graff, The Modern Researcher, 3rd ed. (New York: Harcourt Brace Jovanovich, 1977); also for a more advanced study, see George C. Iggers and Harold T. Parker, eds., International Handbook of Historical Studies: Contemporary Research and Theory (Westport, Conn.: Greenwood Press, 1979).

6. For a list of criteria in industry cases, see Everett E. Hagen, Handbook for Industry Studies, Cambridge, Mass.: Massachusetts Institute of Technology, 1953.

7. Charles J. Stokes, Managerial Economics (New York: Random House, 1969), pp. 181-86.

8. M.S. Feldstein, "Cost Benefit Analysis and Investment in the Public Sector," Public Administration, 42 (Winter 1964), 351-71.

9. Charles J. Hitch and R. McKeen, Economics of Defense in the Nuclear Age (Boston: Harvard Univ. Press, 1961).

10. F.J. Roethlisberger and W.J. Dickson, Management and the Worker (Cambridge, MA. Harvard Univ. Press, 1939).

11.   D. Kershaw and J. Fair, eds., The New Jersey Income Maintenance Experiment, Vol. 1 (New York: Academic Press, 1976); H.W. Watts and A. Rees, eds.,   The New Jersey Income Maintenance Experiment, Vols. 2 and 3 (New York: Academic Press, 1977).

12.   In the equation, $y = a + b\,x$, a and b are parameters; x and y are variables.

13.   Carl Christ, "Econometric Models, Aggregate," International Encyclopedia of the Social Sciences, Vol. 4, pp. 344-50.   This article has a good bibliography of basic works in the field.

14.   Charles W. Churchman, et.al., Introduction to Operations Research (New York: Wiley, 1957).

15.   Robert Dorfman, "Operations Research", American Economic Review, 50 (September 1960), 575-623.

16.   For a simple introduction, see William H. Miernik, The Elements of Input-Output Analysis (New York: Random House, 1965).

17.   Charles W. Churchman, The Systems Approach, rev. ed. (New York: Dell, 1979).

18.   William C. House, ed., Business Simulation for Decision Making (New York and Princeton: PBI, 1977).

4
RESEARCH DESIGN AND PLANNING

Once the broad topic is chosen and type of method visualized, an efficient plan of procedure is required. Broadly speaking, research is divided into three major activities: 1. the design and planning stage; 2. the execution of the research; and 3. the report of the findings. Each of these is an integral part of the research process, but beginning researchers often are impatient with spending much time on the first phase, which is the wrong attitude. Careful thought and planning at the outset is essential to a viable project. It cannot be emphasized enough how important the first phase is to the success of the whole undertaking.

Research design and planning is a large subject on which a considerable number of books or chapters have been written.[1] As the beginning researcher gains experience, he or she will wish to consult some of these more complex sources. This chapter has a more modest objective: It is designed to acquaint the researcher with some basic ideas and procedural principles involved in designing and planning a project.

What is research design? Basically it is a vision and a plan that plots how the project is to be carried out. In other terms, research design is a mental projection, a strategy and operational plan. It is established to find answers to the research problem, to the key question, or to the questions posed. Any research project requires considerable design whatever its method. As set forth in chapter three, a method may be largely descriptive, utilizing library, materials, case studies, or interviews; or it may be quantitative, deriving data from published statistics or collected in a survey. The data, however gathered, almost always verify or test an hypothesis or mathematical model and are usually processed on a computer using standard statistical methods.

Whatever the method, design is required. Like engineers who design a city metro system, the plan specifies what is to be done, how it is to be carried out, and the allocation of time and resources to attain the desired objectives. Fortunately, while engineering plans are often voluminous, the economic-business researcher's plan is usually stated in a document of reasonable length called a proposal. Developing a proposal even for simple research projects is standard operating procedure and an important step for a researcher. It embodies the design or plan of research that is to be used. The elements of the proposal will be covered in the last section of this chapter. A sample proposal is provided in the appendix.

Formulating the problem is a continuous process beginning with choice of broad area, doing some exploratory research, thinking hard, and narrowing or limiting the subject to some manageable research topic. A key step is to state the problem clearly or to define it; the next step is to set up the key question and the hypothesis to be tested. Then comes more detailed planning of the project, which entails review of relevant literature and other similar projects, collection of data, selection of method of analysis, a time frame of execution, cost estimate or budget, and an examination of the limitations and assumptions of the study.

For most people, however, this sequence is not as linear or straightforward as it sounds. In the first place, it is usually fused with exploratory research. That is, a researcher is thinking about the problem and doing some exploratory study at the same time. The exploratory study is needed as soon as the area is chosen to make the limiting process possible. The selection of the initial subdivision may change as more reading is performed. Moreover, the topic goes through a refining process. More precision in deciding just what one wants to do comes only with more reflection, reading, and discussion.

Sequence

Basically the guiding principles for designing the research are:

1. Choose a good subject.
2. Do broad exploratory research (reading and interviewing knowledgeable people).
3. Develop a set of possible questions, and narrow to a crucial question that poses a problem.
4. Ask more questions about the narrowed question and do some further exploratory work.
5. Identify and state the problem.
6. Phrase the problem as a key or central question with some supporting questions.
7. Set up a hypothesis to be tested.
8. Plan to test the hypothesis according to some systematic or recognized method.
9. Plan details of the work to be done in a time-frame and cost budget.

The first three steps have already been covered in the previous chapter. The importance and method of asking questions have also been stressed and illustrated with reference to identifying the problem of the study; however, asking questions is a continuing tool to develop still further one's thoughts and to make more precise just what one wants to do.

This continuing question concept is important to all research. The author remembers a distinguished graduate school professor reiterating: "If you raise the right questions, you get the right answers." Earlier it was noted that research was largely problem solving; it could equally be called "question raising." At least, the continual question asking is an essential tool in the research process. Questions are often classified as key or crucial questions and secondary or supporting questions. Obviously, in the plan of the research, the first type, usually having only one question, provides the main focus and is closely related to the statement of the problem. The supporting questions are important in the definition leading to, expanding, or amplifying the central idea. They are aimed at greater specificity, precision, and sometimes normative implications and prescriptions.[2]

At some point in the design and planning stage the researcher must identify and state the problem clearly (number five on the sequence list). This step is a landmark in the initial stage of design and planning. It means that the researcher has eliminated many extraneous possibilities and focused on what is a feasible, manageable research effort. In other words, the researcher has formulated the problem and now has enough direction to visualize some of the road ahead. Moreover, the statement of the problem establishes channel markers beyond which the researcher should not sail. A well=formulated statement will also save time and effort in the long run.

Generally speaking, the identification and formulation statement by the researcher is the most important step in the whole planning process. For instance, a researcher may have decided to work on Reverend Sullivan's activities in the Opportunities Industrialization Center (OIC). The statement of the problem might be:

> Reverend Sullivan's OIC program is an effort to develop and train minority group labor for commercial and industrial enterprise. It is spreading to many cities, but it has special problems to be overcome before effectiveness is assured.

On a somewhat more advanced level, another typical statement might be:

> The Small business Administration has helped a number of small business people who have failed. The question what happened to such business people after they went out of business and whether they are again acting as enterpreneurs or might want to try again is important for policy purposes.

A statement involving sales and its responsiveness to advertising expenditure might be:

> The sales of this firm are not responding satisfactorily to expenditures . This inelastic response may be due to a number of factors. This study will attempt to determine the nature and extent of the causes

All of these examples may have been rather general, they they are typical statements in the research design process. They have given the research a more specific identity and advanced it on the road to developing the hypothesis and collecting the data. Moreover, the statement of the probelm is equally important for subjects developed primarily through the use of library materials or based on empirical or original data collected from direct evidence.

HYPOTHESIS BUILDING

Once the statement of the problem has been formulated, the next step is to look further at the materials. Broadly speaking, there are two paths: library research and field study. The first involves examining what others have done, written, or said about the problem; the second involves interviews, questionaires, or direct observation. These two paths are by no means exclusive. Typically, experienced researchers try to survey literature of a problem and study available published statistics, case studies, and other materials before they launch into their field work to collect evidence. These channels and sources will be dealt with more thoroughly in the next few chapters.

At this point we are on the way to forming a working hypothesis. The hypothesis differs from the statement of the problem in that it is an educated guess on the solution or causes of that problem; it is a tentative answer to the key question. To arrive at the hypothesis, the researcher needs more thought, more questions, more preliminary reading, and some interviews in order to make an informed judgment. The researcher is involved in a bootstrap raising effort: with greater familiarity of the subject the more likely the researcher's working hypothesis will be correct; with a good hypothesis the more effective will be his or her research.

Library

Doing library research to collect information means to gather some preliminary materials in which the focus has already been achieved. To begin this method, first check with the reference librarians and tell them what you are doing. They may offer some invaluable suggestions. Conventional tools like the book catlog and the Reader's Guide to Periodical Literature for journal articles may be already familiar to the neophyte, but other more precise information sources are appropriate. In the business and economic field there are specialized tools of research that may be far more useful. The Business Periodicals Index (BPI), the Journal of Economic Literature (JEL) or the Public Affairs Information Service (PAIS) are specialized indexes specifically designed to help the researcher in this field. A more clever approach is to find a bibliography already complied on the subject of your research. It is a good rule of thumb to assume that at least one bibliography on your ballpark subject has already been compiled and published by some other researcher. For example, on the subject of minority business enterprise, the Institute for Minority Business Education at Howard University publishes a bibliography called The Negro in the Field of Business kept current with supplements.[3] If one did not know about this list, it could be found under an appropriate subject heading in an annual list of bibliographies called The Bibliographic Index. The procedure of checking with the librarian first would probably orient one in this direction.

Once you obtain some citations, you should look them over quickly, read and think about the problem, and develop a working hypothesis. It should be noted, however, all this work is preliminary to setting up the formal hypothesis for the full-scale study.

Direct Data Collection Path

A similar quick preliminary investigation aimed to develop a working hypothesis should be conducted if one plans field work. An interview or two with knowledgeable persons in the field may yield a good guess as to the solution or cause of the stated problem. Similiarly, a rough preliminary questionaire tested on a few friends may yield valuable insights. Little by little the hypothesis should take shape.

The Hypothesis

What is the hypothesis? Essentially it is a theory explaining what the causes of the problem are or how the problem can be solved. It is a conjecture, an educated guess on what the solution of the problem or the answer to the key question is. The hypothesis should be distinguished from an assumption, which does not require proof. Economic rationality, for example, that people try to get the greatest yield for the least cost is an example of an assumption in business and economics. In contrast, the hypothesis is a theory to be tested in the course of the investigation. The reader should go back to chapter one and reread the distinction between deductive and inductive theory. In particular, the quotation from Darwin should be very instructive in grasping the role of the hypothesis.

The hypothesis is arrived at often by working through a checklist of possible explanations. Indeed, such a checklist may be called a list of working hypotheses. From this list the most resonable or logical may be taken as the hypothesis that is the key idea or focus in the investigation.

Method

The selection of method develops concomitantly with focusing the problem. Form reading chapters two and three, the researcher should know what types of methods are available. While looking for material, consciously or unconsciously, the researcher thinks of how to attack the problem. As was noted earlier, his or her proficiency in technique will influence the choice. A researcher confident in his or her knowledge of mathematical and statistical tools will seek problems that lend themselves to solution by quantitative means. Without these skills or a shaky command of them, a researcher will try less rigorous methods.

Whatever method is chosen, it must be visualized, specified, and detailed. The researcher design includes both specification of the method of the proposed study and a fairly detailed plan for carrying it out. The planning should be the most efficient way to attain the objectives and obtain a successful research projects. Lastly, the method to be used is incoporated as one important element in the research proposal described in the next section.

Tentative Outline One more step remains in the first phase--the planning and design stage, or the making of a tentative outline to proceed into the full=scale investigation of the subject. This outline should be considered very rough and preliminary and subject to change as more evidence is collected. It may compare to a kind of scaffolding that engineers use to build structures like houses: With scaffolding the house can be erected; may change from time to time and ultimately be removed when the work is completed. So with the outline. It should not be regarded as a fixed Procrustean bed but a flexible tool that will give direction to the research as it proceeds.

Obviously, construction of a more effective outline requires learning more abou the problem and its logical parts. There are some common features of outlines. All have an introduction, a body consisting of some chapters to answer the questions about the problem, and a set of conclusions. The final outline (usually changed a few times) will become the basis for the table of contents and the structure of the paper that reports on the research performed. However,it should be emphasized that the outline is not the same as the table of contents of the final report.

THE RESEARCH PROPOSAL

The research steps in design and planning that have been covered should be summarized for each research project in a research proposal. Sometimes called a prospectus, the research proposal is a statement of the research plan. It serves two functions: first, it is a guide for the researcher in doing the study; second, it is in the nature of an offer that can be accepted by people for whom the research is conducted. These would be the sponsor if funds are solicited or the supervisor for nonfunded research. In a company or agency, proposals may be quite informal, such as a letter or memorandum. If it is an external proposal (solicited or unsolicited), the proposal is carefully set out, often to the specifications of the funding agent.

Student research proposals can be quite elaborate for graduate students planning a master's thesis or a doctoral dissertation. For undergraduate students, constructing a simple proposal is appropriate for practice and familiarity with this universal tool of research projects and "grantsmanship." It is a systematic way to formulate the plans for the project and get them on paper. Writing this blueprint forces the researcher to think and plan ahead.

The proposal should cover some or all of the following elements:

1. Title and backround statement

2. Statement of the problem and its importance

3. Some key questions and supporting or secondary questions

4. Hypothesis

5. The method of research and analysis

6. Limitations and assumptions

7. Resources and time required

8. Results anticipated

9. Budget

10. Qualifications or curriculum vita of the researcher(s)

The proposal is usually accompanied with the tentative outline and a preliminary or working bibliography or a tentative questionaire for gathering information and data. Beginning researchers should be aware that the professional proposal, especially those soliciting external funds, will be much more elaborate. Typically, an introduction sets forth the problem; then selections on methods and techniques, availabilities of space and equipment, qualifications and experience of the researchers, a time frame of execution, and a detailed budget follow. It often takes much time and considerable skill to write such a proposal. The funding agency often specifies just how this document should look. An example of the U.S. Air Force's Office of Scientific Research is provided in Figure 4-1 for the budget, and a sample proposal made to that office is in appendix B.

FIGURE 4-1

SAMPLE COST ESTIMATE

(Each year's cost should be estimated separately. This form
illustrates the degree of detail considered essential for evaluation
purposes. Other formats are equally acceptable provided the same
degree of detail is shown. Departures from the estimate or negotiated
amount for each category are permitted as indicated in the brochure.)

RESEARCH PERIOD _____ to _____	AFOSR Support	Cost-Sharing (Non-Federal Support)	TOTAL PROJECT COST
1. SALARIES & WAGES			
Principal Investigator - Dr. W. T. Doan			
One-fourth time acad. yr. (¼ x $12,000/9 mo.)		$ 3,000	$ 3,000
Full-time summer, 2 mos. (2/9 x $12,000/9 mo.)	$ 2,666		2,666
Research Assistants(2 Grad. Students)	6,750		6,750
One-half time,9 mos.-$225/mo. Full-time summer, 3 mos. – $450/mo.			
Laboratory Technichian - Mr. John Hall			
One-fourth time, 12 mos. (¼ x $6,000 annual salary)	1,500		1,500
TOTAL SALARIES & WAGES	$ 12,916	$ 7,500	$ 20,416
2. PERMANENT EQUIPMENT			
Standard Equipment Signal Generator (ABC Model 606A)	$ 1,350		$ 1,350
H.F. Receiver (ABC Model 880)	1,575		1,575
Oecilloscope (XYZ Model 130C)	695		695
Transistor Curve Tracer (Specific model not yet determined. This is best estimate based on present knowldege).	1,075		1,075
Special Equipment None			
TOTAL EQUIPMENT	$ 4,695		$ 4,695

3. EXPENDABLE SUPPLIES AND
MATERIALS
If such a relationship is
feasible, substantiate this
area from experience gained
over a previous grant or
similar project.

RESEARCH PERIOD ___ to ___	AFOSR Support	Cost-Sharing (Non-Federal Support)	TOTAL PROJECT COST
Liquid helium (60 liters @ $6.00 per liter)	$ 360		$ 360
Glassware (Prior yr. actual expenditure - 300)	320		320
Misc. (based on historical experience)	200		200
TOTAL EXPENDABLE SUPPLIES AND MATERIALS	$ 880		$ 880

4. TRAVEL (indicate destination, number of days per trip, cost per trip, and purpose of anticipated travel.)

	AFOSR		TOTAL
2 trips to AFOSR in Washington D.C. @ $150/trip (to discuss and present results of research	$ 300		$ 300
2 trips to East Coast @ $175/trip (to attend the American Physical Society meeting)	350		350
TOTAL TRAVEL	$ 650		$ 650

5. PUBLICATION & REPORT COSTS

8 pages in Physical Review Journal @ $60/page	$ 480		$ 480
TOTAL PUBLICATION COSTS	$ 480		$ 480

6. COMPUTER COSTS (Show name and model number of computer, number of hours, hourly rate and indicate if rate has approval of DCAA Auditor)

IBM 7094, 20 hours @ $210/hr. Auditor approved	$ 4,200		$ 4,200
TOTAL COMPUTER COSTS	$ 4,200		$ 4,200

7. EMPLOYEE BENEFITS (Indicates rate and basis for estimate)

7.2% of Salaries & Wages (Rate was approved by DCAA Auditor)	$ 930	$ 540	$ 1,470
TOTAL EMPLOYEE BENEFITS	$ 930	$ 540	$ 1,470

8. OTHER DIRECT COSTS (Itemize and show basis for anticipated direct costs not included above)

RESEARCH PERIOD _____ to _____	AFOSR Support	Cost-Sharing (Non-Federal Support)	TOTAL PROJECT COST
Consultant (4 days at $50 per day	$ 200		$ 200
TOTAL OTHER DIRECT COSTS	$ 200		$ 200
TOTAL DIRECT COSTS	$24,951	$ 8,040	$ 32,991

9. INDIRECT COSTS (Indicates percentage and base)

Current provisional rate – 55% of Salaries & Wages AFOSR Support 56% x $12,916	$ 7,233		$ 7,233
Cost Sharing 56% x $7,600		$ 4,200	
TOTAL ESTIMATED COSTS	$32,184	$ 12,240	$ 44,424

One element from the more elaborate professional proposal can be recommended for beginning researchers: the time plan or time schedule. A reseacher should try to lay out a plan of the time required, dated from when the work began. The accompanying schedule, called the GANTT chart after the American engineer H.C. Gantt who devised it, is a handy device to visualize (see figure 4-2) tasks and time involved. The PERT diagram also serves this function but is used for larger projects.

FIGURE 4-2
GANTT CHART SCHEDULING
RESEARCH

WEEKS OF THE PROJECT

0 2 4 6 8 10 12 14

1. Choosing the Problem
2. Statement of Problem
3. Preliminary Work to Hypothesis
4. Plan Research/Develop Proposal
5. Develop Questionaire
6. Pre-Test and Revise Questionaire
7. Apply Questionaires
8. Record and Analyze Results
9. Write Up Results
10. Rewriting to Final Typing

CHAPTER SUMMARY

The research process is divided into three phases: 1) design and planning; 2) carrying out the research; and 3) reporting the research. The first phase is the most important, but it is also the most neglected by beginning researchers.

The research design-plan usually embodied in a formal, written proposal--consists of several items that formalize and focus the research problem; it also plans what is to be done to solve this problem over the time span alloted to accomplished the job. After some exploratory research and interviews with knowledgeable persons, the researcher should have a possible focus on a significant research problem from the large subject. When the researcher discovers this focus, he or she should write a proposal. Though proposals may be simple or very elaborate, they should contain some or all of the following elements:

1. Backround or setting showing importance of the proposed study

2. Statement of the problem

3. Key question and supporting questions

4. Hypothesis to to tested

5. Method of procedure and analysis

6. Time plan

7. Likely results anticipated

8. Budget

9. Vita(e) of the researcher(s) showing qualifications to do the work.

Proposals may contain some plan for the execution fo the project in a time frame, accomplished by dividing the work into phases: Phase I, lasting so many weeks or months, might be devoted to a literature search; Phase II, data collection and computer processing; Phase III, analysis and report writing. A GANTT chart or PERT diagram may be shown to plan and control the execution of the research effort.

DISCUSSION QUESTIONS

1. What does exploratory research mean? How does it differ from the research testing the hypothesis?

2. What is meant by model building in research? How does it differ from hypothesis testing?

3. Why is the BPI such a useful tool for exploratory research? What other such handy tools exist?

4. Should your proposal include a statement of the need of your effort? Why?

5. Why are questions so important in research? Is it true that questions can be formulated differently, more sharply or pointedly?

6. What does the term empirical mean? How does it relate to the deductive-inductive method dichotomy discussed in chapter one?

7. What are the advantages and disadvantages of a GANTT chart?

NOTES

1. See, for example, Robert Ferber and P.J. Verdoorn, Research Methods in Economics and Business (New York: McMillan, 1962), pt.3 ch.2; Edwin E. Nemmers and J.H. Myers, Business Research (New York: McGraw Hill, 1966), ch.2; Paul H. Rigby, Conceptual Foundations of Business Research (New York: Wiley, 1965), especially ch. 5.

2. The term normative refers to the idea of a norm or standard and what should be done to meet that standard. Normative contrasts with the word "positive," which emphasizes an objective approach treating social and economic phenomena like a machine without making value judgements. Milton Friedman, Essays in Positive Economics (Chicago: Chicago Univ. Press. 1953).

3. Thelma Halliday, Negro in the Field of Business (Washington, D.C.: Howard University, 1971). This source is kept up to date by periodic supplements.

5
SEARCHING THE LITERATURE

> When I want to discover something, I begin by reading
> everything that has been done along that line in the
> past; I see what has been accomplished by great labor
> and expense in the past; I gather the data of many
> thousands of experiments as a starting point, and
> then make many thousands more.
>
> Thomas A. Edison[1]

If America'a most famous inventor attached such importance to searching literature, any researcher should likewise do careful searches on what others have done. Logically it is the better to do a broad literature search first to be sure that the proposed research is not duplicating any work already completed. This literature falls into two categories: nonstatistical materials or literature and statistical data. The first category involves locating and reviewing other studies appearing in written treatises, textbooks, journal articles, newspaper accounts, government documents, miscellaneous pamphlets, company reports, and even unpublished materials. The second includes various statistical data collected by government or private agencies. Therefore, this chapter will explain the search of analytical materials other than statistics, popularly called, the literature search. The next chapter will cover important statistical sources.

LITERATURE SEARCH

The advantages of a literature search are clear. The researcher may find studies or sufficient data that make further expenditure of time and expense unnecessary, or he or she may discover methods and techniques used by others. Ideas and aspects that have not occured to the researcher may also be turned up. In addition, data sources, more up=to=date information, and the ideas of recognized authorities are obtained by the literature search; or blind alleys found by others may be avoided.

Searches of sources may be divided into unpublished and published data. Unpublished data exist as records in firms, government agencies, or even belong to private persons. The records are often overlooked or neglected in research, but such internal records can be very important. They are, however, difficult to obtain, often being classified as confidential, proprietary, or privileged information. Firms frequently fear that competitors will use this kind of information against them, and the management's permission to use these records may not easily be obtained. Unpublished data from trade associations, government agencies (federal, state, and local) and nonprofit organizations may exist and be more readily available than from firms or individuals. They are often aggregated data that a trade associations releases without disclosure of sensitive firm information.

SPECIAL LIBRARIES

Usually, published data are more important for most research purposes and the library is the principal place to locate such information. But before rushing blindly into the nearest library, it is wise to look for one devoted to the broad subject area in which your topic falls. Every metropolitan area has special libraries that may be ideal for concentrated research efforts. These libraries are often not well known but can be easily located by using proper directories. The Special Libraries Association and other sources publish directories of special libraries, indexed geographically and by subject.² They even publish a special volume on business and law libraries.³ The librarian usually grants permission to bonafide researchers to use these special libraries and collections. Ask the reference librarian in your local library about these directories of special collections.

BIBLIOGRAPHIES

If the researcher cannot locate a special library or finds it inconvenient to use the next best method is to try to locate a bibliography on the subject of the proposed research at your general or public library. If a bibliography is already compiled, reasonably up-to-date, and easily located, the researcher is miles ahead of slowly compiling his or her own list. At least for a preliminary survey, an existing bibliography, especially if annotated, is an excellent start.

Reference librarians may suggest how to find such bibliographies. More directly, book-length bibliographies may be located in the card catalog under the subject heading followed by the word "bibliography." For example, Technology Transfer--Bibliography could be found behind the cards with only the main subject heading. Another way is to use the Bibliograhic Index, a bibliography of bibliographies, which is in virtually every library. Often bibliographies are in textbooks or treatises on the subject. Encyclopedia articles, always a good introduction to any subject, usually have short lists of leading authorities at the end of the articles. The more scholarly or scientific journals contain articles with additional heavy documentation. In a nutshell, the fastest way to collect research is to begin looking for existing bibliographies at the outset of any research effort. Obviously, it is wasteful to compile your own bibliography separately, if much of it can be taken from one already compiled.

The one big drawback in using a published bibliography is it may be out-of-date. This flaw can be offset by finding the publications made before the publication date. Normally, a list issued in say, 1975 would have been compiled a year or two earlier. Hence, to supplement a 1975 bibliography, one would try to go to a 1973 issue or even an earlier one for a large work.

The location of an up-to-date bibliography is good, but the researcher must select references and build his or her own. Each book that appears revelant should be entered on a three-by-five card in complete bibliographic form. It is very annoying to try to cite a reference in the writing stage and find incomplete information on the card. Also, the book's library call number should be written accurately on the corner of the card so that it can be found again if needed, which often happens.

HOW TO USE A LIBRARY

Assuming that the researcher is not so lucky as to have found a special library or a special bibliography in the proposed field of investigation, then the researcher must develop his or her sources from scratch. Broadly speaking, four major categories exist to aid this search: periodical or newspaper articles, government documents, and research reports, such as theses. Each of these categories has its indexes and special subcategories about which the researcher must have at least some rudimentary knowledge. The researcher must also employ a search strategy: decide which category to explore first. Most people typically begin by going directly to the card catalog, which may not always be the best first step; still let us examine this method first.

Book Catalogs

To locate books or to discover whether a book has been published, we can use three systems: the library catalog, the Cummulative Book Index, and the National Union Catalog. The library catalog shows what books are available in the library being used; the others indicate whether a book has been published and a copy exists in another library in the United States.

Whether in card file or in book form, the library catalog shows the books available in the library or the library system of which it is a part. Each book is usually listed in three ways: by author, by title, and by subject. Typically the researcher is initially interested in the last category; later, he or she may need to spotcheck an author or title for verification or to see what other books that author may have published. An example of an author card (Library of Congress system) is shown below in Figure 5-1:

```
BV 5083
   .M29
    1973   Martin, Francis, 1930-
                When God speaks to His people : the communal gift of dis-
            cernment / by Francis Martin. — Gloucester : Fellowship Press,
            1973.

                35 p. : 18 cm. — (Flame series ; 2)          GB73-18385

            Reprinted from Donum Dei, Ottawa.
            ISBN 0-9500814-2-6 : £0.13




                1. Discernment of spirits.    I. Title.
            BV5083.M29   1973              234'.1              75-320770
                                                                 MARC

            Library of Congress              75
```

Note that the form is close to the simplified form recommended by style manuals for bibliographies.

It is not necessary to discuss Library of Congress cards in connection with note-taking for bibliographies and annotations and other minutiae, but at this point a word of caution on subject headings may be offered. Professors of research classes often hear the sad story that the student could find nothing in the library catalog on his or her investigation subject, because often the student had been looking under the wrong subject headings. The Library of Congress publishes a list of subject headings, cognate subject headings, and cross references used in most library catalogs in this country.[4] but if the subject is highly specialized or very new, there may be no books on it either in the available library or even published in English.

To check whether any books in English exist on a particular subject, the researcher next consults the Cumulative Book Index[5] This authoritative publication lists all books in the English language not only in the United States but in the rest of the English-speaking world. As in the library catalog, books are categorized by author, by title, and by subject.

If a researcher finds a book he or she wants and the local library and other nearby libraries do not have it, how can it be obtained? the National Union Catalog is a compilation of books in major libraries all over the United States.[6] It is possible the desired books can be obtained from a nearby big library on interlibrary loan. It should be stressed that reference librarians should be consulted in this and other efforts of this kind. There are other important catalogs--such as Books in Print, Subject Guide to Books in Print, and Publishers Weekly--which show if a book is still in print (in other words, the publisher still sells it) or if a new edition has been published.

Articles in Periodicals and Newspapers

For up-to-date subject matter the researcher is often advised to find some good articles rather than books. Articles will often review certain essentials pertaining to the field (referred to as "reviews of the literature"), and frequently they have citations from leading studies. Broadly speaking, periodical literature may be divided into three groups: (1) popular and news articles; (2) scholarly or scientific contributions; (3) specialized literature. Indexes exist to all three classes. All these tools are essential keys for anyone undertaking a research project.

For popular literature the well-known Readers Guide to Periodical Literature is found in every public and university library. It indexes by subject the articles in popular magazines such as Time and Newsweek and includes business and economic journals such as Business Week and Fortune. If one knows nothing about the topic, the Reader's Guide may be a good place to start; but its journalistic and popular articles limit its use in serious research.

For newspaper accounts, which can include quite lengthy articles, The New York Times Index has the widest coverage; but these reports are often superficial. Like Facts on File, it helps establish the date some event happened.[8] Other newspapers have indexes, two of the best known being the Washington Post and The Wall Street Journal.

The Vertical File Index is a general index guide for pamphlet materials. It is named after a file often maintained by reference and research librarians covering clippings, pamphlets, and other ephemeral materials, which can often be had for the asking.[9]

For scholarly publications in business, economics, and public affairs--the index closest to the popular category is the Public Affairs Information Service or PAIS, as it is often called.[10] This index is also found in most libraries and covers smaller, less-known journals in English--books, government documents, pamphlets, and other more specialized materials. One drawback to this source is that the journal articles or pamphlets indexed may not be easily available in general libraries.

The Social Sciences Index is one of two new indexes superceding the Social Sciences and Humanities Index (formerly International Index).[11] Found in larger and specialized libraries, it covers more scholarly or scientific periodical articles. It is good for economics, public administration, area studies, and other social science fields. These articles are often the most thoughtful and original ones available, but they may be exceedingly technical for the beginning researcher.

The Social Sciences Citation Index is subtitled: An international multidisciplinary index to the literature of the social, behavioral, and related sciences.[12] This heavy title is matched by heavy coverage of about 2,500 journals, making it the widest indexing of any service. It lists publications cited as well as original articles, and with this source researchers can trace the influence of given writers in their fields. The SSCI is found only in the largest and richest research libraries.

Specialized Fields

The third category, the specialized indexes, may be of most interest to the researcher. There are a large number of indexes to periodical literature in many specialized fields such as art, education, engineering, and technology. The special fields considered in this book, economics and business, are also well represented.

For economics a basic source of older articles appearing between 1896 and 1968 is the The Index of Economic Journals which has both subject and author indexes.[13] The Journal of Economic Literature, also published by the American Economic Association, is the more current journal index.[14] Though it has several sections, the third section, formally called Journal of Economic Abstracts, lists the Tables of Contents for 200 current economic journals and all the articles (some with abstracts) in them. The International Bibliography of Economics is a comprehensive listing of articles from several thousand journals all over the world, including books and government publications. However, it may be too scholarly for beginning researchers.[15]

For business administration the most important index is the Business Periodicals Index[16] Published monthly and cumulated quarterly and annually, it indexes English language periodicals in major business fields. it is the first source for looking into any business subject; but for advanced work in any subfield, it will be necessary to consult specialized scholarly bibliographic and abstracting research tools. For example, if one was working on an accounting topic, the Accountant's Index[17] or Accounting Articles[18] might be used. For the personnel field, it would be wise to check the Personnel Management Abstracts, which has both abstracts and an index of periodical literature.[19] Librarians will help the researcher in locating such keys to specialized fields.

For current topics, the Wall Street Journal Index[20] provides an entrance into the most inportant business newspaper. This newspaper's report may be quite lengthy and as valuable as the New York Times accounts, but more business-oriented. Like all newspaper accounts, however, they tend to be journalistic, impressionistic, and not very scholarly. It must be used only as one source of information.

F & S Index of Corporations and Industries (F & S)[21] is the best index for current information on companies and industries. It also covers articles on companies; foreign companies are listed in its companion index, F & S Index International. These indexes are available as computerized data bases, called Predicasts Terminal System.

Government Documents   There are another basic class of literature sources for the researcher. For a systematic approach to what the Federal government has done on the subject studied, the researcher should start with the Monthly Catalog of U.S. Government Publications, which indexes documents from all branches of the Federal government.[22] For current research topics, it is advisable to begin with the current year or month and work backwards. It is arranged alphabetically by the issuing agency, but the researcher typically looks in the subject index. There is a subject for each month and a cummulative annual index for each year. There are also indexes for every ten years, and in the future, there may be five-year indexes. For older documents Carrolton Press, a commercial firm, publishes a subject index covering the period 1893-1971.[23] In these subject indexes one uses the Superintendent of Documents number and the publication date as the key to find the documents (similar to a library call number).

As an illustration, suppose a researcher is searching the topic "Technology Transfer." As he looks in the Carrolton Press subject index, he finds an entry, "Technology Transfer, bibliography (1971), 8477." Remembering how valuable a bibliography already compiled can be, he then goes to the year 1971 of the Monthly Catalog and finds that the number 8477 falls in the May 1971 issue on page 73, where the full citation of the bibliography is found.[24]

Several observations must be made about the Monthly Catalog as an approach to government documents. First the Monthly Catalog does not list or index every federal government document ever published. For publications before 1895, there are other indexes. Even currently, for one reason or another, the publications of some government agencies are not listed. Government documents processed by mimeo-graphing, multigraphing, and other non-print methods might be found easier by writing to the information section of the government agency generating the documents.

Many government agencies issue their own catalogs and indexes of what they publish. For business and economics, one of the most important indexes is issued by the Department of Commerce, United States Department of Commerce Publications.[25] For other agencies, A Directory of Information Resources in the U.S. Federal Government can give much information on what is available.[26]

These suggestions barely scratch the surface of government documents as a research source. State governments also issue documents with indexes. There is the NTIS or National Technical Information Service, which is a control center for all unclassified government-sponsored research reports. Its basic publications, <u>Government Reports Announcements</u> and <u>Government Reports Index</u>, provide entry into the world of the latest research in a particular area.[27] The researcher who seeks government publications should find a good documents librarian and a depository library of government documents located in universities and major libraries in every region of the United States.

Dissertations

An often neglected source of original research are doctoral dissertations. Two dissertation sources exist: <u>American Doctoral Dissertations</u>,[28] which is a complete listing of American and Canadian doctoral dissertations by subject matter; and <u>Dissertation Abstracts International</u>, which as its name implies, lists the abstracts.[29] The <u>Comprehensive Dissertation Index</u> is also an excellent many-volume index through 1972, of which volumes 25-26 are <u>Business and Economics</u>[30] There are also specialized lists of dissertations, such as the one published annually in the University of Chicago's <u>Journal of Business</u> and the <u>American Economic Review</u>, both arranged by subject. Other specialized lists on transportation, finance, industrial relations, and others exist.[31]

As an approach to sources, this dissertation study is probably best used in conjunction with other approaches. Yet if the researcher can locate such a study on a subject close to his or her own research, there is the advantage of easily obtaining a bibliography and probably a literature review. It goes without saying, that any dissertation cited must be credited in the same way as a published document.

Other Sources

The five main research approaches to large classes of literature--books, articles, government documents, dissertations, and research reports--do not exhaust the types of sources and research approaches possible. There are also encyclopedias, handbooks, directories, and miscellaneous pamphlets--which may be an additional approach for some special type of research. Lastly, general guides to reference books may uncover very valuable guides.

Encyclopedias are a useful approach to research. In addition to general encyclopedias (<u>Britannica</u>, <u>Americana</u>, etc.), specialized encyclopedias are of great value. For economic research, the <u>International Encyclopedia of the Social Sciences</u> is very good for almost any topic in this area.[32] The older edition, <u>The Encyclopedia of the Social Sciences</u>, published in the 1930's is still a valuable source for many subjects, especially of an historical nature.[33]

In the general business field, there is no encyclopedia comparable to these large sets, but there are dictionaries that may have lengthy articles in each field. Prentice Hall's <u>Encyclopedia Dictionary of Business Finance</u> is a good example of a one-volume effort that contain many entries of considerable length.[34] It is, however, specialized in business finance. Perhaps the most general book for business is the <u>Encyclopedia of Business Information Sources</u>, though this book is not an encyclopedia but a guide to sources.[35] It lists basic sources of information under each topic heading, including source books, periodicals, organizations, directories, bibliographies, handbooks, and guides.

Handbooks and Guides

Handbooks is another category of volumes useful to the researcher, particularly at the outset of the research. One example is McGraw-Hill's Dictionary of Modern Economics, which is subtitled a handbook of Terms and Organizations.[36] There are handbooks in almost every major business field that usually offer a good first approach to a subject. Typically, this class of literature provides not only a brief introduction to the subject but also some basic references. For example, if one were interested in the concept of "Automation," the McGraw-Hill Dictionary refers us to a half=dozen citations, among which Norbert Wiener's The Human Use of Human Beings is a standard book. Thus, the researcher would have acquired a basic source early in his or her research effort.

If the researcher does not know or cannot easily find a handbook in a field, he or she can use several general guides to literature in business and economics. In addition to Wasserman's Encyclopedia of Business Sources, any researcher should know and use two general guides: Eugene Sheehy's Guide to Reference Books and Carl White's Sources of Information in the Social Sciences.[37] Both of these books contain major divisions on the field of economics and business.

There are also several special guides to business information, the best known being Edwin Coman's Sources of Business Information[38], which includes a more up-to-date successor volume by Lorna Daniells. Up-to-date is a relative term. As new books and editions that supersede those listed in the guides are always being published, the researcher should be very conscious of the date on the volume being used.

More Approaches

A researcher may still use other approaches to sources--as, for example, directories, atlases, company reports, business and financial services, marketing guides, and pamphlets collected in a vertical file.[39] However, these techniques are not so general an approach to the literature as the foregoing. Figure 5-2 provides a summary of the paths into the literature search. In practice, most people will use some combination of the approaches.

Supplemental Bibliography in the Appendix

The researcher will find a further list of selected basic sources of business and economic information in Appendix B. The reference librarians of the Main Reading Room of the Library of Congress prepared this list.[40] Though it duplicates some sources covered in this chapter, this supplemental bibliography provides many other fields and fundamental books not covered in the text. It is especially good for finance and investment, and the annotations for all sources are frequently more extensive than comparable discussion in the text. We may conclude by commenting that if a source is not on this list frm our national library, the researcher probably has not missed much.

FIGURE 5-2
ALTERNATIVE PATHS TO LITERATURE SEARCH

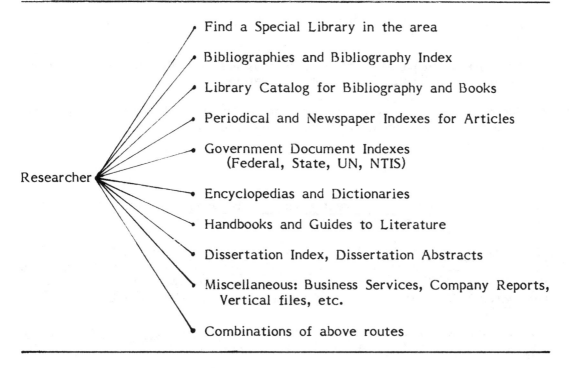

Researcher

Find a Special Library in the area

Bibliographies and Bibliography Index

Library Catalog for Bibliography and Books

Periodical and Newspaper Indexes for Articles

Government Document Indexes
(Federal, State, UN, NTIS)

Encyclopedias and Dictionaries

Handbooks and Guides to Literature

Dissertation Index, Dissertation Abstracts

Miscellaneous: Business Services, Company Reports,
Vertical files, etc.

Combinations of above routes

CHAPTER SUMMARY

For all types of research, searching the literature is a mandatory first step. Though several reasons for doing this search first are given, clearly "reinventing the wheel" is honored nowhere. Special libraries, special bibliographies, and bibliographic indexes are excellent seven=league boots for researchers. Other standard routes are the library catalog and periodical or newspaper indexes. Books may be outdated, up-to-date articles may be too fragmentary, and newspapers may be superficial journalism. Government document indexes are gold mines if understood. Handbooks and encyclopedia articles are often a good way to start. Dissertation indexes and miscellaneous channels of annual reports, telephone books, vertical files, and pamphlets are frequently good channels. Some combination may be best. Above all, use your reference librarians--their knowledge is encyclopedic.

DISCUSSION QUESTIONS

1. When should you go to a special library? How do you know where they are? If after finding one you want, you discover it is in a city 50 miles away. What can you do?

2. Published bibliographies are supposed to be preferred first step. How are they found?

3. One student says, "What's wrong with going to the encyclopedia as I used to do in high school?" What is wrong or right with this procedure?

4. At one point this chapter discusses <u>dissertation indexes</u>. If a researcher finds a dissertation, is there a danger of plagiarism?

5. Discuss the use of unpublished data. What types are found and where? Are they easy to use?

6. The <u>PAIS</u> is supposed to be good for obscure or little known publications? Is that an ambivalent value for a researcher? Why?

7. Suppose your office wants you to find out data on the decline or growth of American productivity. Where would you start?

NOTES

1. J. Eigelberner, <u>The Investigation of Business Problems</u> (New York: McGraw-Hill, 1962), p. 116.

2. <u>Directory of Special Libraries and Information Centers</u>, 3rd ed., 2 vols. (Detroit: Gale Research, 1974); <u>Subject Collections</u> (New York and London: R.R. Bowker, 1974); American Library Association, <u>Amercian Library Directory</u>, 29th ed. (New York and London: R.R. Bowker, 1974).

3. Section on business and finance libraries in <u>Subject Directory of Special Libraries and Information Centers</u> (Detroit: Gale Research 1974).

4. U.S. Library of Congress, <u>Subject Headings</u>, 9th. ed., 2 vols. (Washington, D.C.: Library of Congress, 1980).

5. <u>Cumulative Book Index: World List of Books in the English Language</u> (New York: H.W. Wilson, 1928-date).

6. <u>The National Union Catalog</u>, (Washington, D.C.: Library of Congress, 1958-date).

7. <u>Books in Print</u> (New York: Bowker, 1948-date); see also annual and companion volume, <u>Subject guide to Books in Print</u>; <u>Publishers Weekly</u> (New York: Bowker, 1872-date); and companion volume, <u>Publishers Trade List Annual</u>.

8. <u>Facts on File</u> (New York: 1940-date) A looseleaf weekly, with annual volumes.

9. <u>Vertical File Index</u> (New York: Wilson, 1935-date).

10. <u>Public Affairs Information Service</u> (New York: 1915-date). Weekly cumulations, annual volumes. <u>Cumulation Index</u> (1915-1974), 15 vols.

11. <u>Social Sciences Index</u> (New York: Wilson, 1974-date) a quarterly with annual cumulations.

12. <u>Social Sciences Citation Index</u> (Philadelphia: Institute for Scientific Information, 1973-date).

13. American Economic Association, <u>Index of Economic Journals</u>, 10 vols. (Homewood, Ill.: Irwin, 1961-68).

14. American Economic Association, Journal of Economic Literature (Nashville: 1963-date). Volumes 1-6 , 1963-68 are called Journal of Economic Abstracts.

15. International Bibliography of Economics (Chicago: Aldine, 1962-date).

16. Business Periodicals Index (New York: H.W. Wilson, 1958-date).

17. Accountant's Index (New York: American Institute of Certified Public Accountants, 1921-date).

18. Accounting Articles (Chicago: Commerce Clearing House, 1965-date).

19. Personnel Management Abstracts (Ann Arbor, Mich.: Univ. of Michigan Press, 1955-date).

20. Wall Street Journal Index. (Princeton: Dow Jones, 1958-date). It is divided in two sections: one alphabetically by the name of the corporation; the other by a subject index.

21. F and S Index of Corporations and Industries. (Cleveland: Predicasts, 1960-date).

22. U.S. Superintendent of Documents. Monthly Catalog of United States Government Publications. (Wash., D.C.: Govt. Printing Office. 1895-date).

23. Cumulative Subject Index to the Monthly Catalog of United States Government Publications, 15 vols. (Washington, D.C.: Carrolton Press, 1975).

24. The citation reads: "8477-Technology Transfer, selected bibliography; by Terry Sovel Heller, John S. Gilmore and Theodore D. Browne. Rev. ed. Feb. 1971. 175 pp." This was a NASA Contractor Report, CR Series No. 1724 (a second number, not to be confused with 8477).

25. U.S. Department of Commerce Library, United States Department of Commerce Publications (Washington, D.C.: Government Printing Office, 1952). Annual supplements (1951-date).

26. U.S. Library of Congress National Referral Center, A Directory of Information Resources in the United States: Federal Government (Washington, D.C.: Library of Congress 1974).

27. Of special interest is the SCIM (Selected Categories in Microfiche) whereby selected documents on microfiche are sent to researchers with special interest in a particular field.

28. American Doctoral Dissertations (Ann Arbor: Xerox, University Microfilms, 1955/56-date).

29. Dissertation Abstracts International (Ann Arbor: University Microfilms, 1938-date).

30. Comprehensive Dissertation Index, 1861-1972, 37 vols. (Ann Arbor: Xerox, University Microfilms, 1973).

31. For such special lists, see the PAIS (Public Affairs Information Service) under "Dissertations-Bibliography."

32.   International Encyclopedia of the Social Sciences 17 vols. (New York: MacMillan, 1968).

33.   Encyclopedia of the Social Sciences 15 vols. (New York: MacMillan, 1930-35).

34.   Encyclopedia Dictionary of Business Finance, (Englewood Cliffs, N.J.: Prentice Hall, 1961)

35.   Paul Wasserman, ed., Encyclopedia of Business Information Sources, 3rd ed. (Detroit: Gale Research, 1976).

36.   The McGraw-Hill Dictionary of Modern Economics: a Handbook of Terms and Organizations, 2nd. ed. (New York: McGraw-Hill, 1973).

37.   Eugene P. Sheehy, Guide to Reference Books 9th ed. (Chicago: American Library Association, 1976); Carl M. White, Sources of Information in the Social Sciences, 2nd. ed. (Chicago: American Library Association, 1973).

38.   Edwin T. Coman, Sources of Business Information (Berkeley: Univ. of California Press, 1964). Lorna M. Daniells, Business Information Sources (Berkeley: Univ. of California Press, 1976).

39.   If, for example, one is analyzing a particular industrial company, Moody's Industrial Manual and its supplemental looseleaf service is the place to start. There are important business services in other fields like banking, finance, public utilities, transportation, and many specialized business fields. For an annotated list of Information Services, see Directory of Business and Financial Services, 7th ed. (New York: Wiley, 1979).

40.   This bibliography in both format and content is based on the work of Margaret Clark of George Washington University Library.

6
IMPORTANT STATISTICAL SEARCHES

In contrast to the literature search developed in chapter five, another kind of search is important for researchers in economics and business--the search for appropriate quantitative data or, as it is popularly called, just "data." The objective in this chapter is to describe some useful guides, summary volumes, and famous or well-used sources of data.

Before we proceed, an important distinction should be made between primary and secondary sources. Most of us know intuitively what the difference is, but there are many variations in making the distinction more precise. Strictly speaking, primary data may be defined as only that generated originally by the researcher, but most of us accept the U.S. Census and other first-hand government statistics as primary. Secondary sources refer to those that are one or more removed from original work. Researchers try to get the data from primary sources if possible. If unfamiliar with the original sources, researchers go to guidebooks, summaries, or other lists. The emphasis in this chapter will be on these types of guides rather than the primary sources.

This chapter is short, the material confusing, even boring; but it is important. To present this subject matter as simple and attractively as possible, this chapter is divided into two parts with subdivisions that are beneficial to the researcher yet relatively easy to grasp and use as tools in the research. For clarity, the chapter outline is reproduced as follows:

    I. General Statistical Sources
        A. First Place to Look
        B. Statistical Indexes
        C. Summary Source Volumes
        D. Important Statistical Periodicals
        E. Bureau of the Census

    II. Specialized Statistics
        A. Agriculture and Food Sources
        B. Labor Statistics
        C. International Statistics

The initial sections are the essentials for any researcher. The Bureau of the Census material is so important, it deserves an entire chapter in itself, but this is obviously not possible in a summary book of this kind. In its place, to epitomize and dramatize what the Census Bureau can do for the researcher, a copy of Fact Finder for the Nation, the Bureau's popularizing information sheet, is reproduced verbatim. From the example, which is on minority statistics, a researcher should be able to see applications of the Census materials to his or her own work.

The second part of the chapter dealing with specialized statistical sources is also sugestive rather than detailed. Three or four types of specialized fields are selected to illustrate what is possible for any specific field. The readers are expected to exercise their imaginations in applying the type of source material to their own problems.

GENERAL STATISTICAL SOURCES

The division between general and specialized sources is somewhat artificial; it is merely a rough-and-ready classification referring to those data sources that cover all fields as opposed to those limited to a particular area. The terms comprehensive and specific are also used for this contrast. both kinds of data are collected in three major ways: census, survey, or administrative records. The Bureau of the Census, the most important of the data-generating government agencies, does the national censuses, now eleven in number. It also does surveys based on probability sampling for other government agencies. Government and private agencies collect data routinely, termed administrative records, and also do surveys.

It is important for researchers to be aware of data limitations from whatever sources. However collected, for example, all data are subject to questions of reliability. The 1980 Census made us aware of such problems as reporting errors in the data for individual units, incomplete coverage, and nonresponse. For statistics based on samples, sampling variability is a source of error. As researchers know from their own experiences there are also processing errors that creep into any scholarly or scientific effort.

There are other design and method problems in the collection of statistics. Each agency's survey and collection techniques are to some extent unique. The work of Jean Namias, an economist who has specialized in government agency sampling surveys, is an excellent source for sampling methods used as the basis of collecting government agency statistical data.[1]

Researchers are also limited in that the collected data may not be what they want for testing or proving an hypothesis. In such cases they should contact the agency source and see if pertinent unpublished data is available or if rearrangement of the data may be possible.

First Place to Look

The most important single sourcebok for researchers, or at least the best place to begin a data search, is the Statistical Abstract of the United States, a famous volume published annually for over a hundred years. It is the standard summary of statistics on many important topics, provided by about 200 government and private agencies. The sources of the tables are a quick guide to more detailed and current data provided by the referenced agency sources. In addition, there is an appendix, "Guide to Sources of

Statistics," which lists important primary sources of American statistical information.

The Statistical Abstract has several valuable supplements.[2]   Among these, Historical Statistics of the United States provides historical series on thousands of economic topics.[3]   Another, the County and City Data Book presents the latest available census figures for each county and the larger cities in the United States.[4]   The Congressional District Data Book offers the same type of data by Congressional district.[5]

Handbook of Basic Economic Statistics is another authoritative sourcebook to use if one is not familiar with the sources.[6]   It covers 1,800 statistical series in an annual volume with monthly supplements.   The Standard and Poor's Trade and Securities Statistics, a loose-leaf, privately published book with monthly supplements, is a very good source of current statistics on banking, finance, security prices and various important industries.[7]

The World Almanac and other almanacs should not be neglected simply because many people have grown up with a copy in the home library.[8]   It and the other almanacs will answer the same questions as those in the Statistical Abstract and may provide unique information and leads to sources. Unlike the Statistical Abstract these almanacs are privately published.

Indexes to Statistics   Among the guides to statistics, a simple index to use is an alphabetized list of subject headings called Statistics Sources published by Gale Research.[9]   It covers government and nongovernment sources as well as foreign statistics.   A more comprehensive index is the American Statistics Index (ASI).[10]   This is a master index or central catalog of all data available in federal government agencies, U.S. Congress committees, and other statistics producing programs.   It catalogs the publications in which the data appears, describes the contents, and provides microfiche copies of the reports to subscribers.   It is kept up-to-date by monthly supplements that report changes in the included publications and new government data publications coming out.   The ASI is not easy to use, but if one uses the subject index for the topic being researched, one can get substantial references to abstracts and then to data-filled source documents.   Futher, in a subscribing library a researcher can examine a selected document quickly on microfiche reader found in most larger libraries and have a copy of a particular page made with a reader-printer.   This index is undoubtedly the best way to get into obscure sources of government statistics.   It is now available in machine-readable form and on-line computer searching.   There are, of course, other indexes and guides to data sources, but the ASI far surpasses the others as a research tool.[11]

At this point mention should also be made of statistical data bases. While these will be discussed later, the sources providing time series, such as those from the Bureau of the Census or the Bureau of Labor Statistics, are very useful.   Also, the NTIS Directory of Computerized Data Files provides a good index to statistical data bases.[12]

Summary Source Volumes

There are five major sources of basic or primary government statistics in economics, business, and related fields:

Bureau of the Census

Bureau of Labor Statistics

National Center for Educational Statistics

Statistical Reporting Services of the
Department of Agriculture

Bureau of Health Service

Other agencies generate statistics, but most primary data come from these agencies. Several books represent main sources of such data. Business Statistics, published by the Office of Business Economics (OBE), is basic for the data of the Department of Commerce.[13] It gives about 2,500 time series back to 1947, which appear in the well-known periodical Survey of Current Business (discussed in the next section). Predicasts Basebook is the basic volume of the Predicast's system.[14] It gives 18,000 time series of data and is kept current with monthly publications; each time series is numbered with SIC (Standard Industrial Classification) numbers. The system is also on machine readable tapes.

Important Statistical Periodicals

For current business and economic statistics there are four or five well-known journals, of which the most important is the Survey of Current Business.[15] Besides covering general business indicators and a great wealth of industrial series, its National Income Issue is the authority on national income accounting. Another is the Federal Reserve Bulletin, which is the best source of current banking and financial statistics.[16] A third is the Monthly Labor Review, which as its name implies, is the basic source for labor, unemployment, productivity, and labor-management data.[17] Economic Indicators[18] is still another famous monthly source,[4] as is the Business Conditions Digest.[19] Both of these are especially good for forecasting and analysis of the current economy.

Bureau of the Census

The Bureau of the Census is the nation's largest collector of statistics, and it publishes all kinds of basic data. The key to Census data is the Bureau of the Census Catalog, published quarterly and annually, which has monthly updates of new publications.[20] The catalog is divided into two parts: (1) publications; and (2) data files and special tabulations, including unpublished materials. The catalog also notes what is available by geographic location.

The Bureau collects data in its censuses and in its many surveys and, in most cases, issues reports with its findings in these canvasses. The Bureau's Census of Manufactures, the basic source of data on the nation's manufacturing industries, may well be its most valuable contribution to the field of economic activities.[21] Done every five years, it covers such matters as establishments, shipments, payrolls, assets, rents, and inventories. Between its censuses, an Annual Survey of Manufacturing gives statistical estimates for much of the census data.[22] Other Censuses include those done on population, housing, agriculture, construction industries, retail trade, wholesale trade, service industries, transportation, mineral industries, and governments. Most libraries contain printed reports of these censuses. A list of major reports of the most recent ones appears as an appendix in the Statistical Abstract, which gives summary information on coverage frequency and reports. The Bureau of Census Catalog gives complete information on publications of all censuses as well as a list of data files, computer tapes, punch cards, and unpublished material.

The Bureau of the Census also does special surveys and issues reports based on them. These include, for example, foreign trade, international research, and business enterprises such as those owned by women and minorities.

We may illustrate the many materials issued by the Bureau of the Census by letting it speak for itself and describing its activities and their uses. Fortunately, a popular Bureau of the Census series called Factfinder for the Nation exists to do exactly this illustrative job. One of the series, "Minority Statistics," is reproduced in Figure 6-1. Researchers are urged to visualize how they could use materials of type illustrated in their own problems. If not sufficiently stimulated with this example, there are more Factfinders on many other topics equally vivid and easily available. Some of the Factfinder titles are "History and Organization"; "Agricultural Statistics"; "Housing Statistics"; "Population Statistics"; "Retail Trade Statistics"; "Wholesale Trade Statistics"; Statistics on Manufactures"; "Census Bureau Programs and Products"; and "Foreign Trade Statistics." For still more ideas on how to obtain and use Bureau of Census data write or call:

The Data User Division
Bureau of the Census
Washington, D.C. 20233

But first, please study "The Factfinder"(Figure 6-1), reproduced verbatim on the following pages.

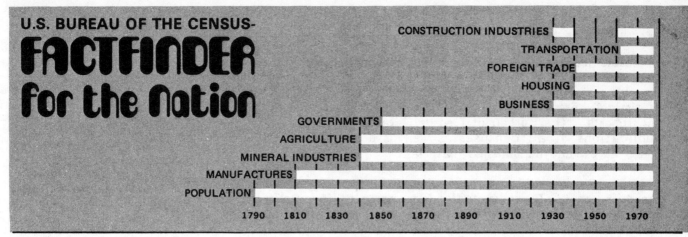

U.S. BUREAU OF THE CENSUS
FACTFINDER
for the nation

CFF No. 1 (Rev.)

Issued February 1978

MINORITY STATISTICS

INTRODUCTION

A "minority" can be just about any group of people that shares a particular economic level, citizenship status, color, national origin, language, physical handicap, sex, age, or any combination of these that gives the group important social significance.

In contemporary usage, the Census Bureau defines the term "minority" to refer principally to Black or Spanish-origin persons, Asian Americans, American Indians, and other racial or ethnic groups.

The Spanish population, recognized by the Census Bureau as an ethnic group rather than a race, is identified variously by "mother tongue," surname, origin or descent, or Puerto Rican birth or parentage.

The Census Bureau has several public advisory committees composed of members and leaders of various minority communities, organizations, universities, and local governments. They review the Bureau's efforts toward improving minority statistics and suggest program changes.

USES OF MINORITY STATISTICS

Do you need statistics to help you show that your community needs—

● An adult education program or a voter registration drive?
The census shows for your area the number of persons by age, race or ethnic background, education, employment (or unemployment), and income.

● Improved housing?
The census has data on the number of housing units that lack plumbing or are overcrowded.

● A daycare center or a playground?
Census statistics include the number

A CHART FROM THE U.S. SUMMARY

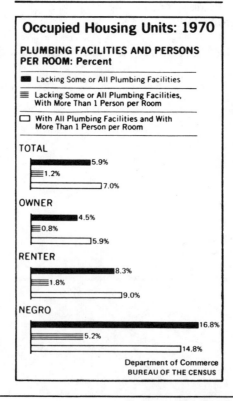

Occupied Housing Units: 1970

PLUMBING FACILITIES AND PERSONS
PER ROOM: Percent

▬ Lacking Some or All Plumbing Facilities

≡ Lacking Some or All Plumbing Facilities, With More Than 1 Person per Room

▭ With All Plumbing Facilities and With More Than 1 Person per Room

TOTAL
5.9%
1.2%
7.0%

OWNER
4.5%
0.8%
5.9%

RENTER
8.3%
1.8%
9.0%

NEGRO
16.8%
5.2%
14.8%

Department of Commerce
BUREAU OF THE CENSUS

of households headed by women, the number of husband/wife households with children under 6 years old and the number of women in these households either working or looking for work, and the family income levels.

● A change in local hiring patterns?
Check the census reports for the racial and ethnic composition of your area, as well as sex, education, and occupation characteristics.

Detailed data are published for neighborhood-sized areas (called census tracts) specifically for the Black and Spanish-language populations whenever there are 400 or more such persons in the tract.

In combination, census and local statistics can pinpoint the location of many types of needed facilities and provide evidence needed in making applications for grants.

Census minority statistics are used by numerous individuals, agencies, and organizations, either directly or through secondary sources:

Federal, State, and local governments study them in connection with employment, housing, and educational programs and legislation, and health systems and public services.

The statistics are useful to religious or community organizations that aid the elderly, teach English to foreign-born persons, provide recreation facilities, or are concerned about political representation.

U.S. Department of Commerce
BUREAU OF THE CENSUS

For sale by Subscriber Services (Publications), Bureau of the Census, Washington, D.C. 20233, or any U.S. Department of Commerce district office. Postage stamps not acceptable; currency submitted at sender's risk. Remittances from foreign countries must be by international money order or by draft on a U.S. bank. 25 cents per copy. A discount of 25 percent is available on orders of 100 copies or more sent to a single address.

Chambers of commerce, industries, and businessmen use these data in marketing, hiring, and in locating new stores and factories.

Sociologists, economists, historians, and other scholars find these figures essential to their studies of, for example, income and education gaps and the movements of minority groups from one part of the country to another.

AVAILABLE CENSUS DATA

Various kinds of statistics about minority groups in the United States (and other areas under its sovereignty or jurisdiction) are available in census reports dating back to 1790, although such data in the earliest censuses are extremely limited.

Demographic censuses. The decennial census has been conducted at 10-year intervals since 1790. The 1970 census included the following items:

- Population Characteristics
  - Age and race
  - Household composition
  - Employment status
  - Occupation
  - Income
  - Education
- Housing characteristics
  - Owner or renter occupied
  - Value or rent of unit
  - Plumbing and kitchen facilities
  - Year structure built
  - Number of rooms
  - Air conditioning
  - Appliances and automobiles

A number of these items are covered in different ways in current surveys.

In the 1970 census, counts of persons classified according to racial groups were produced for cities, counties, and States. Additionally, counts of Black persons were presented for smaller areas, such as minor civil divisions (towns, townships, etc.), census tracts, and city blocks. Counts of persons of Spanish heritage were presented for States, counties, cities, and census tracts.

In addition to the counts of persons of the various racial groups and Spanish heritage described above, 1970 census reports present detailed information about the characteristics of the Black and Spanish-heritage populations, including their income, education, employment status and characteristics, age, and marital status. Data are also published on characteristics of housing owned or rented by these two population groups.

Agriculture censuses. Information on the age and other socioeconomic characteristics of farm operators has been collected and cross-tabulated with farm data in virtually every agriculture census from 1890 on. For example, the number of Black-operated farms is shown for each county in the Southern States. The latest agriculture census was for 1974.

The Census Bureau and the U.S. Department of Agriculture (USDA) cooperatively prepare certain reports, such as the annual *Farm Population of the United States,* series P-27. (The USDA also publishes other useful analyses that are based in part on census statistics and on surveys, such as the Current Population Survey, described on p. 4.)

Economic data. In 1969, the Census Bureau conducted the first Survey of Minority-Owned Business Enterprises (SMOBE). The latest SMOBE reports are based on data from the 1972 economic censuses as well as other Government records. It provides separate reports for businesses owned by (1) Black persons, (2) Spanish Americans, (3) American Indians, Asian Americans, and others. Two further surveys, begun in 1975, cover minority-owned manufacturing firms and businesses owned by women. The published SMOBE data cover the number of firms and paid employees, together with gross receipts, industry, size of firm, and legal form of organization, distributed geographically down to the level of cities with 100 or more such firms.

Sources. Results of the 1970 Census of Population and Housing are published in several major report series. Population data about minorities are found especially in PC(1)-C, *General Social and Economic Statistics,* and PC(1)-D, *Detailed Characteristics.* The PC(2) *Subject Reports* deal with racial and ethnic groups, migration, fertility, marriage and living arrangements, education, employment, occupation and industry, and income. Useful housing data appear particularly in series HC(2), *Metropolitan Housing Characteristics,* and the HC(7) *Subject Reports* (which include senior citizens and selected racial groups and topics). The PHC(1) *Census Tracts* reports and PHC(2) *General Demographic Trends for Metropolitan Areas* contain both population and housing statistics. PHC(3), *Employment Profiles of Selected Low-Income*

A TYPICAL TABLE FROM THE 1970 CENSUS SUBJECT REPORT, PC(2)-1C

Table 17. Housing Characteristics of Households With Head of Spanish Origin for Selected Standard Metropolitan Statistical Areas and Places: 1970 — Continued

[See footnote 1, table 9 for definition of "All family heads of Spanish origin." Data based on 5-percent sample, see text. For minimum base for selected Spanish origin groups, derived figures (percent, median, etc.), and meaning of symbols, see text]

Standard Metropolitan Statistical Areas With 50,000 or More Persons of Spanish Origin Places With 25,000 or More Persons of Spanish Origin	Standard metropolitan statistical areas — Con.											
	Newark, N.J.		Oxnard–Ventura, Calif.		Philadelphia, Pa.–N.J.		Phoenix, Ariz.		Sacramento, Calif.		San Antonio, Tex.	
	Total Spanish origin	Puerto Rican origin	Total Spanish origin	Mexican origin	Total Spanish origin	Puerto Rican origin	Total Spanish origin	Mexican origin	Total Spanish origin	Mexican origin	Total Spanish origin	Mexican origin
HOUSEHOLDS												
Total	21 394	9 181	13 290	11 099	21 344	10 105	24 745	20 917	14 345	10 761	74 886	67 952
In owner occupied units	3 946	816	6 596	5 326	9 696	3 395	14 162	11 839	7 621	5 491	46 967	42 857
Percent	18.4	8.9	49.6	48.0	45.4	33.6	57.2	56.6	53.1	51.0	62.7	63.1
In renter occupied units	17 448	8 365	6 694	5 773	11 648	6 710	10 583	9 078	6 724	5 270	27 919	25 095
ROOMS												
1 room	602	331	132	112	261	134	486	442	235	235	750	707
2 rooms	1 320	558	688	582	1 031	577	1 627	1 439	652	500	4 000	3 734
3 rooms	4 339	2 043	1 912	1 737	2 706	1 437	3 275	2 918	1 890	1 468	11 005	10 121
4 rooms	6 250	2 731	3 120	2 627	3 274	1 732	6 847	6 016	3 331	2 594	21 529	19 597
5 rooms	5 096	2 221	3 876	3 319	4 037	2 040	6 912	5 779	4 647	3 606	21 320	19 400
6 rooms or more	2	991	2 424	1 846		2 442	3 641			1 687	11 573	10
			1 138				1 957				4 709	

Areas, and a variety of supplementary reports and maps all provide minority data. The *Urban Atlas* series, GE-80, displays data in map form for large metropolitan areas.

Agriculture census results are found in the Volume I *Area Reports* by State, and economic data are found principally in the *Survey of Minority-Owned Business Enterprises*—SMOBE *(Special Reports),* series MB.

In addition to the printed volumes (also available in microfiche), the Bureau furnishes data in even greater detail in the form of summary tapes for use on computers. These tapes cover popula-

tion, housing, agriculture, and economic census data.

The Bureau will retabulate its basic information on special order.

The Bureau also publishes graphic and pictorial brochures in its *We, the Americans* series. The subjects include women, Black persons, the elderly, Indians, the foreign born, homes, incomes, and youth. "Nosotros" ("We, the Spanish Americans") was published in English and Spanish; "We, the Asian Americans" was printed in English as well as in Vietnamese for refugees who have come to this country.

Users interested particularly in time series compiled by the Census Bureau

and other statistical agencies will find them collected in the Bureau's *Statistical Abstract of the United States* (annual, since 1878), the popular paperback *Pocket Data Book, USA* (every other year), and *Historical Statistics of the United States from Colonial Times to 1970.*

CURRENT SURVEYS AND THEIR REPORTS

Between and even during censuses, the Census Bureau conducts a number of national surveys, some of which are listed below, that include data on

A TYPICAL TABLE FROM THE SMOBE REPORT, SERIES MB72

TABLE 5. **Selected Statistics by Industry Division for Cities With 100 or More Black-Owned Firms: 1972**—Continued

Industry	All firms		With paid employees					Without paid employees		
	Firms	Gross receipts	Firms	Employees	Gross receipts	Average employees per firm	Average receipts per firm	Firms	Gross receipts	Average receipts per firm
	(number)	($1,000)	(number)	(number)	($1,000)	(number)	($1,000)	(number)	($1,000)	($1,000)
SOUTH ATLANTIC										
Delaware										
Wilmington city, total	248	6,716	39	207	4,007	5	103	209	2,709	13
Construction	26	862	7	(D)	(D)	(D)	(D)	19	(D)	(D)
Manufacturing	2	(D)	–	–	–	–	–	2	(D)	(D)
Transportation and public utilities	34	1,503	6	64	1,086	11	181	28	417	15
Wholesale trade	1	(D)	–	–	–	–	–	1	(D)	(D)
Retail trade	48	2,679	16	62	1,839	4	115	32	840	26
Finance, insurance, and real estate	5	79	1	(D)	(D)	(D)	(D)	4	(D)	(D)
Selected services	121	1,404	9	44	551	5	61	112	853	8
Other industries	–	–	–	–	–	–	–	–	–	–
Industries not classified	11	171	–	–	–	–	–	11	171	16
Maryland										
Annapolis city, total	136	1,948	13	53	904	4	70	123	1,044	8
Construction	10	166			(D)			7	(D)	

A TYPICAL TABLE FROM THE CENSUS TRACT REPORTS, SERIES PHC(1)

Table P-6. **Economic Characteristics of the Negro Population: 1970**—Continued

[Data based on sample, see text. For minimum base for derived figures (percent, median, etc.) and meaning of symbols, see text]

Census Tracts With 400 or More Negro Population	Atlanta (part in Fulton County)—Con.														
	Tract 0017	Tract 0018	Tract 0021	Tract 0022	Tract 0023	Tract 0024	Tract 0025	Tract 0026	Tract 0028	Tract 0029	Tract 0031	Tract 0032	Tract 0033	Tract 0036	Tract 0037
EMPLOYMENT STATUS AND OCCUPATION															
Male, 16 years old and over	1 569	1 188	88	869	1 886	1 621	1 759	1 205	758	917	856	176	913	206	213
Labor force	1 100	786	38	568	1 514	1 247	1 266	899	457	631	651	120	547	155	65
Civilian labor force	1 094	786	38	568	1 514	1 242	1 262	899	457	631	651	120	547	155	65
Employed	1 050	757	38	546	1 421	1 214	1 198	835	445	604	632	109	517	152	61
Unemployed	44	29	–	22	93	28	64	64	12	27	19	11	30	3	4
Not in labor force	469	402	50	301	372	374	493	306	301	286	205	56	366	51	148
Female, 16 years old and over	1 850	1 441	153	1 309	2 328	2 234	2 432	1 594	906	1 148	1 096	272	1 576	399	719
Labor force	997	736	87	566	1 310	1 287	1 315	751	545	579	547	116	617	268	316
Civilian labor force	997	736	87	566	1 310	1 287	1 315	751	545	579	547	116	617	268	316
Employed	978	706	80	534	1 236	1 207	1 231	695	511	552	524	116	573	257	297
Unemployed	19	30	7	32	74	80	84	56	34	27	23	–	44	11	19
Not in labor force	853	705	66	743	1 018	947	1 117	843	361	569	549	156	959	131	403
Married women in labor force, husband present	369	243	11	122	512	471	397	276	173	205	238	33	155	58	36
With own children under 6 years	65	34	7	24	180	144	99	43	71	40	69	6	45	27	15
Total employed, 16 years old and over	2 028	1 463	118	1 080	2 657	2 421	2 429	1 530	956	1 156	1 156	225	1 090	409	358
Professional, technical, and kindred workers	87	41	5	49	138	289	146	94	72	37	27	–	33	37	9
Managers and administrators, except farm	39	16	–	–	38	42	25	12	4	23	6	–	17	–	–
Sales workers	42	22	–	6	72	79	60	19	22	34	4	–	8	3	4
Clerical and kindred workers	187	90	28	109	387	425	349	141	105	81	113	12	103	153	45
Craftsmen, foremen, and kindred workers	160	124	6	101	178	131	157	165	63	90	98	33	59	31	9
Operatives, except transport	356	234	–	143	399	311	280	175	199	216	237	50	241	44	61
Transport equipment operatives	116	115	–	110	234	121	132	111	55	102	109	18	79	15	–
Laborers, except farm	303	185	7	72	306	194	313	209	80	90	146	21	77	26	10
Farm workers	6	9	–	–	6	19	8	–	–	17	7	–	13	–	–
Service workers, except private household	477	441	61	355	585	507	638	336	197	274	288	55	265	58	101
Private household workers	255	186	11	135	314		268		159	192		36	188	29	–
				534							511		573	257	

U.S. Department
of Commerce
BUREAU OF THE CENSUS
Washington, D.C. 20233

Official Business

Postage and Fees Paid
U.S. Department
of Commerce

Third Class

COM-202

minority persons or groups. These surveys are designed to measure broad trends by means of sampling, and usually do not yield data below the national level. Results are published by the Bureau or by sponsoring Federal agencies.

● The Current Population Survey, which originated in 1942, samples the entire U.S. population every month through interviews at about 57,000 households. Data are collected on different subjects each month. Various socioeconomic characteristics then are cross-classified by race and published in the Current Population Reports series: *Population Characteristics,* P-20 (about 15 reports a year, including Spanish-origin data), *Population Estimates and Projections,* P-25 (monthly and annual), *Farm Population,* P-27 (annual), *Special Censuses,* P-28 (twice a year), *Consumer Income,* P-60 (several times a year), and *Consumer Buying Indicators,* P-65 (occasional reports published through 1974). A Survey of Purchases and Ownership for 1973 and 1974 (report issued in 1976) provides statistics on minority households' appliances and automobiles. The consumer income series includes characteristics of the low-income population, and the buying indicators series shows expenditures by age and race of the household head, by income. Recent reports in the *Special Studies,* series P-23, have covered such topics as literacy, ethnic origin, migration, voting, household and farm workers, persons of Spanish origin, aging, and female family heads, and included an annual report on the Black population. A Survey of Income and Education was begun in 1976 to obtain State-level data based on 200,000 households.

● Other Federal agencies sponsor and publish the results of a number of surveys conducted by the Census Bureau. Of particular interest, with regard to minority statistics, are those surveys sponsored by the Departments of Health, Education, and Welfare; Housing and Urban Development; and Justice.

● The Annual Housing Survey, series H-150 and H-170, was begun in 1975 to provide annual and occasional reports that include neighborhood conditions, the physical condition of housing units, and socioeconomic characteristics of occupants and recent movers. Results are published for the United States, its regions, and selected standard metropolitan statistical areas (SMSA's).

● The Census Employment Survey, carried out in 60 urban and 7 rural low-income areas in 1970-71, obtained detailed socioeconomic information on employment-related problems in approximately 250,000 households. The results were published in 76 reports in the 1970 census series PHC(3).

● In 1975, when Congress was extending the Voting Rights Act of 1965, the Bureau tabulated information from the 1970 census on years of school completed for specified racial and ethnic groups in counties with 5 percent or more of any given language minority. Data concerning language minorities and voting participation in certain areas in the November 1976 elections were published in the P-20 series.

WHERE CENSUS BUREAU DATA CAN BE OBTAINED

In addition to census and survey statistics that appear in Bureau publications, and in journals, textbooks, newspapers, and other secondary sources, the data are available in a variety of places. Public libraries across the country have or have access to the printed reports, and an increasing number have them in microform. The publications are kept for reference and order at the U.S. Department of Commerce's 43 district offices and the 12 Bureau of the Census regional offices. Copies of the Census Bureau's and other agencies' publications can be purchased from the Superintendent of Documents, U.S. Government Printing Office, Washington, D.C. 20402, or through its bookstores located in other parts of the Nation.

Microfiche copies of published reports can be ordered from the Library, Bureau of the Census, Washington, D.C. 20233, and summary tapes and special tabulations can be obtained from the Data User Services Division, at the same address. There also are a number of private and academic summary tape processing centers, located throughout the United States, which are able to provide tape copies and services to their customers.

DATA USER SERVICES

The Census Bureau assists its data users in a number of ways. It publishes a catalog and a monthly *Data User News* and issues guides to particular segments of its statistics. Two of these guides, which deal with demographic data on minorities and show the geographic level of detail available, are *Data Access Descriptions* No. 40, "Data on Selected Racial Groups Available From the Bureau of the Census," and No. 41, "Data on the Spanish Ancestry Population Available from the 1970 Census of Population and Housing." The Bureau also conducts workshops on the availability and use of statistics. Its National Services Program offers exhibits and resources for the conventions of interested national minority organizations, while its Community Services Program works at the regional and local levels.

Inquiries and suggestions about the minority statistics program and other Bureau activities are invited. Write or call—

Director
Bureau of the Census
Washington, D.C. 20233

FACTFINDER FOR THE NATION

General information about the history and operation of the Census Bureau, including its various statistical programs, is contained in the publication in this series entitled "History and Organization."

SPECIALIZED STATISTICS

Leaving the general statistics guides and sources, we can discover a plethora of specialized statistical sources for each area, industry, and specialized field. The following are a few representative books to illustrate specialized statistical materials available.

For the agriculture and food-producing area there is a Census of Agriculture (reachable through the ASI index). A summary annual volume, called the Agricultural Statistics, also exists.[23] It is a kind of Statistical Abstract for agriculture and contains hundreds of tables of the most important data series. Beyond this summary volume, for each important subdivision of agriculture and food, there are often specialized books with statistics. For example, the American Frozen Food Institute publishes the Frozen Food Pack Statistics.[24]

For the labor field there is the Handbook of Labor Statistics, another summary volume of great value.[25] Tables cover the major series produced by the Bureau of Labor Statistics. Each major industry has some basic volume. For example, statistics on the petroleum industry (on production, refining, marketing, etc.) are given by the American Petroleum Institute, a trade association that publishes Petroleum Facts and Figures[26] and current supplements. Other sources in this field are available, such as the Oil and Gas Journal and its special issues; but the American Petroleum Institute is basic for industry statistics.

International Statistics

Lastly, the international and foreign sector is a world in itself, or better, worlds in themselves. It would take another chapter to adequately describe all the sources available for this sector. Each country usually has its own statistical sources. India, for example, though low in per capita income, has a very impressive national system of data maintained by its Central Statistical Organization. India's Statistical Abstract is a basic entry volume; so too is the India: A Reference Annual.[27]

But it is better to use the international sources of the United Nations before exploring the statistical data of an individual nation. The United Nations' World Economic Survey is an annual survey reviewing trends in various countries.[28] International Financial Statistics is a basic source on exchange rates, reserves, and financial statistics of all kinds.[29] The Statistical Yearbook, kept current by the Monthly Bulletin of Statistics, is a basic data book on all United Nations' countries.[30]

Selected Sources of Data

Finally, a list of selected government and private agencies that generate source data, taken from the Statistical Abstract of the United States, is provided for researchers who have not been helped in their work by the books treated in this chapter (see Figure 6-2). It may offer a suggestive idea beyond what has been said. A section on statistical information sources, reproduced from the Library of Congress bibliography, is also available in the Appendix B of this book.

SOURCES OF DATA

U.S. GOVERNMENT:

Agency for International Development: Foreign economic and military aid.

Arms Control and Disarmament Agency: Worldwide military expenditures.

Board of Governors of the Federal Reserve System: Mortgage and credit market debt; money market rates; consumer credit; common stock indexes; mining production index; industrial productivity; gold stock; reserve assets.

Bureau of the Census: Population; households; families; education (enrollment, school years completed); law enforcement expenditures; State and local government finances, employment, and payroll; money income; poverty; lumber and woodpulp production; construction—value, composite cost index, price index; housing units—number, new starts, sales, median sales price, vacancy rate; manufactures—value added, shipments, inventories, new orders, capital expenditures; retail and department store sales; merchant wholesalers sales and inventories; exports; imports; merchandise trade balance.

Bureau of Economic Analysis: National and capital expenditures for pollution abatement; GNP; national, personal, and disposable income; personal saving; industrial stock index; business capital expenditures; corporate profits; capital consumption allowances; value of farm output; investment in foreign minerals; retail trade inventories; balance of trade; foreign commerce and aid; international investment position.

Bureau of Labor Statistics: Medical care price indexes; defense-related employment; labor force; unemployment; productivity and compensation indexes; union membership; work stoppages; purchasing power of dollar; prices and price indexes; construction materials price index; building-trades union wage index.

Bureau of Mines: Mineral production.

Corps of Engineers: Waterborne commerce.

Council of Economic Advisers: Labor output and compensation; average weekly earnings; profit rates; private liquid assets; balance on current account.

Dept. of Agriculture: Federal food programs; farms—population, land, employment, assets, income, productivity, exports, crop production.

Dept. of Defense: Defense expenditures; military personnel; foreign military assistance and sales; outlays for veterans benefits.

Dept. of Energy: Energy production and consumption; petroleum exports and imports; coal, gas, and petroleum production; nuclear capacity; electricity; electric utility revenues.

Dept. of Housing and Urban Development: Low-rent public housing.

Dept. of the Treasury: U.S. gross debt per capita.

Employment and Training Administration: Insured unemployment.

Environmental Protection Agency: Air pollutants.

Federal Aviation Administration: Air transportation.

Federal Bureau of Investigation: Crimes—number and rate; police officers killed.

Federal Communications Commission: Telephone system revenues; broadcast stations and revenues.

Federal Deposit Insurance Corporation: Banks—number, assets, deposits.

Federal Highway Administration: Highways—total miles, State and local highway debt; motor vehicle travel; registrations; fuel consumption.

Federal Home Loan Bank Board: Savings and loan associations; first-mortgage interest rates.

Federal Trade Commission: Largest manufacturing corporations—share of assets; mergers.

Forest Service: Pulpwood production.

Health Care Financing Administration: Health expenditures; Medicare.

Immigration and Naturalization Service: Immigrants.

Internal Revenue Service: Income tax per capita; proprietorships and partnerships; corporations.

Interstate Commerce Commission: Intercity passenger and freight traffic; operating revenues—railroads and motor carriers; railroads.

Law Enforcement Assistance Administration: Law enforcement expenditures; police and corrections personnel; prisoners.

National Aeronautics and Space Administration: Space program outlays.

National Center for Education Statistics: School expenditures; public school teachers; pupil-teacher ratio; graduates; higher education costs.

National Center for Health Statistics: Births; deaths; marriages; divorces; life expectancy; health care personnel; bed-disability days; motor vehicle fatalities.

☆U.S. GOVERNMENT PRINTING OFFICE: 1980—311-046:1170

SOURCES OF DATA—U.S. GOVERNMENT (Continued)

National Institute of Mental Health: Mental health patient care.
National Oceanic and Atmospheric Administration: Fisheries.
National Science Foundation: Research and development funds; scientists and engineers; science doctorates.
Office of Management and Budget: Pollution control and research and development obligations; Federal budget; Federal aid; defense expenditures; military personnel; outlays for veterans' benefits.
Office of Personnel Management: Federal employment and payroll.
Postal Service: Postal revenues and deficit; pieces of mail.
Securities and Exchange Commission: Stock and bond sales.
Social Security Administration: Social welfare expenditures; social insurance enrollees and payments; public aid recipients and payments.
Veterans Administration: Veterans.
Water Resources Council: Water use.

NONGOVERNMENT AGENCIES:

A.C. Nielsen Company: Households with TV sets. (Copyright.)
American Council of Life Insurance: Life insurance; assets of insurance companies.
American Gas Association: Gas utility industry—revenues, proved reserves. (Copyright.)
American Hospital Association: Hospitals—number, beds, patients, expenses. (Copyright.)
American Iron and Steel Institute: Steel production. (Copyright.)
American Medical Association: Newly-licensed physicians. (Copyright.)
American Public Transit Association: Local transit passengers.
American Telephone and Telegraph Co.: Households with telephones.
Dun & Bradstreet, Inc.: New business incorporations; industrial and commercial failures.
Editor & Publisher Co., Inc.: Newspapers. (Copyright.)
Health Insurance Institute: Health insurance.
Investment Company Institute: Mutual funds.
McCann-Erickson Advertising Agency: Advertising expenditures. (Copyright.)
Moody's Investors Service: Corporate bond rates.
Motor Vehicle Manufacturers Association: New passenger car retail sales.
National Education Association: Teachers salaries. (Copyright.)
Waring, John A.: Horsepower.

CHAPTER SUMMARY

Searching for data or statistics appropriate to the research problem is another task for which researchers must equip themselves. Every researcher should own or become very familiar with the Statistical Abstract of the United States, the first place to look for data and data sources. Beyond this excellent Abstract many other good statistical sources and indexes exist; however, probably the next best place to look is the privately published ASI or American Statistical Index which covers most government agencies. Subject indexes usually will disclose data on almost any subject; and many libraries subscribe to microfiche documents, which can be found quickly and copied with the microprinter.

In addition to this general approach, every field (for instance, agriculture, food, labor) has special sources of statistical data, which researchers should be alerted to seek. For specialized and obscure data sources, reference librarians and Daniells' Business Information Sources should be consulted. Lastly, business and economic researchers should know the five periodical sources of statistics, especially the Survey of Current Business.

DISCUSSION QUESTIONS

1. Where would you find a series of annual data on job openings and placements and help-wanted advertising for the entire United States? For individual states?

2. Suppose you had a problem to determine how much TV advertising was sold in two major cities--say, Baltimore and Boston--over the last five years. Discuss approaches to be used.

3. Suppose you were working on a problem of how much the dollar fluctuated against foreign currencies in recent years. Where would you go to find these kind of data?

4. You wish to use census data on a particular topic. What major census sources would you consult first?

5. It may happen that you find there is unpublished data on your subject that the Census Bureau has not published. How could you obtain these data for research purposes?

6. What kind of research data would you find in Standard and Poor's Trade and Securities Statistics? Consult this source and suggest a research project based on its data.

7. You want data on the appliance industry, specifically factory sales of appliances, housewares, and plumbing fixtures. Would a trade publication do any good or would the Bureau of Census be a better approach? Discuss critically.

8. Name and discuss the five periodicals of statistics. Which is best for what types of research?

NOTES

1. Jean Namias, Handbook of Selected Sample Surveys in the Federal Government (New York: St. John's Univ. Press, 1969). Has excellent examples of samples.

2. U.S. Bureau of the Census, Statistical Abstract of the United States (Washington, D.C.: Government Printing Office, 1871-date). Consult the most recent year, which usually appears in the early part of the calendar year following the year covered.

3. U.S. Bureau of the Census, Historical Statistics of the United States, Colonial Times to 1970, 2 vols. (Washington, D.C., Government Printing Office, 1975).

4. U.S. Bureau of the Census, Historical Statistics of the United States, Colonial Times to 1970, 2 vols. (Washington, D.C., Government Printing Office, 1975).

5. U.S. Bureau of the Census, Congressional District Data Book (Washington, D.C.: Government Printing Office, 1949-date).

6.   Handbook of Basic Economic Statistics (Washington, D.C.: Economic Statistics Bureau, 1947-date).

7.   Standard and Poor's Trade and Securities Statistics, (New York, 1941-date).

8.   World Almanac and Book of Facts (New York: Newspaper Enterprise Association, 1868-date).

9.   Statistics Sources, 6th ed. (Detroit: Gale Research, 1980)

10.   American Statistics Index: A Comprehensive Guide and Index to the Statistical Publications of the United States (Washington, D.C.: Congressional Information Service, 1973-date).   Monthly, with annual cumulations.

11.   For other important indexes, see Daniells, Business Information Sources, pp. 50-53.

12.   National Technical Information Service, A Directory of Computerized Data Files, Software and Related Technical Reports (Springfield, Va.: NTIS, 1978).

13.   U.S. Office of Business Economics, Business Statistics: The Biennial Supplement to the Survey of Current Business (Washington, D.C.: Government Printing Office, 1932-date), biennial.   1977 edition was published in March 1978.

14.   Predicasts Basebook (1973-date).

15.   U.S. Department of Commerce, Survey of Current Business (Washington, D.C.: Government Printing Office, 1921-date). Monthly.

16.   U.S. Board of Governers of the Federal Reserve System, Federal Reserve Bulletin (Washington D.C. 1915-date). Monthly.

17.   U.S. Bureau of Labor Statistics, Monthly Labor Review (Washington, D.C.: Government Printing Office, 1915-date). Monthly.

18.   U.S. council of Economic Advisers, Economic Indicators (Washington, D.C.: Government Printing Office, 1948-date). Monthly.

19.   U.S. Bureau of Economic Analysis, Business Conditions Digest (Washington, D.C.: Government Printing Office, 1900-date). Monthly.

20.   U.S. Bureau of the Census, Catalog (Washington, D.C.: 1974).   annual supplements.

21.   U.S. Business of Census, Census of Manufactures (Washington, D.C.: Government Printing Office, 1947-date).   Latest 1972 published in August 1976. 3 vols.

22.   Annual Survey of Manufactures, (Washington, D.C.: Government Printing Office, 1952-date).

23.   U.S. Department of Agriculture, Agricultural Statistics (Washington, D.C.: Government Printing Office, 1936-date).

24.   American Frozen Food Institute, Frozen Food Pack Statistics (Washington, D.C.: 1900-date).

25.   U.S. Bureau of Labor Statistics, Handbook of Labor Statistics (Washington, D.C.: Government Printing Office, 1927-date). Annual (1976 Handbook is BLS Bulletin, 1910).

26.   American Petroleum Institute, Petroleum Facts and Figures (Washington, D.C.: 1971). Current statistics in their Annual Statistical Review and Weekly Statistical Bulletin.

27.   India Central Statistical Organization, Statistical Abstract (New Delhi, India: 1950-date); Ministry of Information and Broadcasting, India A Reference Annual (New Delhi, India: 1978 is latest at this writing).

28.   United Nations Bureau of Economic Affairs, World Economic Survey (New York: 1945-date).

29.   International Monetary Fund, International Financial Statistics. (1948-date).

30.   United Nations, Statistical Yearbook (1949-date).

7
COMPUTERIZED SEARCHES

INTRODUCTION

In addition to conventional search methods, a new method of researching by computer is becoming available. The researcher can go to large libraries--like the Library of Congress in Washington or the Ohio State University Library in Columbus, Ohio--and use a computer terminal free to the public. Alternatively, for a fee the researcher may employ the services of a search center often located on a large university campus. For example, the University of Maryland College Park Libraries offers a Computerized Literature Search Service. An early pioneer, Ohio State University provides the students not only free reading room terminals that search the library catalog but also a Mechanized Information Center with access to data banks not located on campus. Besides libraries commercial services provide searches directly for researchers. For example, ERIC, a data base provided by the Educational Resources Information Center in Washington, D.C., can be directly contacted. This service is also available through the University of Maryland or Ohio State's Search Service and is subscribed to by other large research libraries or centers offering computer searches.

For the researcher who wants to begin to use the computer as a method of research, it is well to recognize that this field is quite complex and changes rapidly, almost from day to day. Yet it is wise to learn something about computer-based information services, for they may well be the wave of the future. Computerization in libraries started only a few years ago as a device to lower the cost of cataloging books. Now some fifty-seven major libraries have such services, and a plan exists to put the Library of Congress catalog on a computer in the 1980s.

This chapter offers some orientation on searching the literature by computer. It is certainly true there is no substitute for an hands-on experience in using a library computer terminal. Yet if one has some fundamental ideas and guidelines before approaching the terminal or the commercial service, the researcher is less apt to waste time or to lose money.

SOME COMPUTER IDEAS AND RULES

The first distinction to make is the one between computer terminals and the data banks to which they are connected. The terminal is the typewriter-type machine that appears in the reading room of the library offering this service. It is connected to a cathode ray tube (CRT) and the user carries on a dialog, reproduced on the screen, with the computer. Following a set of provided instructions, the user gives commands to the computer and the computer responds by finding the information designated in its data bank and displaying it on the screen. Information retrieval is the broad term for this computer searching, and the hands=on relationship is said to be in an interactive, conversational mode. It is also referred to as on-line searching.

The data bank accessed by the terminal may contain only the library's materials, and thus the researcher could find the same information by conventional searches of book catalogs, periodical indexes, and so forth.[1] The computer's advantage is that it is taped, and if a printer is attached to the terminal, a printout of what appears on the screen can be secured. Data bases, however, should be understood as separate from the particular library or institution that houses the terminal. Data bases exist all over the United States and in many foreign countries. They cover many diverse subject matters, including business and economics. These data bases, referred to as machine-readable data bases, are named with distinctive acronyms or titles, usually having some reference to their subject matter.

One example of a machine-readable data base is the AGRICOLA (previously called CAIN) generated by the National Agricultural Library; it corresponds to its printed publication, the Bibliography of Agriculture. CHEMCON is the data base for Chemistry derived from Chemical Abstracts published by the American Chemical Society. PA is the data base from Psychological Abstracts published by the American Psychological Society. The field of medicine is very advanced with a data bank based on the U.S. National Library or Medicine in Bethesda, Maryland. Its data bank, called MEDLARS, has a terminal system called MEDLINE (Medlars On-Line) with terminals in 200 medical libraries across the United States. Typically, these include books, reports, and journal articles in on=line files going back to the late 1960s.

For business and economics data bases, no comprehensive data bases comparable to the above fields is now available. The New York Times Information Bank is probably the best known, but besides economics and business it contains much general data. The Lockheed Aircraft Corporation Data Base and the Systems Development Corporation (SDC) files are also well known, but they likewise cover other technology oriented matters in addition to the economics-business field. Other data bases are Funk and Scott Business Data Bank based on the F and S Index to Corporations and Industries published by Predicasts in Cleveland, Ohio, and a new Bibliographic Retrieval Service (BRS), located in New York. The Institute for Scientific Information in Philadelphia provides a service of keeping a researcher current in specialized economics topics, as, for example, input-output, balance of payments, or demographic economics.

There are some directories of machine-readable data banks, but unfortunately these quickly become out-of-date--KRUSAS's Encyclopedia is probably the best known.[2] The American Society for Information Science, publishes a directory of data banks popularly referred to as the ASIS directory.[3] For the social and behavioral sciences, a directory by Sessions is useful for economic and business topics.[4] Though all of these directories are far from complete, the bigger problem is they soon become out-of-date in this rapidly changing field. For those interested in studying and keeping up with this voluminous field, annual review volumes (<u>ARIST</u>) published by ASIS are the best single introduction to the field and its new developments.[5]   Of particular interest to researchers is the review article on education for on=line systems in volume 14 of <u>ARIST</u> (1979), which has a cumulative index to all volumes.

SCORPIO: A Case Study

This intriguing word <u>SCORPIO</u> refers to the Library of Congress system of computerized information retrieval, which is likely to become national in scope.   In any case, it is the system our national library uses; and while it is somewhat experimental and changing, it can be taken as representative of what big libraries are doing with computers for researchers.   Almost nobody remembers what <u>SCORPIO</u> stands for, but its authors tell us it is "an interactive, conversational system for computer searching."[6]   With some modesty they say its objective is merely to supplement the traditional search methods however, its proponents maintain it allows users to develop creativity and unique search strategies, by combining sets of stored information under the logic of Boolean algebra theory.[7]

Files and Commands

To use <u>SCORPIO</u> or other such systems, the unfamiliar user must understand two concepts central to the construction and use of computerized search equipment: <u>File</u> and <u>Command</u>.   The computer file is like an office file but its information is stored electronically in a tiny space instead of in file folders.   This data can be "retrieved"; that is projected on the CRT screen by typing specific commands at the terminal typewriter.   These commands are common English words like "begins," "browse," "search," "find," and "display," which are abbreviated into three or four letters (<u>bgns</u>, <u>brws</u>, <u>dspl</u>, etc.) or even the first letter or two on the newer model terminals.   A command tells the computer to do something to the stored data.

As of June 1980, there were eight <u>SCORPIO</u> files, all except one available to the public:

FILE NAME	SEARCH ABBREVIATION
Legislative Information for the 96th Congress	<u>cg</u>96
Legislative Information for the 94th Congress	<u>cg</u>94
Legislative Information for the 95th Congress	<u>cg</u>95
Bibliographic Citation	<u>bibl</u>
*Major Issues	<u>issu</u>
National Referral Center Resources	<u>nrcm</u>
Library of Congress Computerized Catalog	<u>lccc</u>

*Not available to the public.

The most important file for the researcher is the Library of Congress Computerized Catalog File (lccc) extracted from the Library's MARC (Machine=Readable Catalog) data base. This base consists of about 700,000 library books primarily in English published since 1968 or cataloged since 1969. Books can be found by author, title, and subject. The subjects are virtually the same as those found in the Library of Congress Card Catalog. Periodical or journal articles are not available through this machine search file.

How to Use a Computer

Figure 7-1 shows the main steps in using the computer. The researcher sits at a typewriter computer terminal and begins his or her search by typing the begin search command (BGNS) with the file designation lccc and the term enter, which is required in commands. The video screen computer makes an appropriate reply:

```
xxxLCCC--THE LIBRARY OF CONGRESS COMPUTERIZED CATALOG,
        WHICH WAS UPDATED ON 03/28/77 AND CONTAINS 698,400
        RECORDS IS NOW AVAILABLE FOR YOUR SEARCH
        THE INDEX FILE, UPDATED ON 03/28/77, CONTAINS 1,561,954
        TERMS.
        THE CONGRESSIONAL RECORD INDEX FROM THE 95th
        CONGRESS IS AVAILABLE.  TO ACCESS IT, ENTER
        BGNS  CR95.
        READY FOR COMMAND:
```

This begin function is followed by appropriate commands to browse, select, display, and print out what is in the data banks.

FIGURE 7-1
LCCC BASIC SEARCH INSTRUCTIONS

IF YOU WANT TO:	TYPE:	FOLLOWED BY:	EXAMPLE:	PRESS:
BEGIN an LCCC search	**bgns**	**lccc**	**bgns lccc**	ENTER key
BROWSE a subject, author or title	**b**	your subject, author, or title	**b** solar energy **b** haley, alex **b** humboldt's gift	ENTER key ENTER key ENTER key
SELECT desired term	**s**	line number beside term	**s** b6	ENTER key
DISPLAY desired set in **SHORT FORMAT**	**d**	set number	**d** 2	ENTER key
display **NEXT** page in **SHORT FORMAT**				ENTER key
DISPLAY desired set in **FULL FORMAT**	**d**	/item	**d/item**	ENTER key
display **NEXT** page in **FULL FORMAT**			**n**	ENTER key
PRINT the display	**PRINT** key	d	**PRINT d**	
END your search	**ends**		**ends**	ENTER key

Source: Library of Congress.

To start an author search, type BRWS (browse), an important selection function command. Typing BRWS, followed by the author's name and ENTER, is a command to show books by a particular author. For example:

The Command: BRWS Spencer, Daniel Lloyd ENTER (yields two books displayed on the screen):

Books

> 67-25249:Airlie House Conference on Transfer of Technology.
> The transfer of technology to developing countries.
> LC CALL NUMBER: HD82. A546 1966
> 70-118987:Spencer, Daniel Lloyd. Technology gap in
> perspective strategy of international technology
> transfer.
> LC CALL NUMBER: T20.S65
> READY FOR NEW COMMAND:

Older books by the same author (for example India's Mixed Enterprise, 1957) would not be displayed because the Machine-Readable Catalog (MARC) was started only with books cataloged in 1968.

Subject Search. Entering BRWS followed by the subject heading is the same as looking under the subject heading in the card catalog. The user enters the full or partial word describing his or her interest, which will summon up the subject and some others on lines before and after. As an example, the subject "Technology Transfer" may be searched.

Command:
> BRWS   TECHNOLOGY TRANSFER ENTER

Response:
BRWS FILE: LCCC; ENTRY TERMS: TECHNOLOGY TRANSFER
B01 TECHNOLOGY OF WOODWORKING// (TITL=i)
B02 TECHNOLOGY PROBLEM IN RURAL SMALL-SCALE IND//
(TITL=i)
B03 TECHNOLOGY RESEARCH BUREAU// (CORP=i)
B04 TECHNOLOGY SERVICES, INC.//(CORP=i)
B05 TECHNOLOGY TODAY///(TITL=i)
B06+TECHNOLOGY TRANSFER--//(TITL+5; INDX=116)
B07 TECHNOLOGY TRANSFER AND DEVELOPMENT//(TITL=i)
B08 TECHNOLOGY TRANSFER AND INNOVATION CAN HELP//(TITL=I)
B09 TECHNOLOGY TRANSFER AND THE DEVELOPING NAT//(TITL=I)
B10 TECHNOLOGY TRANSFER AND U.S. FOREIGN POLICY// (TITL=I)
B11 TECHNOLOGY TRANSFER BY PEOPLE TRANSFER//(TITL=i)
B12 TECHNOLOGY TRANSFER IN CONSTRUCTION//(TITL-i)
B13 TECHNOLOGY TRANSFER IN PACIFIC ECONOMIC DEV//(TITL=I)
B14 TECHNOLOGY TRANSFER IN THE PHARMACEUTICAL I//(TITL=I)
B15 TECHNOLOGY TRANSFER TO PAST EUROPE//(TITL=i)
B16 TECHNOLOGY TRANSFER TO THE ORGANIZATION OF// (TITL=I)
B17 TECHNOLOGY TRANSFER; A SELECTED BIBLIOGRAPHY//
(TITL=I)
B18 TECHNOLOGY TRANSFER-A SELECTED BIBLIOGRAPHY//TITL=I)
B19 TECHNOLOGY TRENDS//(TITL=i)
B20 TECHNOLOGY UNBOUND: TRANSFERRING SCIENTIFIC//(TITL=I)
READY FOR NEW COMMAND (FOR NEXT PAGE, XMIT ONLY):

This display lists the files under the subject being searched and adds subjects on either side of the subject.[8]   The user selects the file B06 with the command: SLCT B6 ENTER.   The computer response is:

SET 1   5: SLCT TITL/TECHNOLOGY TRANSFER
SET 2   116: SLCT INDX/TECHNOLOGY TRANSFER
READY FOR NEW COMMAND:

This response says there are two sets; one with 5 items and the other with 116 items.   The user then commands the machine to display set 1: DISPL 1 ENTER   The computer response is:

68-60276:United States. Congress. Senate. Committee on
          Small Business.
          Subcommittee on Science and Technology.
          Technology transfer.
          LC CALL NUMBER: T174.3.U54
73-92090:Technology transfer.
          LC CALL NUMBER:T174.3.T4
73-606570:United States. Congress. Senate. Committee on
          Small Business.
          Subcommittee on Science and Technology.
          Technology transfer
          LC CALL NUMBER: KF26.5.S635. 1970
75-314260:NATO Advanced Study Institute on Technology
          Transfer. Technology transfer.
          LC CALL NUMBER:T174.3.N37. 1973
79-133786:TTA Information Services Company. Technology
          transfer.
          LC CALL NUMBER:T174.3.125
READY FOR NEW COMMAND:

When the video-screen displays this set 1, those items in which the subject is a title, the machine is given the command PRINT.   The printer then prints this list of books.

It remains to request set 2, which is quite long with 116 items.   The same command is issued with set 2 request: DISPL 2 ENTER.   The machine's response is to give the first seven items in the set as follows:

File; LCCC;title/Line--Set 2
66-62210:LESHER,RICHARD L. Assesing technology transfer.
          LC CALL NUMBER:T176.1.38
67-25249:Airlie House Conference on Transfer of Technology
          The transfer of technology to developing countries.
          LC CALL NUMBER: HD82.A546. 1966
67-60040:Symposium on Technology and World Trade. Technology
          and world trade.
          LC CALL NUMBER: QC100. U57 no.284
67-61550:United States. Library of Congress. Science Policy
          Research Div. Policy planning for technology transfer.
          LC CALL NUMBER:T174.3.U56
67-62467:Conference on Technology Transfer and Innovation.
          Proceeding.
          LC CALL NUMBER:T174.3.C6. 1966

68-59148:Rivkin,Steven R. Technology unbound; transferring
            scientific and engineering resources from defense to
            civilian purposes.
            LC CALL NUMBER: T174.3.R5. 1968
68-60276:United States. Congress. Senate. Committee on Small
            Business Subcommittee on Science and Technology.
            Technology Transfer.
            LC CALL NUMBER:T174.3.U54
READY FOR NEW COMMAND OR NEW ITEM NOR (FOR NEXT PAGE,
EMIT ONLY):

Again, if the user wishes, this list is printed out on an attached printer by the command PRINT. Then, the user can continue with more items of the 116 in set 2 by commanding the machine to display the next batch with the command NEXT or, on newer machines, by pressing some suitable key (e.g., key PF). After NEXT is pushed, the second batch (items 8-15) appears and may be printed out. The user continues until he or she has printed out the full bibliography of 116 items and tears it off the machine. The search is terminated by typing ENDS, and the machine indicates it took 21.97 minutes to complete this search using the SCORPIO system.

The advantage over manual searches will be perceived by all who have ever used a library book catalog. To get a printed list of 116 books on a subject in less than a half hour is a remarkable feat. Another big advantage is accuracy. Everyone makes mistakes in bibliographic copying, but the machine does not make mistakes, provided it is programmed correctly. Also, the detail with which each entry comes through is usually greater than most human efforts. In short, the computer service renders a fast, accurate, and comprehensive list.

There are, however, drawbacks. First, the machines are always breaking down. At the present state of the technology, the system is not very reliable. Second, there may be lines in the reading room waiting to use the machines. Third, as is well known, the computer is an idiot that requires instructions. A user or even one with some modest experience with the machine may waste time merely learning to press the right keys. Pressing the wrong keys severely penalizes the user by forcing him or her to end the search and begin again. The programmers who designed the system did not pay enough attention to the public's needs and limitations. In the future, rumors depict horror stories about whole tapes being erased in the data bank and the records permanently lost because some wrong key was pressed. In contrast, the library catalog, whether card or book, is an old reliable institution, always available, easy of access, and easy to use. With the library catalog there is little chance of basic records disappearing.

The above SCORPIO examples show only some very basic and elementary usages of the computer search. Many more commands yield specialized uses. Thus, one might order the machine to display any item in the long form, which, in contrast to short form of the set, gives all the bibliographic information found on the Library of Congress card catalog. Another possible usage is to command the machine to display an item by LC call number or LC card number, if for example, the user had only the number, having lost the other bibliographic information. For more complicated uses, the command combine (COMB) enables users to create their own sets recombining data pulled from various files. Figures 7-2 and 7-3 explain combining concepts.

FIGURE 7-2
COMBINING COMMANDS

SCORPIO GENERAL REFERENCE

System Availability:

      7:00 a.m. to 9:30 p.m., Monday through Friday
      8:30 a.m. to 5:00 p.m., Saturdays and holidays (if neither chamber in session)
      8:30 a.m. to 9:30 p.m., Saturdays and holidays (if either chamber in session)
      1:00 p.m. to 5:00 p.m., Sunday

Training and Information:

Library Users	— CRS Information Systems Group	426-6447
Senate Users	— Sergeant at Arms	224-1517
House Users	— User Assistance and Training Group	225-6002

To Report Problems:

Library Users	— Telecommunications Technical Control	426-6237
Senate Users	— Sergeant at Arms	224-1517
House Users	— User Assistance and Training Group	225-6002

    ● Report terminal location and identification number
    ● Describe problem

COMBINE COMMAND

The searcher can create a new set of documents from existing sets by using the three conjunctions (and, or, not) in the **Combine** command. The diagrams below depict the operations possible with the **Combine** command (comb). Suppose that two sets have been selected and that each set has five documents represented by letters.

    SET 1: A D F G Q
    SET 2: B D F K R

The sets are shown as circles enclosing the documents belonging to each set. In the example, two documents (D and F) appear in both sets, so the circles overlap. The shaded areas show the result of the Combine operation:

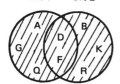

Set 1   Set 2

1 or 2
Result = (ABDFGKQR)

combine 1 or 2
comb   1 or 2
c   1 r 2
comb   1 + 2

Result: A new set containing all documents
           in set 1 or set 2

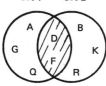

Set 1   Set 2

1 and 2
Result = (DF)

combine 1 and 2
comb   1 and 2
c   1 a. 2
comb   1 * 2

Result: A new set containing all documents
           in both set 1 and set 2

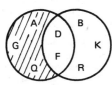

Set 1   Set 2

1 not 2
Result = (AGQ)

combine 1 not 2
c   1 not 2
comb   1 n 2
comb   1 - 2

Result: A new set containing all documents
           in set 1 but not in set 2

June 1977

FIGURE 7-3
MORE COMBINING COMMANDS

COMBINING MORE THAN 2 SETS

In the diagrams below, suppose that three sets have been selected and that each set contains documents represented by the following letters:

     SET 1:   A   Q   D
     SET 2:   B   R   D
     SET 3:   C   Q   D   R

In these diagrams, 1 document (D) appears in all three sets, as the overlapping circles demonstrate. Shaded areas show the results of typical Combine operations:

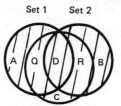

Set 3
1 or 2 or 3
Result = (ABCQDR)

comb	1 or 2 or 3
c	1 or... or 3
combine	1 o 2 o 3
c	1 + 2 + 3

Result: A new set containing all documents in sets 1, 2, or 3

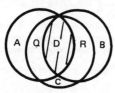

Set 3
1 and 2 and 3
Result = (D)

comb	1 and 2 and 3
c	1 an 2 an 3
combine	1 * 2 * 3
c	1a 2a 3

Result: A new set containing all documents common to sets 1, 2, and 3

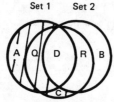

Set 3
1 or 3 not 2
Result = (ACQ)

comb	1 or 3 not 2
c	1 o 3 n 2
combine	1 or 3 not 2
c	1 + 3 - 2

Result: A new set containing all documents in sets 1 or 3 but not in set 2

ORDER OF COMBINE OPERATORS

In complex **Combine** commands, the order in which the operators are processed can affect the results. The order of priority is: NOT, AND, OR. For example, the expression "comb 5 or 3 not 1" implies a two-step operation. First the "not" is processed (3 not 1) yielding an intermediate result which is then combined with set 5. This operation produces a final result set, which is returned to the user.

USING PARENTHESES

The order of the operators used in the **Combine** command can be altered by enclosing portions of the expression in parentheses. The innermost parenthetical expressions are processed first. In the expression "comb (5 or 3) not 1" the "or" is processed (5 or 3), yeilding an intermediate result set which is combined with set 1, yeilding the final result set, which is returned to the user. Parentheses may also be enclosed within other parentheses: comb ((1 or 2) and 3) not 4. In this example the order of processing is: or, and, not, because of the double sets of parentheses.

STATISTICAL DATA BASES

The revolution in storing and retrieving of literature by computer is paralleled by the development of machine-readable data files for statistics. Some of these data bases have already been mentioned in connection with important statistical sources in book form or government tapes. In this section, these data bases will be treated more systematically.

There are three kinds of statistical data bases: The first refers to financial data banks emphasizing the investor's needs; the second deals with marketing data bases; and the third , and perhaps most important, is the statistical time series, such as the types offered by the Census Bureau. The financial statistical data base, an expensive service used by investors, is exemplified by Compustat tapes.[10] These cover 3,500 American and Canadian companies with 20 years of data. The marketing type is of interest to marketing researchers for data on population, income, business location, sales, and others. For example, Market Statistics in New York maintains this kind of data bank. Survey of Buying Power, a special annual issue of Sales and Marketing Management, is also drawn from it.[11]

The most important type of data base, the economic and business time series, deserves more attention than the other two. For it, the government has a vast collection of data dases available. The Census Bureau not only publishes the volumes of the various censuses but also has much information stored on computer tapes. The annual Catalog of Census Publications publishes a list of those available in its Part II Data Files and Special Tabultions.[12] The Census data files are of two types: (1) confidential records of individual respondents, and (2) summary files containing statistical totals or summarizations for small areas or detailed subject classifications. It is the second type of tape that is for sale by the Census Bureau and of interest to researchers.

There are many machine-readable data files available from other government agencies. Some years ago, the National Technical Information Services Directory of Computerized Data Files listed 500 data banks available from 60 federal agencies. The Bureau of Labor Statistics data bank for labor matters is quite famous. Another is the data bank from the Social Security Administration called: Continuous Work History Sample (CWHS), which provides a 1 percent sample of the work history of selected individuals. The CWHS sample may be used to illustrate briefly how the researcher may use such data bases.

The CWHS survey provides data on individual income,age, sex, race, location, and many other important variables since 1960. If the question of what sort of migratory patterns of the labor force for 1960-73 were raised, this data base could provide an answer. Again, if the question of what factors relate to the success or lack of success of workers, this sample data could develop regression analysis giving some answers.

In addition to the government data banks, researchers should be aware that some commercial services incorporate many of these data banks and perform statistical services for industrial firms, banks, and other sophisticated moneyed users. Such services are very expensive for individuals doing their own studies; but if one is a member of a company research staff, these services might become possible. Figure 7-4 from Kruza's Encyclopedia

FIGURE 7-4

ENCYCLOPEDIA OF INFORMATION SYSTEMS AND SERVICES, 4th Edition

Scope and/or Subject Matter: Data entry into computers including keypunching, key to disc and voice operations, OCR, online, distributed processing, and word processing.

Publications: Newsletter (10 issues each year). Also published are special reports and equipment, compensation, and statistical surveys.

Contact: Marilyn S. Bodek, Executive Director, Data Entry Management Association.

★394★
DATA PROCESSING MANAGEMENT ASSOCIATION (DPMA)
505 Busse Highway   Phone: (312) 825-8124
Park Ridge, IL 60068   Founded: 1951
Edward J. Palmer, Executive Director

Staff: 33 Total.

Description of System or Service: DATA PROCESSING MANAGEMENT ASSOCIATION develops research and education programs related to data processing hardware, software, and management techniques for the benefit of its members. In addition to educational programs, DPMA sponsors an annual conference and business exposition.

Scope and/or Subject Matter: Data processing management.

Publications: 1) Data Management (monthly); 2) Compu-Fax (bimonthly). DPMA has also issued a number of monographs related to data processing. Publications are available to nonmembers.

Contact: Edward J. Palmer, Executive Director, Data Processing Management Association.

★395★
DATA PUBLISHING INTERNATIONAL (DPI)
TOEGEPAST VIEWDATA SYSTEMEN (TVS)
N2 Voorburjwal 225   Phone: 020 228022
Amsterdam, Netherlands   Founded: 1978
Frans Uoopmans, Manager

Staff: 2 Management professional; 3 clerical and nonprofessional.

Related Organizations: The parent organization of DPI is United Dutch Publishers (V.N.U.).

Description of System or Service: TOEGEPAST VIEWDATA SYSTEMEN (TVS) provides the business community with viewdata consultancy and publishing services. It assists clients in input, structuring, and layout of information; consults in the application of viewdata for both public and private use; and undertakes viewdata publishing projects.

Scope and/or Subject Matter: Viewdata services and consultancy.

Computer-Based Products and Services: The company is an information provider on private and public viewdata networks. TVS has developed various data bases for clients such as Subsidies for Dutch Industries, Jobdata (vacancies for higher education employees), and Distrifood (for food traders). Consulting in public and internal communication or closed user group viewdata use is also offered.

Clientele/Availability: Primary clientele is the business community.

Contact: Mr. Akjaan Everts, Toegepast Viewdata Systemen, phone 020 263327.

★396★
DATA RESOURCES, INC. (DRI)
29 Hartwell Ave.   Phone: (617) 861-0165
Lexington, MA 02173   Founded: 1968

Staff: 600 Total.

Related Organizations: Data Resources, Inc. recently became a subsidiary of McGraw-Hill, Inc.

Description of System or Service: DATA RESOURCES, INC. (DRI) relates developments on the national and international economic scene to detailed product, company, industry, and regional results. It combines online computer access to forecasts, data banks, models, and software with individual consulting, educational programs, and contract research to meet the particular needs of each customer. The DRI user group includes over 600 companies, financial institutions, government agencies, and research centers. DRI provides complete time-sharing support of econometric applications including:

conversational software for statistical analysis and modeling; professionally managed models and forecasts of the U.S. and foreign economies; online up-to-date data bases of several million series; a technical education program; and consulting services to assure the successful application of quantitative techniques. Also offered are forecasting conferences, a complete program of educational seminars covering the theory and application of econometrics to world problems, and a computer telecommunications network covering major cities in the United States, Canada, and Europe.

Scope and/or Subject Matter: Aspects of national and international economics as applied to corporate planning, regional analysis, investments and marketing, and insurance and banking industries.

Input Sources: Input is received from various financial and statistical sources including: the International Monetary Fund, Standard & Poor's Corporation, Investors Management Sciences, and individual researchers and economists.

Holdings and Storage Media: DRI's real-time data banks include over 5 million economic, industrial, and financial series of figures about the U.S. and 127 other countries.

Computer-Based Products and Services: The primary function of the system is the computerization of data collected for online access. DRI's software packages are designed for statistical analysis, modeling, decision-making, and report writing, and its telecommunications network provides access to the data bases through a wide variety of terminal devices. Its EPS programming language provides direct access to both DRI and private-user data banks, and offers extensive time series capabilities, including standard transformation and data creation techniques. Data acquired and offered online by DRI include the following files: 1) Agriculture—contains approximately 2000 series of farm income and balance sheet data. 2) Cost Forecasting—provides data on the construction trade. 3) DRI Capsule—contains more than 3000 time series data from 1947 on major U.S. economic indicators. 4) DRI Central—provides 20,000 macroeconomic series dealing primarily with the U.S. economy. 5) European National Source—time series on member nations of the European Economic Community and Switzerland. 6) Exrate—data on exchange rates, price and production indexes for 15 countries. 7) Forsim—data supporting the DRI Forest Products Model. 8) Pro Forma—contains annual sales and net income for 700 companies and 81 industries from the last ten years. 9) State and Area Forecasting—historical and short-term future values available at the SMSA, state, regional, and U.S. aggregate levels. 10) U.S. Regional—contains more than 35,000 time series on economic indicators in various regions of the U.S. 11) Canada—produced with Statistics Canada. 12) Platt's Oilgram Price Data Bank—produced with McGraw-Hill Publications Company. 13) Oil and Gas Journal Data Bank—produced with the Petroleum Publishing Company; offers over 2000 annual time series from the International Petroleum Encyclopedia and the Gas Journal. 14) Best Executive. 15) California Data Bank. 16) Census Tract. 17) Commodities. 18) COMPUSTAT. 19) Conference Board. 20) Consumer Expenditure Survey. 21) Current Population. 22) Energy. 23) FDIC. 24) Flow of Funds. 25) International Monetary Fund. 26) OECD. 27) Paper and Pulp. 28) Securities. 29) Steel. 30) Standard & Poor's. 31) Target Group Index. 32) U.S. Weekly Banking. 33) Value Line. 34) Weather. 35) World Debt. 36) World Tables.

Other Services: In addition to the services described above, DRI provides forecasts, simulation models by special contract, consulting, large scale research studies, and related services.

Clientele/Availability: Services are available by special arrangement.

★397★
DATA RETRIEVAL CORPORATION OF AMERICA
5600 W. Brown Deer Rd.   Phone: (414) 355-5900
Milwaukee, WI 53223   Founded: 1964
James K. Heller, President

Staff: 8 Information and library professional; 12 management professional; 54 technicians; 13 clerical and nonprofessional.

Description of System or Service: The DATA RETRIEVAL CORPORATION OF AMERICA designs and implements automated systems to meet the needs of the legal information and text processing community, especially the state legislatures. Working to of Information Services describes a firm of consultants called Data Resources Industry. (DRI), well known for econometrics forecasts on the economy.[13] The listing for Data Retrieval Corporation of America, working in the legal field, is also shown for contrast.

The contrast between these two companies highlights the distinction between a statistical data base, which provides the data itself on tapes, and the bibliographic data base of literature and source material, which locates the references. The company providing the tapes may, for a fee, manipulate the data for the researcher in some specific statistical method such as regression analysis. The above distinction is valid for most commercial services, but exceptions can combine elements of both types. For one, Predicasts Terminal System (mentioned in chapter five) offers a combination of bibliographical and statistical data bases.

If one looks at the two types from the standpoint of the researcher, the main difference between them is one must understand statistics to use a bibliographic data base. For business and economic researchers, understanding regression analysis as a statistical technique is very important. This method will be discussed in later chapters.

FUTURE OF COMPUTER SEARCHES

Research use of computer data bases, whether bibliographical or statistical, is only a beginning. Younger readers may expect a tidal wave of computer usage in their lifetimes. Advances in computer technology have resulted in more efficient methods of working with inputs and outputs. Costs are still high, but will undoubtedly decrease on a unit basis, as standardization, wider markets, and greater understanding take place.

The researcher today is faced with a curious public-private sector dichotomy. On the one side is the traditional library, which is beginning to develop computer services for bibliographical searches, such as the Library of Congress SCORPIO system. Such systems have no fee to the library user, the costs being borne by taxation. In contrast, private sector companies offer services for fees or subscriptions, usually too high for the individual, though they can be bought by companies or sponsored research. Nothing is wrong with this state of affairs. Indeed, it has been traditionally American to maintain public libraries side=by=side with commercial private information services. But it is to the researcher's advantage to know about both types of services.

In the foreseeable future it is likely that as unit costs decline with volume, private sector offerings may become more resonable. Also, the tradeoff between money and time may become so that the researcher cannot resist spending money on such conveniences as a quick bibliography or a monthly mailing with up-to-date news on his or her selected field. Finding time series and processing elaborate regressions are also saleable products. Indeed, a new industry called "information brokers" is already here.[14]

Home Information Systems

Beyond computer searches more startling developments are looming. Some commercial companies are working on projects to turn the home TV terminal into a computer terminal that can retrieve information from data banks and display it in the living room.[15]   Home information systems call "TV Text" or "teletext" are in use on a small scale in some foreign countries.   The British have systems called CEEFAX and ORACLE that broadcast much information to those who own a decoder with the set, currently priced at $200.   There is another kind of home information system known as Viewdata or Videotex.   Viewdata enables the subscriber to interact with the broadcast station by telephone.   Fees can be at $1,000 or more.   Some American TV stations are experimenting with this idea, the most extensive being done in Coral Gables, Florida, by some newspapers.   The price of the decoder must decrease substantially, however, before widespread adoption of this innovation takes place.

Many people talk of the computer revolution.   Actually, it is more an information revolution made up of a combination of telecommunications and computers.   Increasing access to the store of human knowledge by quick efficient systems such as those being developed will greatly accelerate and simplify the research process in the future.   Today's students should prepare themselves well for the future in this rapidly developing research potentiality.

CHAPTER SUMMARY

Most people think a literature search is confined to a library effort using the familiar tools of book catalogs, bibliographies, periodical indexes, and other such devices of the printed word.   These indices are still in use, but now a new dimension, based on computer use, has been added with the advent of mechanized information retrieval.   Data banks are available for computerized searches in many fields.   These data banks are available through libraries, usually at no cost, and commercial vendors, often quite expensive.

The advantages of a computerized search include the speed and accuracy inherent in computer usage.   Also, the computer can develop search strategies that combine subjects, a feature unique to computers.   However, serious disadvantages likewise exist: the unreliability of the technology, the high cost of private vendors, and the waiting period to use the few available public facilities.

Statistical data bases embody the same principles of computer storage and retrieval as bibliographical data bases.   They differ in that bibliographical data bases list only references to books and articles on the subject studied; whereas statistical data bases provide the actual data.

The future of the computer as a research tool is growing rapidly.   Information brokers for a fee will find data and even process it for the researcher.   Not far down the road, the home TV set may become a data retrieval terminal.   The information and telecommuncations revolution is moving so fast, it seems clear that research work will be greatly simplified and expedited in the lifetime of the present generation.

DISCUSSION QUESTIONS

1.   Compare and contrast bibliographical data bases and statistical data bases. Which seems more useful?

2. Consult The Wall Street Journal, on which the text is based, for the future of home TV information systems. Can you add anything to the prospects suggested?

3. How would you find a data base applicable to your problem?

4. Can you obtain access to another data base like ERIC through SCORPIO?

5. Why are commercial vendors of data bank services so expensive? How can one obtain a low-cost computer service? Alternatively, can research fund computer services? How?

NOTES

1. However, the computer can search in ways that conventional methods cannot (e.g., the combining of sets and key words in the adjunct MUMS system).

2. Anthony T. Kruzas, ed., Encyclopedia of Information Systems and Services, 3rd ed. (Ann Arbor, Mich.: Anthony T. Kruzas Associates, 1978).

3. John H. Schneider, Survey of Commercially Available Computer=Readable Bibliographic Data Bases (Washington, D.C.: American Society for Information Sciences, 1973). Updated by Computer Readable Bibliographic Data Bases (1976-date).

4. Vivian Sessions, ed., Directory of Data Bases in the Social and Behavior (New York: Science Associates, 1974).

5. American Society for Information Science, Annual Review of Information Science and Technology (Washington, D.C.: 1966-date).

6. SCORPIO means Subject Content Oriented Retriever for Processing Information On=Line.

7. U.S. Library of Congress Information Systems Office, SCORPIO (1979); Reference Guide to SCORPIO (1977).

8. These added "subjects" may be titled (TITL) or corporate authors (CORP) and are so designated.

9. To date, librarians declare that, to their knowledge, this has never happened. Moreover, there are back=up tapes for such emergencies. The system is constantly being improved over the years and made easier to learn and handle.

10. Investor's Management Sciences, Compustat (Denver, Col.: 1962-date).

11. Sales and Marketing Management, Survey of Buying Power (New York: 1974-date) in July and October issues each year.

12. U.S. Bureau of the Census, Catalog.

13. Anthony Kruzas, Encyclopedia of Information Services.

14. American Society for Information Science, Bulletin (February, 1976), pp. 1-20.

15. "Video=Frontier," The Wall Street Journal, 24 July 1979, p. 46.

8
INTERVIEWS, SURVEYS, AND QUESTIONNAIRES

INTRODUCTION

The collection of one's own original data--primary data--is an exciting prospect for a researcher. Getting out of printed sources in libraries, away from what others have said or concluded, is an important part of many research efforts. At minimum, even one interview with an acknowledged authority or even a knowledgeable person is a great way to guide one's thinking in the design and planning stage as well as to provide invaluable insights in the operational phase. For a bigger research effort a well-designed survey based on carefully constructed questions may be the heart of the project. But whatever the prospect yields from this field work, it is important to remember at the outset that these yields come only as the result of much planned effort. Thoughtless contact with people wastes time. This chapter will concern itself with proper methods of data collection by direct field approaches and attempt to point out obvious misuses and pitfalls of direct approaches.

In terms of the choice of method discussed in chapter three, if the researcher elects to do a field survey, he or she is moving toward quantitative research methods. If using diagnostic interviews, the researcher is still in a qualitative mode; but with the design and execution of a planned survey, the researcher is in the realm of numbers. Of course, the researcher would normally use quantitative analysis with data obtained from statistical sources described in previous chapters; with his or her own field survey, the researcher is committed to at least some quantitative analysis.

Thus, this chapter may be a turning point in the researcher's thinking, and he or she should be planning ahead to use statistical procedures and computer manipulations of the data, covered in the succeeding chapters. In any case, this chapter puts the researcher in the quantitative direction. The chapter outline is as follows:

A. Interviews
   1. Diagnostic Interviews
   2. Survey Interviews
   3. Some Do's and Don'ts

B. Sample Survey
   1. Types of Samples

2. Size of Sample
3. Survey Administration

C. Questionaires
   1. Construction
   2. Administering Questionaires

A word of caution about field surveys may be added. There are undoubted advantages if a researcher elects to develop his or her own data through a well-planned survey. The data are fresh, up-to-date, and often can suit the problem more exactly than data from statistical sources. Yet the costs to the researcher in money and time are heavy, and the survey should not be undertaken lightly. Existing source data should be found first and carefully examined before rushing into a survey. One authority puts it beautifully when he says that a survey is like surgery: It should be done only after other courses of action are ruled out.[1]

This chapter is of necessity highly compressed. Fortunately, for researchers who wish to pursue any of the subject materials in greater depth, an excellent bibliography by William Belson and B.A. Thompson on survey methods covers over 2,000 select and sometimes classic articles with a detailed subject index.[2]

INTERVIEWS

There are, of course, several types of interviews. For example, there are job interviews when one seeks employment or counseling interviews when one has a problem. The type of interview considered in this chapter is the research interview, which is basically of two types: a <u>diagnostic</u> and a <u>survey</u> interview. The diagnostic interview is used to understand the scope or incidence of a problem and is conducted with a knowledgeable person or expert in the field. The survey interview is focused on eliciting systematic information from a group or class of people, usually with a set of carefully formulated questions.

The diagnostic or exploratory interview can be very helpful in starting a new investigation through suggestions of sources, guidelines, and other products of "brain-picking." It may even be used with people who help judge the nature, scope, and incidence of problems in which they are involved, as for example in structuring personnel problems in a factory.

The survey interview, certainly better known, is more frequently used. It aims to collect information and is structured on planned questions--often in questionaire form, though it may be a checklist of questions. However, some flexibility may be built-in with room for "other" type answers. The survey interview is part of the planned sample survey, considered in the next section.

Diagnostic Interviews

The research interview should be clearly distinguished from a mere casual conversation. First and foremost, it has a purpose--a clear objective or goal formulated before the meeting. Second, it has structure. Third, it has certain formal dynamics of interaction. Last, it must be thought of as a scientific method with defined steps of acquiring information, data, or leads.

The nature of the interview will be clear on some reflection. An essential decision at the outset is who to interview. It wastes time to ask someone for an interview and discover that this person does not know or is unwilling to give information. Some attempt must be made at the beginning to assess the potential interviewee's capabilities and attitudes before contacting him or her. Another consideration is whether the interviewee has a representative opinion of the group being studied. Also, one must decide how many people must be interviewed.

After the preliminary questions are settled, the objective of the interview is formulated. Just what do we want to learn from the interview? Even a graduate student seeking to interview a professor regarding the student's research must have a clear idea of what he or she wants to ask. It is still more essential to define objectives if the student contemplates visiting strangers to get information. For example, if a researcher plans to interview managers of small-service businesses, like barbershops, a checklist of what to accomplish in each interview is essential so time is not wasted, which often means a loss of money for the proprietor.

Another characteristic of the interview is its structure, usually a planned sequence over time. First, the researcher solicits the meeting and setting a date, time, and place. Secretaries or others may act as intermediaries. If possible, a friend or prestigious person may be asked to introduce the person interviewed. In fact, letters of introduction in most foreign research attempts are essential.

Once the interview is secured, the interviewer should arrive with a plan or an outline of what is to be done. Like anything else, the interview should have parts or sections: at minimum, an opening, a body, and closing. One authority on interviewing in the fields of social psychology, social relations, and education tells us the interview breaks into four structural elements: (1) the start; (2) crisis in the trend of discussion; (3) psychological moments; and (4) conclusion.[3]

The start requires an opening that makes clear the purpose of the interview, under what auspices the research is being conducted, and an expression of appreciation for the time the interviewee is generously giving. Crises are those moments in the interview in which a new direction or change of focus occurs. They may be minor or major, the latter in a successful interview being high points or climaxes. If a climax takes place, it is recommended that the interview should be terminated in a courteous and expeditious manner. Psychological moments are points used to effect a change of focus in the interview. These often lead to the climax and the conclusion. The conclusion should convey repeated thanks for taking the respondent's time and include some suggestion of providing a copy of the finished research report if the interviewee would like one.

The interview should permit observation of the individual or group being interviewed in a way that might prove valuable to the researcher. Interaction involves sensitivity to the other person's reaction. The interviewer must cultivate the ability to respond such that the purpose of the dialogue is served. For instance, allowing the interview to ramble wastes time, but skillfully steering it in productive directions yields useful information. It often happens that resistance, negative feelings, or even hostility develops in the interactive process of the interview. The interviewer needs to understand that there are many possible reasons for such developments and have some resources to cope with such eventualities. Smiling, maintaining friendly behavior, acting interested, refraining from dogmatic assertions, and being a good listener are talents to be cultivated.

Pretesting one's interview plan on friends or family is a good idea. A dry-run or two may smooth out some rough questions and help the researcher improve his or her technique. Also, responses from friends may prepare one for responses in the actual situation.

Survey Interview

Having covered some elements of diagnostic interviews, we may glance at the survey interview. Interaction between the researcher and the interviewed person follows many of the principles set forth in the diagnostic interview (planning, pretesting, friendly behavior, etc.), but there is a difference. The respondent learns quickly that he or she is being sought out not as a unique individual but as one in a chain of people interviewed in the survey. For this reason, the survey interview is bound to be somewhat more impersonal than the diagnostic or exploratory interview. The survey instrument or questionaire, which is simply handed to the interviewed person, also contributes to the impersonality. Of course, this impersonality may be diminished by the interviewer reading the questions aloud or asking them from memory, picking up responses with a tape recorder; but even these techniques are formal and impersonal. Such impersonality is still more true of telephone interviews and questionaires mailed to the respondents. Thus, great care must be taken in developing the questionaire, whatever method of contact is used. The advantages and disadvantages of personal interviews as a method of administering questionaires in surveys will be covered in the section on questionaires.

Some Do's and Don'ts of Interviewing

In an interview one should be very careful about the sensitivities of the person interviewed. An obvious rule is to keep the number of questions short. Another is to place the sensitive questions later in the interview, with openers that are less likely to offend. When recording information, one should use the tape recorder only with permission. If it distracts or stiffens the interviewee, forget it. Even note-taking may upset people, and some authorization should be asked. Filling in a questionaire from the person's responses may cause boredom and should be done with quick notes. These notes should be transcribed as soon as possible after the interview, together with any impressions fresh in the mind of the researcher. Finally, some attempt should be made to assess the person's responses for truth, accuracy, and consistency. People sometimes tell the researcher what they think he or she wants to hear, whether from ignorance, malice, or just to be rid of him or her. Naiveté is not an asset even in a beginner.

The interview is a good tool in the researcher's kit, but like other tools, it must be used intelligently. Its big limitation is it takes time, and it should not be undertaken if adequate time cannot be programmed for it. It also can be expensive, and it may not pay off for reasons such as lack of skill, churlish respondents, and other reasons previously suggested. Yet if the researcher has some awareness of the hazards and drawbacks, it can provide insights superior to printed data, mailed questionaires, or even telephones. Picking another person's brains in direct personal contact can be stimulating and rewarding.

SAMPLE SURVEY

Turning from interviews and their techniques to the sample survey--or contact of people in person, by mail, by telephone, or by some combination of these channels--it is first essential to consider briefly the concept of sampling. Though judgmental samples exist, underlying all scientific studies by sample surveys is the assumption that this sample is representative--in other words, that the distribution of answers from a small segment of the studied population will be the same or similar to the distribution obtained if the whole popluation or universe were questioned.[4] If one had a 1,000 marbles--500 of which were red and 500 blue--mixed them thoroughly in a box, and then withdrew 100 at random, this sample would approximate a distribution with half of each color. Thus, the famous random sample would be secured.

TYPES OF SAMPLES

When randomness is applied to people, each individual in the collection should have an equal chance of being selectecd for questioning. In practice this method is not always so easy to carry out. When the universe is documented, as in a telephone book, it is easy to select every tenth, twenty-fifth, or fiftieth name--usually a practical method for a telophone or mail survey. Such selection may also be used in house-to-house interviewing when the field worker goes to every fifth house, for instance; but there are difficulties such as the fact that people may not be aт home. While conceptually easy to grasp, the random sample is often hard to apply.

Stratified Sampling

In stratified sampling the researcher uses his or her judgment or knowledge to divide the population into sub-populations or strata. These strata are then sampled in a random manner. People understand this idea of stratification intuitively when they buy a basket of apples and examine the bottom as well as the top layer. Stratified sampling is used when identifiably different characteristics for sub-groups are evident. In the marble example, if it were known that 700 marbles were large and 300 were small, a total of 70 large and 30 small might be withdrawn under controlled or stratified sampling. Put more generally, when a characteristic of the universe is known, the sample is selected so that this feature will be distributed in proportion to the known information. For example, in studying buying behavior for certain products, the researcher notes the teenage strata is identifiably different from the older persons. The researcher thereby selects members of each strata in the same proportion as their relationship to the total sample. This approach is called Proportionate sampling, a variant of stratified sampling. If teenagers constitute 20 percent of the group studied, this is the proportion that should be taken in the sample.

Area Sampling

Area sampling is similar to stratified sampling. It obtains samples representative of various geographic areas. In the minority enterprise study referred to earlier, we might wish to divide the population of the enterprises into smaller sample areas, for instance districts of the city selected to study. Each district could be given a number, and from these numbers a random sample would be drawn.

Clustered Sampling

A clustered sample is the process of selecting cases by arranging the sampled items in groups instead of singly. Thus, interviews may be obtained in two residences side=by=side in every twentieth block rather than one residence in every tenth block. Alternately, the researcher might select a random sample of several city blocks and visit every household in them. The idea of this type of sample is to reduce costs because less travel or fewer stops and starts are involved. Usually costs in time and money must be balanced against the accuracy and reliability of the sample.

Size of Sample

Basically a problem with sample surveys is deciding if the sample is typical of the population. Ideally a 100 percent--or total universe--sample is best; but for obvious reasons of cost, time, and physical magnitude, such a complete sample is usually not possible. Generally, the sample is of adequate size when it sustains no more possible range of variation or error than can be accepted by the researcher. The dispersion of the sample varies in direct proportion to the dispersion of the population from which it is drawn. It also varies inversely in proportion to the size of the sample.

There are various statistical formulas for computing the size of the sample for estimating the mean of a universe, the proportion, and the significance tests. These formulas may be found in standard statistical textbooks; but generally, the size of the sample is determined in respect to the degree of confidence level required, as, for example, 95 or 99 percent confidence level. Thus, the formula for computing the size of a sample for estimating a mean of a universe is as follows:

$$n = \left(\frac{\sigma}{\dfrac{\overline{X}_s - \overline{X}_p}{z}} \right)^2$$

where n = size of the sample

σ = standard deviation of the population (known or estimated)

$\overline{X}_s - \overline{X}_p$ = estimated deviation of sample mean from population mean or one half the estimated confidence interval

z = standard normal deviate (2.576 for 99%, 1.96 for 95% confidence levels)

This reasoning is covered in numerous statistical textbooks that deal with the principles of statistical inference and the confidence limits of probable deviation of sample characteristics from true population characteristics. Chapter nine also provides further discussion of this subject.

Survey Organization and Administration

A survey must be organized and administered. First the objectives of the survey must be clearly stated. Who are the targets? How will they be contacted? What is the exact character of the questionaire? When precisely is the survey to take place? Is it necessary to hire and train interviewers? Much of this thinking should occur in the design and planning stage; but human beings, being what they are, typically leave such matters to the last minute. What then are the key procedural steps in collecting and processing data? The following sequence or checklist is recommended:

1. Set forth the plan of data collection
2. Develop the questionaire
3. Select the sample
4. Apply the questionaire
5. Edit the returns
6. Tabulate the data
7. Analyze and interpret results

Plan of Collection   Surveys on the subject may have been done already by others. If so, they should be checked to compare results, to use as models, and to discover warnings on mistakes made. In any case, the researcher should make a plan of collection, which includes such matters as: what are the objectives, who is to be contacted, how it is to be done, when will it take place, who will do it, and many more such details. Even in a simple one-man survey, this plan should be a written document.

Development of Questionaires   The questionaires are the heart of the sample survey. Their careful development is so important that the entire last section in the present chapter is devoted to them. Suffice it to say, the researcher should first make a rough list of what questions he or she wants to ask. The researcher will then establish a priority system ascertaining which questions are most important to the research problem. Then comes some decisions on how to administer the instruments: interviewing, mailing, telephoning, or some combination.

Selecting the Sample   The concept of sampling has already been discussed. Obviously, the researcher must make some hard decisions on the nature and size of the sample.   He or she must weigh the size of the sample and scientific purity against the time and money involved. Ease of execution is another big factor to be considered. Consulting experienced researchers for advice is good.

Applying the Questionaires   The next section covers the advantages and disadvantages of each channel for applying the instruments. If the interview is chosen, the interviewer must be schooled in the kinds of interpersonal problems likely to occur in such situations. If a mail or telephone survey is chosen, the problems of each must be understood. Whatever is decided, forethought, care, and common sense are major aides.

Editing the Returns   When the samples are completed, they should first be checked for completeness. If some entries are missing or incomplete, the editor-researcher marks them appropriately with some code, typically "N.R." or "not reported." Then handwriting must be deciphered for anyone who will tabulate or code the material. Coding is another task of the editor, but matters are greatly simplified if the schedule has been precoded. The editor is responsible for catching and treating mistakes, omissions, or flaws of any kind before tabulating.

Tabulating the Data   Tabulating data has been greatly simplified with the coming of the computer and the development of simplified software systems like the Statistical Package for the Social Sciences (SPSS), most researchers will try the computer. The old hand-tally sheet with marks like a picket fence (卅卌 //) are now used only with very small samples. The computer is a genie and will do almost anything the researcher needs, provided the researcher knows what to ask for. Chapter ten will demonstrate the role of the computer in modern research data tabulation and analysis.

Analysis and Interpretation   Again the computer has made this task much easier than could have been imagined even a few years ago. The computer program, for most research tasks, is already made up or "canned." It has most of the basic statistical routines, which are available to the researcher directly with little help from the computer technicians and programmers. Frequency distribution, tables, even charts are printed out. In addition, there are important statistical analyses such as cross=tabulations, correlations, and regression analyses. The computer can almost give too much. The big requirement is that the researcher must know some statistics and a little of the SPSS program--or at least be willing to learn about them. The next two chapters attempt to fill in this gap if it exists or refresh those already initiated in statistics and the computer.

THE QUESTIONAIRE

The questionaire sometimes called the schedule or instrument is the basic tool of developing data. It is a list of questions designed to collect data and may be filled out at the survey interview, though often it is mailed to the respondent. After the researcher decides what the survey's objective is and who the people questioned will be, the questionaire is designed, redesigned, and pretested. At the outset, questions are usually written in crude form as a sort of checklist. Sometimes they are put on cards so that they can be rearranged into the most effective grouping. Initial questions, for example, may be more general and less apt to provoke antagonism in the respondent.

All questions should have a cover letter or an introductory statement, which, at minimum, contains the title of the questionaire, the purpose of the survey, the sponsorship of research, and where the questionaire is to be returned. The cover letter is important and careful wording must be used so that the information solicitation is in no way offensive. A self-addressed stamped envelope or postcard on which the questions are listed is also essential. Appendix C provides a classic example of a good cover letter and proper mailed questionaire procedure.

Questionaire Construction

Questionaire construction methods fall into two basic categories: open=end and checkbox answers. The first type provides blank lines in which the respondent writes the answers. The second type requires the respondent to answer by checking an appropriate box. Sometimes the two methods are combined, especially when the series ends with "other" or "other (explain)" and provides lines for the answer. Figure 8-1 shows these two types of questionaires and how they can be combined.

An example of the open-end type is question number 2: "If you come for a particular exhibition or event, how did you learn about it?" Question number 3 in the same figure exemplifies the checkbox answers, and question number 1 illustrates the mixture of both.

FIGURE 8-1
MUSEUM CAFETERIA PATRONAGE SURVEY

1. *What is the main purpose of your visit today?*

   ☐ Current temporary show *(Which?)*

   _____

   ☐ A particular collection *(Which?)*

   _____

   ☐ A class, tour, film, lecture
   ☐ Seeing the Museum in general
   ☐ Cafe, lunch, art shop
   ☐ Some business with the Museum itself

   *Anything else?*_____

2. *If you came for a particular exhibition or event, how did you learn about it?*

   _____

3. *Did you come to see this in the capacity of a*

   ☐teacher,   ☐student,   ☐artist, or   ☐none of these?

4. *Have you been to the Museum before?*   ☐Yes   ☐No

   If yes, *how long ago did you* <u>*first*</u> *come to the Museum?*

   ☐Within 5 years   ☐10-20 years
   ☐5-10 years   ☐20 years or more

   About how many other times have you been to the Museum in the past 12 months?

   ☐None   ☐3-5 times   ☐10 times
   ☐Once or twice   ☐6-9 times   or more

5. *Sex:*   ☐Male   ☐Female

6. *Age:*   ☐Under 18   ☐25-29   ☐35-44   ☐55-64
            ☐18-24   ☐30-34   ☐45-54   ☐65 or over

7. *Local residence:*

   ☐ Baltimore City   ☐ Baltimore County

   Other county in Maryland_____

   If permanent residence elsewhere, *where?*

   _____

8. *Are you a* <u>*member*</u> *of the Baltimore Museum of Art?*

   ☐ Yes   ☐ No

The open-end questionaire has the disadvantage of taking longer for the respondent to complete. In fact, he or she may refuse to fill out such questions. Besides being difficult to tabulate and summarize, its answers may ramble, be incorrect, or fail to report something the respondent would have mentioned had a list of options been provided. On the positive side, it gives the individual a sense of freedom of expression.

They give a truer picture of feelings, attitudes, and subtleties of the respondent. On balance, the open-end type is more suitable for personal interviews or telephone surveys.

The checkbox question is similar to the objective test. It may be merely a yes-no, true-false choice, or it may be somewhat more extensive. The answer or answers are selected among three or more alternatives and are checked off in the appropriate box. As in multiple-choice testing, answers may also be indicated by circling the correct choice. The advantage of this checkbox testing is its simplicity and speed of response. For busy people who are asked to respond to a questionaire, the researcher is asking them for only a small commitment of time and trouble. Because it is fo fast to use, it is low in cost both to the respondent, who wastes little of his regular working time, and to the researcher who obtains the replies quickly and tabulates the answers more efficiently. Furthermore, the multiple-choice arrangement provides a guide of possibilities for the respondent. He or she does not have to think laboriously through each answer, and the list may give the respondent an option he or she might not have considered.

Scaling   The multiple=choice form also permits scaling. Scaling is a method of social science that permits the assignment of quantitative values to attitudes, feelings, and other subjective concepts. For example, if the question is; Do you feel confident that a business recovery will occur after January 1--a multiple=choice answer might be:

1.__ Extremely confident
2.__ Very confident
3.__ Confident
4.__ Not Confident
5.__ Extremely unconfident

A variant of this technique is used for rating a person in personnel work, as for example in references. Another usage is to gauge intensity of feeling, as in asking such a question as, "How strongly do you feel that inflation, not unemployment, is the worst economic evil?"

Mixed Objective and Open-end Questions   The disadvantages of rigid objective questions include difficult, time-consuming efforts to construct a good set of questions. The yes-no, true-false statement must be constructed precisely so no ambiguity exists. If there is a possibility of a third choice, such as, "I don't know," it must be listed. Often such dual-choice questions are followed by related questions as in question 4 in Figure 8-1; "Have you been to the museum before?" The yes-no choice here is unequivocal, but it doest not provide much information. The follow-on, amplifying question provides more specific information of dates and times. The multiple-choice type has less of the rigidity of the yes-no answer, but it also requires much care in providing unambiguous choices. Overlapping alternatives are the bane of researchers who construct such questionaires.

The combination of a checkbox (see question 1 in Figure 8-1) with a fill-in questionaire is also a possibility, but clearly it adds to the problems the researcher faces with the open-end method. No doubt the last option in question 1 ("anything else?") is necessary for flexibility, but the open-end questions of the first two choices may add more effort to the questionaire than is justified in the response.

Pretesting and Common Sense   Pretesting is the key word to keep in mind while creating a first questionaire. For reasons indicated, it is wiser to think in terms of a multiple-choice formulation. In order to develop these multiple-choice questions, first formulate some open=end questions and pretest them on a few friends. Ideally, it would be better to test on persons similar to those to be surveyed, but this is often not possible. From the answers, you can make a set of multiple-choice questions. Then pretest this second questionaire to create more choices and to avoid overlapping choices. Finally, the revised questionaire should be ready.

Some other rules governing questionaire construction include the following: The number of questions should be brief--eight or ten questions are all many people can tolerate. For longer questionaires three pages are probably a maximum. The questions should be clear and fairly simple. Choose words with precise, unbiased, or not leading (loaded) meanings. Include the option "other" or "others (explain)" liberally. Use double spacing and easily read typed lines on clean white bond or xerox paper. Set up some kind of question numbering (precoding) system that can be used easily for tabulation either by machine or by hand. Pretesting should determine the question order of the questions. Usually easy, interesting, and noncontroversial questions should be first, with the more complex, sensitive questions last. Common sense is obviously an indispensable aide.

Administering Questionaires

Distributing questionaires may be done by interviewing, mailing or telephoning. Obviously interviewing imposes heavy time requirements on the researcher. Mailing is quicker, and telephoning accomplishes much in quite a short time. Each mode has advantages and disadvantages. Each channel will be discussed below in considerable length and summarized in Figure 8-2.

Personal Interviews   The advantages of the personal interview are many. First, the personal interview permits the use of questionaires of wider scope and the acquisition of better responses. The face-to-face nature of the interview makes it hard to brush off the interviewer. More complicated questions can be asked, and a skilled interviewer can probe foolish or superficial answers. Since the identity of the respondent is usually known, there is likely to be more responsibility to his or her replies. The interpersonal interaction of a skilled interviewer can overcome hostilities and get cooperation from people who would not bother to complete a mailed questionaire. Discussion questionaires, impossible with mail or telephone survey, can be answered even tape recorded. Nonresponse rates are very low, and, generally, the interviewer has a lot of control. He or she can not only focus the interviews on people of this or that category (age, sex, income, etc.); but also the interviewer can influence and control the interviewing conditions. Thus, experienced survey people consider the interview method to be superior to the mail or the telephone survey.

Disadvantages, however, also exist. This method is likely to the most expensive of the available methods. If the researcher does his or her own interviewing, the opportunity cost of the days foregone from other work and the daily travel expenses quickly mount up. If interviewers are hired, the expense of training and sending them into the field are high. Interviewers can cheat the researcher, deviate from instructions, be incompetent, and allow bias to creep into their interviews. The headaches of training, supervising, and controlling of interviewers can be imagined.

Mailing   The mailed questionaire is suitable for surveys under certain conditions. First, the group surveyed should be literate--on a well-designed document. People like lawyers, teachers, college students have little trouble in making choices. They can follow written instructions on the instrument or in the cover letter. But if a researcher were surveying the buying habits of ghetto families, an interview survey would be preferable. Another condition is homogeneity of the group. College seniors would be more homogeneous than people with some college. A third consideration would be the time needed for a mailing. People do not answer questionaires in sufficient volume on the first mailing, thus making successive requests necessary to obtain an adequate set of responses. Lastly, mailing charges, including stamped-return envelopes, can mount up very quickly so that the researcher must be ready to commit considerable funds to the effort or else be able to secure outside funding.

If the conditions are met, the advantages of the effort must be cost-benefit against the disadvantages. Advantage include assurance in reaching people directly without the time and trouble of personal interviews. Mail is picked up at the address (home or business), and people can answer more efficiently. They have more time to read and think what their answer will be in a privacy undisturbed by the presence of the interviewer or by the immediate demand of a telephone question. If the questionaire is to be returned unsigned, people will answer more freely and honestly than in a personal or telephone interview. Indeed, some data are so sensitive they are difficult to obtain with any method but the anonymous questionaire.[6]

On the negative side, the mailing survey faces the apathy of the receiver. If a third of the questionaires are returned with the first mailing, it would be propitious. In a survey on retired or resigned officers conducted for the author through Air Force Channels and under official auspices, it was lucky to receive a 50 percent return from a homogeneous, dedicated, and interested population, even after several follow-up mailings.[7] Another drawback is that people do not answer all the questions. Similarly, the may answer incorrectly, because they misunderstand, read hurriedly, or act mischievously. Moreover, no personal check on honesty and accuracy might be obtained from the interview.

As noted earlier, the mailed questionaire requires a cover letter, stating the purpose of the survey, the auspices under which it is being conducted, and to whom the questionaire should be returned. Some of this information should be at the top of the first page of the questionaire in case the cover letter is lost.

Telephone Survey   This survey may be looked on as a "quick and dirty"' method because it is handy for securing some reaction in a hurry. Its big advantage is the speed of response. With a short set of questions, a researcher may amass may answers in a few hours. It is also a low-cost method: if one has unlimited calls, the additional cost is only in the time spent performing the survey. Phone calls may also be used to supplement the other methods--if one does not have enough responses.

On the negative side, it assumes those people being questioned have telephones, which means they tend to be at least middle income. In 1936 a famous popular magazine The Literary Digest conducted a pole based on people in the telephone book. It forecast Alf Landon, the Republican opponent of Franklin Roosevelt, to be the winner in the coming presidential election of that year. Unfortunately, after the election the magazine was out of business, and the lesson that telephone surveys are biased toward higher income, more established people has never been forgotten.

Other disadvantages include the limitation on the information obtainable and the need to keep the questions more simple than in mailed questionaires or personal interviews. The telephone conversation must be confined to a few minutes with only a few questions possible--say, up to a half dozen. Even these must be simple, tending to yes-no answers. For example, in a business study designed to ask upper-income housewives about their needs for domestic help, such questions as, "Do you have a maid?" or "Are you planning to hire a maid this year?" offered yes-no choices. In just a few minutes the harvest of information from such inquiries is limited. Nevertheless, the well-designed telephone survey has its place in garnering some essential information in a hurry. It is frequently employed in market research studies where speed is an essential ingredient.

The merits and demerits of the three methods are summarized in Figure 8-2; three other minor methods of data collection are discussed briefly in the following sections.

FIGURE 8-2
MERITS AND DEMERITS OF MAIN DATA COLLECTION METHODS

I. Personal Interviews

Advantages
1. Distribution of instruments is very controlled
2. Interviewer meets respondents and has eye-to-eye contact.
3. It is the most flexible method. The interviewer can probe and ask complicated questions not possible with other forms.
4. The non-response rate is low because the interviewer can get cooperation from people who would not bother if other methods were used.

Disadvantages
1. Labor involved makes it the most expensive of methods.
2. Interviewers may be biased unless carefully trained.
3. Interviewers may cheat and falsely fill out data; they may often hurry the respondent to answer.
4. Supervision to prevent such flaws in the system is difficult and expensive.

II.   Mailing

Advantages
1. It reaches people directly without much time and trouble.
2. Expense of mailing is cheaper than sending interviewers out.
3. It is possible to reach a larger, more representative sample.
4. People can answer more efficiently. They have privacy to read and think about their answers.
5. It is particularly good to question educated or loyal bodies of people.
6. If the questionaire is annonymous, people answer more freely and honestly.

Disadvantages	1.	Non-response rate is usually very high unless loyal body of people, like alumi, being studied.
	2.	People do not answer all the questions; some answer incorrectly or mischieviously.
	3.	The interviewer has no control over questionaires.
	4.	No lengthy probes or in-depth questions are possible.
	5.	People are slow to reply; therefore, mailing is often the slowest of methods.

III. Telephone

Advantages	1.	It is the quickest way to obtain some response.
	2.	Low-cost method (if one has a phone with unlimited calls).
	3.	The non-response is generally quite low.
	4.	Call backs are possible and not expensive.
	5.	Random selection of telephone subscribers can be easily made (every twentieth, fiftieth, or hundreth name selected).

Disadvantages	1.	There is a limit of a few minutes for the interview; people will not talk very long to the interviewer.
	2.	Questions must be short, factual, to the point or the respondent will hang up. The probing questions are at a minimum.
	3.	People without a telephone and non-listed numbers cannont be contacted.
	4.	People will tell the caller anything to get rid of him or her. Little control is possible.

Group Interview Questionaire Application

Another method of collecting data is distributing a questionaire to a group--a club, an association of people such as a teachers, or students in a college classroom. With support of the officers in charge, the management, or the professor, information can be obtained expeditiously and at low cost. In fact, for the individual researcher, this method is the cheapest way to obtain a sample of responses from a homogeneous group in a short time and is recommended to beginning researchers. Clearly, it is also good for opinion research. However, proper sampling is difficult with this method; the researcher must simply take the group as it is.

Mixed or Combination Methods

Often a combination of several methods may be useful. Thus, one method might be used to get cooperation for a second method. For example, letters might be sent asking for a personal interview, or a telephone call might be made requesting an unanswered questionaire, recently mailed to a respondnt, be filled out and returned. The double sampling technique is reported for cases in which a sample obtains basic information while a subsample probes more specific information. For example, a researcher might use a mail survey to examine the general characteristics of purchasers of imported cars and follow it up with intensive interviews of a subsample for more in-depth information.

Direct Observation is still another method for gathering data--for instance, store-patronage, pedestrians, and automobile-traffic counts. Many of these can be done by mechanical devices such as traffic counters or motion picture devices. They yield accurate facts, but the information is usually quite limited.

Sometimes, direct counting is combined with other methods. For example, the author was stopped in a city tunnel for an interview on where he was going, from where the trip had begun, and why he was traveling. The car was obviously selected at random for the interview; other cars were merely counted. This survey was probably the double sampling technique.

CHAPTER SUMMARY

This chapter covers field research, an exciting prospect for developing primary data, though it should not be undertaken lightly because of costs and time involved. Two kinds of research interviews exist. The diagnostic interview is conducted with knowledgeable persons who have experience in the field being investigated. The survey interview is used as a method of eliciting information in a sample survey.

To be credible, sample surveys must be based on scientific principles of sampling design. A sample represents the population being studied. There are various concepts of sampling, the random sample being most basic. The size of sample can be established by a formula based on several variables, including the standard deviation of the population (can be estimated) and the confidence level acceptable to the researcher.

Design of survey instruments or questionaires should be done thoughtfully, bearing in mind such considerations as types of questions (open-end or closed), wording sequencing, bias, clarity, and pretesting. Methods of distributing survey instruments include direct interviewing, mailing, or telephoning. Each method has its own advantages and drawbacks.

DISCUSSION QUESTIONS

1. Why does the researcher need diagnostic interviews? Why bother busy people when presumably you can obtain all information by exploratory research? Or can you?

2. Compare and contrast the diagnostic interview with the survey interview. Which requires more planning? Which is more difficult to do? Defend your answers.

3. The press or the TV media is always "doing a survey" by having an interviewer stop a few people and (say, maximum 15 or 20) on the street and ask them questions off the top of th interviewer's head. Is this procedure valid? Is it helpful or misleading? Discuss.

4. If the government and other organizations collect so much data, published and unpublished, in books, reports, or data bases (as demonstrated in chapters six and seven), why does a researcher need to do his or her own survey?

5. Discuss the advantages and disadvantages of:

       a. interview method
       b. mailed questionaires
       c. telephone survey

6. What is pretesting? Why is it necessary?

7. Identify and discuss briefly the following types of sampling:

       a. random
       b. stratified
       c. area or geographic
       d. proportional
       e. clustered

8. What is scaling? Give some examples.

NOTES

1. Robert Ferber and P.J. Verdoorn, Research Methods in Economics and Business (New York: McMillan, 1962), p. 208.

2. William A. Belson and B.A. Thompson, Bibliography on Methods of Social and Business Research (New York: Halstead Press, 1973).

3. Anne F. Fenlason, Essentials in Interviewing (New York: Harper, 1952), p. 102.

4. A judgmental sample is simply collected from enough persons, in the judgment of the researcher, to adequately represent the group studied. The newspaper and TV media use it a good deal to get some kind of opinion.

5. See for example, A.L. Edwards, Techniques of Attitude Scale Construction (New York: Appleton-Century, 1957).

6. The public is becoming aware of some branches of privacy in which supposedly anonymous questionaires have secret markings revealing the respondent. Such unethical practices are against the very nature of honest scientific enquiry and should be avoided.

7. Daniel L. Spencer, "Value Transfer of Military-Acquired Skills to Civilian Employment," KYKLOS (Basle), 12, Fasc. 3 (1969), 467-92.

9
QUANTITATIVE TECHNIQUES

At this point information has been collected from either data sources or original sources such as company records or a questionaire survey. Now this gathered information must be organized. Some logical classification is required either to present the material directly or to prepare the information for statistical manipulation and analysis. Nowadays, this analysis is conducted usually with a statistical computer program, the subject of the next chapter.

This chapter proceeds from simple summarizing devices to more complex statistical methods. The objective is to provide the uninitiated researcher with some step-by-step quantitative techniques as well as offer a refresher guide for those knowledgeable in the subject. It is also an easy referral source for a researcher planning to run his or her data through a computer program, complementing the next chapter on computer usage. It is not, however, a substitute for a statistics textbook or a statistics course.

The main subjects covered in this chapter are the traditional ones of basic, descriptive, statistics: frequency distribution, measures of central tendency and dispersion, statistical estimation, standard error of the mean, and some measures of relationship as the scatter diagram and linear regression analysis. For more advanced matters the researcher should consult standard statistical works.

SIMPLE SUMMARIZING DEVICES

One of the simplest methods of tabulation is simply to record the answers of the questionaire on a blank questionaire form. The resulting "Summary Questionaire" can be used in the report, probably as an appendix, and the appropriate statements drawn from it for presentation in the text. For instance, in an evaluative survey of the MANDAT Project, a training project directed by the author the questionaire results were set forth in an appendix; while interpretation was made in the text. A typical text statement in the report read as follows:

27 percent of the students in our courses are experiencing their first post-high school education. 11 percent have some 11 percent have some technical education but no college work; 8 percent have less than one year's college credits prior to MANDAT participation. 15 percent say they have one year of

college. Thus, of those who did not leave the answer blank, 61 percent have 1 year of college or less. 38 percent of our students never went to college. Put in more dramatic, rounded terms, almost two out of five students have only one year of college or less.

If the text reader wanted the tabulation, he or she could turn to the appendix.

Another basic device for summarizing data to present information is the humble table. Though the old joke says, "When reading, I look the tables straight in the eye and then go around them,"--the table is an essential tool. They organize information showing basic relationships, trends, class frequencies, and other characteristics of collected data. Of special interest is the frequency table, a basic summary device that reduces large quantities of data to manageable proportions. For even the least quantitative subjects, tables usually can be constructed. They enhance any study and should almost always be included even if only in the appendix. Care should be taken to number each table , to give it a correct title, and to document it with a source. Tables should be numbered sequentially, and a list of tables should be provided in the beginning of the text after the table of contents.

Other devices of descriptive statistics include graphs, bar charts, pie diagram, and statistical maps. Essentially, they are largely refinements of the table or tabular concept, but they have the advantage of an attractive visual form. Some examples of these are provided in any statistics text. Any research effort dealing with numbering should have at least a few of these devices. Beyond simple tables and charts, if data have been acquired from some agency or by a sample survey, two methods of setting up the data for analysis can be used: the array and the frequency distribution.

The Array

The array, as its name suggests, is simply an arrangement of the data from smallest to largest or vice=versa. If, for example, a researcher had collected data on a sample of ten minority business enterprises in his or her home town and a volume of sales figure for each business, the researcher might array these data as follows:

FIGURE 9-1
Sales of Minority Business
(in dollars)

Name of Business	Numerical Array of Sales per year
A	20,500
B	25,000
C	30,000
D	31,000
E	38,000
F	49,000
G	49,000
H	62,000
I	75,000
J	89,000
K	93,500

Source: Hypothetical data for illustration.

The array is a simple but useful research device. We can see the range and measures of central tendency (mean, median, mode) are either evident or easily calculated. (These terms will be explained further in the text; these are mean: $51,091 median: $49,000 and mode: $49,000.)

The Frequency Distribution

For large quantities of data the frequency distribution is the essential tool. It arranges the data in classes or equally spaced intervals. The number of items in a class is called the class frequency. Applicable to a sample or the entire universe, the frequency distribution can be constructed for many types of data. Figure 9-2 is an example of data taken from the field of agriculture in a study done by the research unit of the Department of Agriculture.[2] It gives the yield of corn, varying in one state, Iowa, over a long span of years. The years, 1866-1943, are, however, classified by yield per harvested acre.

FIGURE 9-2

Corn: Frequency distribution of years classified by yield per harvested acre, Iowa, 1866-1943

Yield per harvested acre Bushels	Frequency of years Number
15.0-19.9	2
20.0-24.9	1
25.0-29.9	5
30.0-34.9	15
35.0-39.9	23
40.0-44.9	24
45.0-49.9	7
50.0-54.9	1

Source: Department of Agriculture

Each class shows the number of years in which the yield fell in the defined class interval. In 15.0-19.9 bushels class, for example, only two years had low yields. The frequency distribution approaches a normal distribution or bell=shaped curve, seen when the distribution is plotted on graph paper as in Figure 9-3. The shaded area, also called a histogram, shows the number of years when the yields fell in each class as given in the previous table. The smooth curve was imposed by free-hand methods but can be computed mathematically from formulas available in standard statistics books or manuals. In this case the curve is skewed or slanted, to the left. It is also of interest to note that the data in the later years were adjusted to allow for the famous innovation of hybrid corn, which caused the yields to jump.

Figure 9-4 provides a typical normal curve--the symmetrical, bell shaped curve--which contrasts with the skewed or slanted curve of Figure 9-3. In statistics, this normal curve is a very important curve, which will be discussed later in connection with statistical estimation.

FIGURE 9-3
Frequency Distribution Plotted on Graph Paper

Corn: *Yield Per Harvested Acre, Iowa, 1866-1943* ✳

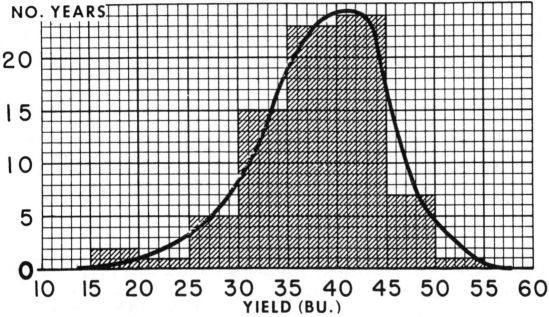

✳ *ADJUSTED FOR ESTIMATED EFFECTS OF HYBRID SEED*

Source: U.S. Department of Agriculture.

FIGURE 9-4
The Normal Curve

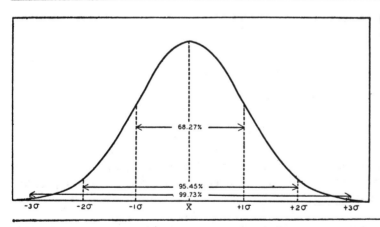

(Shows percentages of area subtended under the curve for 1,2, and 3 standard deviations)

MEASURES OF CENTRAL TENDENCY (AVERAGES) AND DISPERSION

Measures of Central Tendency

Measures of central tendency--the mean, median, and mode--summarize the data and permit comparisons with other batches of data or other research studies. Perhaps the most useful and widespread method of summarizing quantitative data is the arithmetic <u>mean</u>, though its close relatives--the <u>median</u> and <u>mode</u>--are also worthy of examination. More technical measures, geometric and harmonic means, can be found in standard statistics books. The arithmetic mean is the term for everyday concept, <u>average</u>. It is simply the sum of the values divided by the number of observations. Thus, if three girls are 5'6", 5'4", and 5'8" in height, the average is (66" + 64" + 68") /3 = 66" or 5'6". The median is simply a place average, the midpoint of the distribution when arrayed in sequence. In the height example, it would be 5'6". Lastly, the mode is the value that occurs most frequently or is most typical of the items in a distribution.

Beginning researchers should concentrate on using the mean and median. Though the mean is useful in samples and is more widely used, it is sometimes influenced by extreme values in the distribution. The median is not so influenced. For example, in income comparisons between two commodities, the median is better because it is less influenced by extreme values. It is often a good idea to calculate both measures, specifying them exactly with their proper terms and avoiding the popular term, "average."

Measures of Dispersion

Closely associated with the measures of central tendency are <u>measure of dispersion</u>--the idea of deviation or spread of the observations away from the average. <u>Standard deviation</u> measures the spread or scatter of the data on either side of the central value and tells us how representative of the data is the mean or median. Obviously, if the spread is large, the average is less representative of the batch than having a small standard deviation. If the spread is small, the opposite is true. The mean and the standard deviation are perhaps the most widely used measures in statistical analysis.

The formula for the <u>arithmetic mean</u>:

$$\overline{X} = \frac{\Sigma X}{N}$$

where

$\overline{X}$ = the arithmetic mean

Σ = summation sign

$\underline{X}$ = values of the variable

$\underline{N}$ = number of observed values

With this formula, the arithmetic mean can be calculated from the raw data or from an array. For example, the arithmetic mean for the data given in the array in Figure 9-1 is $51,091.

When the data is given in the form of a frequency distribution, also called <u>group data</u>, the formula for the arithmetic mean is as follows:

$$\overline{X} = \frac{\Sigma(\underline{fm})}{\Sigma \underline{N}}$$

where

$\overline{X}$ = the arithmetic mean

Σ = summation sign

$\underline{f}$ = frequencies in each class

$\underline{m}$ = midpoint of each class

$\underline{N}$ = total number of cases

The mean for the data in Figure 9-2 is calculated to be 37.77 (see also Figure 9-5).

<u>Weighted Mean</u>   In the preceding computation of the arithmetic mean, each observation has the same weight. However, some observations have more weight than others in the computation. In this case, the weighted average formula has to be used:

$$\overline{\underline{X}} = \frac{\Sigma\, \underline{wX}}{\Sigma\, \underline{w}}$$

where

$\overline{\underline{X}}$ = arithmetic mean

$\underline{X}$ = values of the variable

$\underline{w}$ = the weight

For example to calculate a student average score in a statistics course, we compute as follows:

Examinations	Scores $\underline{X}$	Weight $\underline{w}$	Weighted Score $\underline{wX}$
1st Test	80	20	1,600
2nd Test	70	20	1,400
Final	90	60	5,400
		100	8,400

$$\overline{\underline{X}} = \frac{8,400}{100} = 84$$

That is, the student's weighted average is 84.

<u>Median</u>   The method of finding the median for arrayed data is simply to locate the middle item or, if there are an even number of items in the array, to average the two middle items. When the data are given as a frequency distribution, the formula for the median is:

$$\underline{Md} = \underline{L}_1 + \left(\frac{\frac{N}{2} - \Sigma_1}{\underline{fm}_1} \times \underline{\underline{j}} \right)$$

where

$\underline{Md}$ = median

$\underline{L}/1$ =   the median class lower limit

$\dfrac{N}{2}$ =   total frequencies halved

Σ =   Cumulated frequencies to the median class

$\underline{fm}/1$ =   number of frequencies in medican class

$\underline{i}$ =   size of the medican class interval

The median for the frequency distribution in Figure 9-2 is computed by this formula to be 38.43 (see also Figure 9-5).

<u>The Standard Deviation</u>   To calculate the data organized in an array, we use the formula for the <u>standard deviation</u>:

$$= \sqrt{\frac{\Sigma \underline{x}^2}{\underline{N}}}$$

where

σ =   the standard deviation

Σ =   the summation sign

$\underline{x}^2$ =   squares of the data from the mean, $(\underline{X}-\overline{\underline{X}})^2$

$\underline{N}$ =   total number of values

Standard deviation: $\sigma = \sqrt{\dfrac{\Sigma \underline{f}(m-\overline{X})^2}{\underline{N}}}$

σ =   the standard deviation

Σ =   the summation sign

f =   frequencies appearing in the classes

$(\underline{M}-\overline{X})^2$ =   squares of the deviations of the midpoints in each class from the mean

$\underline{N}$ =   total frequencies

Figure 9-5 is an sample calculation of mean, median, and the standard deviation. It will be noted that the mean and median are not the same as would be true of a normal distrbution or bell-shaped curve. The standard deviation is small--less than one third the value of the mean, which makes the mean a good average of the data. That is, since there is not too much dispersion, the arithmetic mean is fairly representative of the data. Had the

FIGURE 9-5

CALCULATION OF MEAN, MEDIAN, AND STANDARD DEVIATION

X	f	cf	m	fm	m-X̄	(m-X̄)²	f(m-X̄)²
15.0-19.9	2	2	17.45	34.90	-20.32	412.90	825.80
20.0-24.9	1	3	22.45	22.45	-15.32	234.70	234.70
25.0-29.9	5	8	27.45	137.25	-10.32	106.50	532.50
30.0-34.9	15	23	32.45	486.75	-5.32	28.30	424.50
35.0-39.9	23	46	37.45	861.35	-0.32	0.10	2.30
40.0-44.9	24	70	42.45	1,018.80	4.68	21.90	525.60
45.0-49.9	7	77	47.45	332.15	9.68	93.70	655.90
50.0-54.9	1	78	52.45	52.45	14.68	215.50	215.50
Σ	78			2,946.10			3,416.80

$$\overline{X} = \frac{\Sigma(fm)}{N} = \frac{2,946.10}{78} = 37.77$$

$$Md = L + \frac{\frac{N}{2} - \Sigma_1}{fm_1} \times i = \frac{\frac{78}{2} - 23}{23} \times .5 = 34.95 + \frac{16}{23} \cdot .5$$

$$= 34.95 + 3.48$$

$$= 38.43$$

$$\sigma = \sqrt{\frac{\Sigma f(m - \overline{X})}{N}} = \sqrt{\frac{3,416.80}{78}} = \sqrt{43.8051} = 6.62$$

standard deviation been larger, the mean would not be as good a representative of this collection of data.

Normal Curve   The normal curve or bell-shaped curve illustrated in Figure 9-4 and mentioned briefly before is the basis for statistical inference or estimation. The normal curve represents the normal distribution, which is a mathematical phenomenon describing values of a variable occurring in large numbers. The properties of the normal curve are of special note and make possible scientific inference or estimation on the basis of probability theory.

These properties are (1) that the arithmetic mean is at the maximum of the normal curve; (2) that the mean is always equal to the median and the mode; (3) that the mean plus and minus one standard deviation includes 68.27 percent of the area subtended under the curve; (4) the mean plus or minus two standard deviations includes 95.45 percent of the area subtended under the curve; and (5) the mean plus or minus three standard deviations (σ) includes 99.73 percent of the area subtended under the curve.

The probabilities in statistical inference are based on these relations of sigma (σ) and the area under the normal curve. The term confidence level is used to indicate our confidence that our sample is representative of the universe. Any confidence level can be related to a multiple of sigma, but 90, 95, and 99 percent confidence level are typically used in statistical work. Thus, a 90 percent confidence level equals 1.645σ; 95 percent confidence level equals 1.96σ; and a 99 percent confidence level equals 2.576σ. With these equivalences in mind, statistical estimation is next.

Statistical Estimation

In the corn-yield example the data given are not a sample but are all the values of the actual years considered. In fact, this data could be a sample of a longer series of years than those given, and it will be used in this way later. The principles for frequency distributions already set forth apply to samples as well, but there is a further consideration. The sample represents the universe, but the question of how representative it is must be faced. This is the subject of statistical estimation or inference. Statistical inference is the process of estimating properties of a population from the data in a random sample.

The data in the sample are analysed to give a single estimate (point estimate) of the population's characteristics (mean, standard deviation, etc.). The chances are that this sample will not give the true mean. Indeed, sample means will clearly vary from sample to sample. So, some likely estimate of the sample mean deviation from the true population mean is needed. Within what range would we expect the true value to be?

The Sampling Distribution

To cope with this variation on the sample mean, statisticians have developed the concept of the sampling distribution, a hypothetical large number of sample frequency distributions, which, in theory, could be taken from a universe. Each of these samples would have a mean, a standard deviation, and other characteristics. The sampling distribution would be a frequency distribution of the characteristics--say the mean of these samples. In other words, a new frequency distribution could be constructed from these arithmetic means of the many samples. This sampling distribution means would be normally distributed and come out in the shape of the bell=shaped curve, or normal curve. The mean of these sample means would approximate the true mean of the universe. The areas under the normal curve would then give use the probabilities in inferring the arithmetic mean of the universe from the mean of the sample.

In practice, there is usually only one sample, because it would be too time consuming to take hundreds of samples and calculate their means. However, we can calculate a value called the standard error of the mean, which sets confidence limits to the deviation the sample mean can depart from the mean of the sample means or from the true mean of the universe. The standard error of the mean is computed as follows:

$$\sigma_{\overline{X}} = \frac{s}{\sqrt{n}}$$

where

$\sigma_{\overline{X}}$ = standard error of the mean

$\underline{s}$ = sample estimate of the standard deviation of universe

n = size of sample

With this standard error of the mean, the area under the normal curve may be calculated, which can be used as, or transformed to, a probability in making an inference about the mean of the sample as against the mean of the universe.

More specifically, if the researcher wishes to estimate the mean of the universe from the data of his or her sample, the following procedures are followed. First, the arithmetic mean and the standard deviation of the sample are calculated. Second, we compute the standard error of the sample mean, which is used to construct a confidence level desired (say, 95 or 99 percent). Confidence levels stated in percentages correspond to areas under the normal curve according to the standard deviations away from the mean. Any desired confidence level can be converted to standard deviations by using tables of Areas of the Normal Curve, given in appendices of many statistics books; common confidence levels of 95 and 99 percent correspond to 1.956 and 2.576, respectively.

Using the data from the previous example, we can compute the following:

$$\overline{X} = 37.77$$
$$s = 6.62$$
$$n = 78$$

$$\sigma_{\overline{X}} = \frac{s}{\sqrt{n}} = \frac{6.62}{\sqrt{78}} = \frac{6.62}{8.83177} = .7497$$

99% confidence level = 2.576σ

2.576 x .7497 = 1.93; $\overline{X} \pm 1.93 = 37.77 \pm 1.93$

= 39.70 and 35.84.

The resulting interval between 35.8 and 39.7 is an interval in which the means of 99 out of 100 samples would be expected to fall. Put alternatively, the probability that the true mean of the universe falls within the limits is 99 percent.

MEASURES OF RELATIONSHIP

In addition to measures of central tendency (mean, median, mode) and measures of dispersion and variability (standard deviation and others), there is a third important measure for research: the measure of the relationship between two or more sets of values in two or more distributions, the researcher often wants to determine the relationship or association between them. For example, a problem might be: What is the relationship between the price of pork and the amount of the pork's consumption? Or is it true that as the population in a county or city rises so does its per=capita income? Or, Do sales representatives who have high IQs also make big sales for the company and high commissions for themselves.

In each of these problems the researcher would secure data or observations on each of the variables involved; then he or she would try to find the relationship between these variables. If the consumption of pork tended to fall as the price rose (a reasonable hypothesis from economic theory), the relationship would be an inverse one. If the two variables moved in the same direction (as is likely in the second and third problems), the relationship is said to be direct or positive. Variables are also referred to as a dependent and independent according to which determines the other. Sometimes it is easy to see which is dependent, as in rainfall and crop growth. Clearly, the crop depends on the rain, not the other way around. In less clear cases, we arbitrarily designate that one variable is independent and the other dependent. Thus, consumption of pork (dependent variable) depends on price (independent variable), though there is logic also in the growth. Clearly, the crop depends on the rain, not the other way around. In less clear cases, we arbitrarily designate that one variable is independent and the other dependent. Thus, consumption of pork (dependent variable) depends on price (independent variable), though there is logic also in the reverse relationship.

Scatter Diagram

The simplest way to obtain a relationship between two variables is the scatter diagram. Two sets of values of two variables are plotted on a graph with a dot placed so as to represent values for each individual or unit observation. By convention, the x axis is used for the independent variable; and the y axis, for the dependent variable. After a cloud of dots has been plotted, the researcher can learn much by just inspecting and even more by fitting a line or curve through the dot cloud. If it is a linear relationship, the dots or points plotted will tend to follow a diagonal line. Though curvilinear relationships exist, for these examples we will concentrate on linear relationships.

The coefficient of correlation is a single value used to represent the relationship between two sets of collected data. It represents the extent to which one variable (dependent variable) is accompanied be changes in the other (independent variable). When the arrangement of dots on the scatter diagram all fall on a straight line, the correlation coefficient has a value of

1.00 and is said to be "perfect." If there is no relationship between the sets of variables, the coefficient is 0. If the negative or inverse relationship is perfect, the coefficient would be negative 1.00. In practice, a research distribution is seldom perfect, and the coefficient falls somewhere between negative 1.00 to zero (0.00) to positive 1.00. If the coefficient were .90 or higher, a high positive correlation would exist; If negative .90, a high negative (inverse) correlation. If the correlation is in the eighties (.80s), most analysts would say, a "good" correlation exists. The sixties (.60s) and seventies (.70s) would indicate "considerable" correlation. Below .60, the possibility of systematic relationship weakens rapidly.

Consider these diagrams showing possible relationships between values of varible x and variable y:

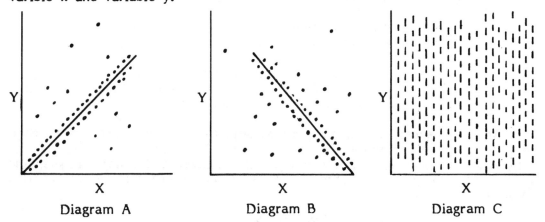

Diagram A   Diagram B   Diagram C

Diagram A shows a high, positive linear relationship; diagram B shows a high negative relationship, and diagram C indicates virtually zero or no relationship between the variables.

There are several methods of calculating correlation coefficients, the most commonly used is the Pearson-Moment Coefficient of Correlation (Pearsonian Coefficient of Correlation) and the Rank Order Correlation Coefficient (Spearman's Rank Correlation Coefficient). For calculation and use of these and other indexes of correlation, the reader should refer to standard textbooks on statistics. However, available canned computer programs often provide the convenient coefficient values as part of the researcher's computer run and printout. Though the computer eliminates the drudgery of calculation, the researcher should still have a clear idea of the meaning and use of these values in research.

Linear Regression Equation   The line imposed on the scatter diagram of dots is called the line of regression. A device used for estimating the value of one variable from the value of the other, it represents the average relationship between the two variables. The term "regression" is close to the term "correlation," but regression implies prediction or forecasting of the dependent variable from the independent while correlation refers merely to the measurment of relationship. In practice, however, the distinction is often ignored.

The simplest way to draw the regression line is by inspection. That is, the analyst draws the line on the diagram by hand so it passes through the center of the dots. While this simple technique can be used, a more scientific method of locating the regression line is the method of least squares. This widely used method takes its name from idea that the "best fit" is the line that minimizes the deviations of the observed points from the line of regression. Since the deviations above the line are positive (+) and those below the line are negative (-), squared deviations are used to eliminate the signs--hence, the name "least squares."

The concept may be explained as follows. Any straight line is represented by the equation:

$$\underline{y}_c = \underline{a} + \underline{bx}$$

where

y_c = the values on the regression line

a = the y intercept, or the value of the Y variable when x = 0

b = the slope of the line or the amount of change in the Y variable that is associated with a change of one unit in the X variable.

To fit a regression line to a set of data by the least squares method requires finding the values a and b for the equation of the straight line satisfying the criterion that the sum of the squared differences between the y_c and the y values be a minimum. These formulas are used to compute the values of a and b.

$$a = \frac{\sum x^2 \sum y - \sum x \cdot \sum xy}{n \cdot \sum x^2 - (\sum x)^2}$$

$$b = \frac{n \cdot \sum xy - \sum x \cdot \sum y}{n \cdot \sum x^2 - (\sum x)^2}.$$

Again reference to standard textbooks may be made for fuller explanation, but standard computer programs can provide calculations with lightening speed and even give computer printout drawings of scatter diagrams.

Multiple regression analysis may be mentioned briefly. It is an extension of simple regression and correlation analysis, but two or more independent variables in such equations make them much more difficult to compute. Fortunately, standardized computer programs are available to do this work quickly. Again reference to standard statistics textbooks may be made for fuller explanation of both simple and multiple types.

CHAPTER SUMMARY

Almost any research project can make use of a few simple statistical presentations and tables. Such numerical pictures enhance any research report on even the least of quantitative subjects. Data should be summarized in the text and given in full in the appendix. Other devices of descriptive statistics, especially the frequency distribution, can be used profitable in reporting and analyzing data.

Measures of central tendency--averages like mean or median--and measures of dispersion around the mean--typically, the standard deviation--are basic tools of analysis for researchers. Statistical inference, meaning inferences about a universe derived from sampling that universe, is another important idea for research. The standard error of the mean is a useful concept that permits us to set confidence limits on how far our sample mean might depart from the true mean of the universe.

Measures of relationship is the third type of statistical treatment useful for researchers. Scatter diagrams, regression analysis, and coefficients of correlation are important tools for research in determining if and how one variable moves systematically in some way with another variable.

DISCUSSION QUESTIONS

1. You are doing case-study research, but you only have a few cases. Can you suggest ways to use quantitative techniques in this project?

2. Distinguish the mean, median, and mode. What are some advantages and disadvantages of each. Which is the most important? Why?

3. Look up some other measures of central tendency in statistical textbooks. Discuss why we should or should not use them.

4. Define standard deviation. Why is it so important?

5. Define the standard error of the mean. What does it relate to confidence limits?

6. Draw a scatter diagram for two variables with which you are working (real or imaginary). Are they highly correlated or not? Why or why not?

7. What is the line of regression and the method of least squares all about? Can you use a computer in their calculation? Explain.

NOTES

1. Some well-known statistical textbooks and monographs include, but are not limited to, J.R. Stockton and C.T. Clark, Introduction to Business and Economic Statistics 5th ed. (Cincinnati: Southwestern, 1975); Morris Hamburg, Basic Statistics: A Modern Approach, 2nd ed. (New York: Harcourt Brace Jovanovch, 1979); Robert Schlaifer, Probability and Statistics for Business Decisions (New York: McGraw-Hill 1959); Jean Namias, Applications of Quantitative Methods for Business Decisions (Jamaica, N.Y.: St John's Univ. Press, 1975); W. Edwards Deming, Sample Design in Business Research (New York:Wiley, 1960).

2. Frederick V. Waugh, Graphic analysis in Research (Washington, D.C.: U.S. Department of Agriculture, 1955), p. 5.

10
COMPUTER DATA MANIPULATION

The development of computer electronic data processing has greatly simplified and aided the handling of data by statistical methods. Before the computer was available, researchers limited themselves to working with only a few variables because of the labor and time involved in hand computations. Now, as researchers have become more familiar with data processing and as computer technology has improved, computers can produce analyses in a few minutes that used to take hours or days. The researcher does not have to program the computer; programmers are available for that task. In fact, for many statistical routines, packaged or canned programs are available. The existence of these packaged programs for researchers who face statistical computations is a great advantage.

In the simplest instance the researcher may take his or her data to the computer room and ask to find a program that will calculate the various statistical measures covered earlier. That is, such typical data characteristics as the range, mean, median, mode, standard deviation, and standard error of the mean can be obtained with the help of computer specialist. Again, the computer technician does not have to develop a special program for this research but has available appropriate packaged programs for the task. One of the most widely used is often referred to as SPSS from its title Statistical Package for the Social Sciences[1]. An introduction to its use for researchers will be given later in this chapter. Another, older but well-known package is the BMD or Biomedical Computer Program, which has many nicely packaged programs but is harder to use than the SPSS.[2] Still another is IBM's STAT/BASIC program discussed later. Mention should be made also of STATPAK, a workbook of computer statistical programs specifically designed to use with statistical textbooks.[3]

This chapter divides into two sections: "Some Computer Concepts" and "Computer Experience for Researchers." The first section covers some essential information on computer terms and ideas, both physical installations (hardware) and general ideas on programs and programming (software). With the second section the reader enters the world of computer usage through the SPSS system and learns by example how a researcher can develop a batch of computer cards for his or her data. Topics treated include types of computer cards, their punching and sequencing. Illustrations from descriptive statistics, such as frequency distribution and cross tabulations, are given, and the more analytical procedures pointed out.

SOME COMPUTER CONCEPTS

The researcher who has not had a course in the computer should have an elementary understanding of what they are and how they work. For research purposes a computer is simply a machine to which the researcher brings his or her assembled quantitative data. The machine performs certain manipulations on the data that are mechanized versions of statistical calculations. That is, the machine calculates the measures of central tendency, measures of variability, and measures of relationship learned in statistics courses. The terms program or computer program are simply glorified expressions for computerized, statistical manipulation of the data collected by the researcher.

However, the computer is a complex machine that must be given detailed instructions. So, a science of computer programming has developed to instruct computers. Basically, from the researcher's standpoint the program is designed to transform the input of research data into the output of desired statistical characteristics. The researcher does not need to become a computer programmer to make use of the computer, but some sense of programmers and their paraphernalia is valuable in using the computer.

Hardware vs. Software

Computer matters usually are divided into software and hardware categories. The program is part of the software area, with which the researcher is more concerned; but a word first on the hardware basics is appropriate. The heart of the hardware or computer installation is the central processing unit (CPU). To this CPU are attached the memory or storage unit and input-output devices. Since computer installations vary from place to place and are constantly changing as new equipment becomes available, it is better to talk of functional "educational exposure" categories, of which one authority identifies five.[4] This classification together with some common hardware units in each category is as follows:

Input units put instructions and data into the computer. Common input units include card readers, paper and magnetic tape readers, typewriters, terminals, disks, and drums.

Storage units are the memory devices that hold instructions, data, and computed or partially computed results until needed. Common storage units are core, disk, tape, drum, capacitor, data cell, semiconductors, thin film, and surface storage media. Others are being developed.

Computation units do arithmetic and symbol manipulation. The computation units comprise the computer (but are of little use without the other units).

Output units provide ways of getting the results out of the computer. Line printers, typewriters, terminals, card punches, cathode ray display tubes, disks, drums, and tape units are among the common output devices.

Control units are perhaps the real heart of the computer. They direct which unit should do what and when. They are the "police officers" and the "administrative executives" of the entire complex.

For the researcher the important input device is the IBM Card or Hollerith Card, which is punched with the data, often by the researcher. These cards are combined with the program cards and fed into the machine. The output typically appears on a printout or resultant sheet that flows from the auxilliary printer. The input data are punched on the card with a key punch machine, the data being assigned to certain columns in an 80=column card. These data from a survey might be punched as follows:

Card Columns	Content
1-21	Last Name of Respondent
22-28	First Name or Initial
29-49	Address
50	Sex
51-52	Age
53-60	Coded Answers to Seven Questions Asked in Survey
61-80	Blank Columns Not Used

How the card looks is shown in the example:

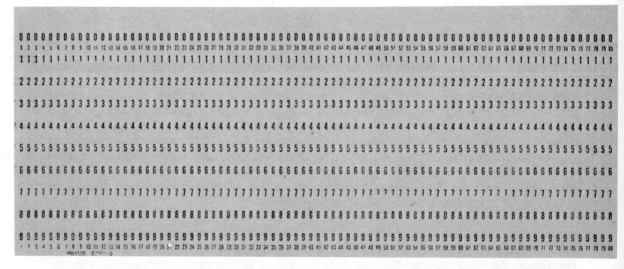

As noted, these data cards are fed into the computer together with the instructions on program cards. The computer performs its manipulations according to the instructions and gives the output or solution to the questions asked in the programmed instructions.

Computer Language

The programmed instructions to the computer are written in a special language. There are a number of these languages with peculiar sounding acronymic names like COBOL, ALGOL, TECO. For the researcher the important program is FORTRAN, which itself has many varieties or dialects. Currently, FORTRAN IV is the most important variant, and special courses (both credit and non credit) are widely available for researchers to learn of it.[5] While desirable, learning FORTRAN IV is not really necessary to use the computer for research, because canned programs and helpful computer technicians permit relatively uninformed use. Still, it is always good to have some knowledge of FORTRAN to comprehend intelligently what is going on. However, it is essential for the researcher to know statistics. Know statistics and you know what program to ask for and how to interpret the output.

There is another language called BASIC or STAT/BASIC for statistical work simpler than FORTRAN. BASIC was designed for time-sharing use and is relatively easy to use as a first language for beginners. Researchers can use it directly in a hands-on experience or, put more technically, in the interactive computer mode. BASIC has many different versions, but for IBM's STAT-BASIC, 40 statistical programs are available.[6]

Of course, many aspects of computers have not been covered in this discussion, which emphasized canned or packaged program usage. There are problems of coding and recoding data to prepare them in such a way that they can be easily represented on the IBM Cards. While some categories in a questionaire like "age" or "sex" are easily coded by appropriate numbers in two or one columns respectively, open-end questions may be quite difficult and time-consuming to represent. Modification of the data, such as creating scales or constructing indexes, may also be necessary. These matters and many others must be left to the researcher, who must read more widely and learn by experience, (lessons toward which the next section contributes).

COMPUTER EXPERIENCE FOR RESEARCHERS

The researcher must plunge into the world of computers. The only way to understand the computer is to do a specific analysis. An old proverb says, "experience is the best teacher"--an admonition even more true of computer use than of most fields. In the past such experience was a considerable chore. Fortunately, there is now a system fairly easy for the beginner: the SPSS or Statistical Package for the Social Science, which is available in primer form. This system is a based on FORTRAN computer language and requires very little knowledge of computers. SPSS is a canned program that manipulates data obtained by researchers in typical analyses used in statistics.

Again it must be repeated that there is no substitute for experimental learning in the computer field; however, this section attempts to set forth some ideas and suggestions to work with the SPSS in an initial effort. These remarks are not a substitute for buying the SPSS Primer or taking a training course.

Broadly speaking, there are two modes in working with computers: the interactive and the batch. The interactive or on-line mode involves a telephone sharing of some remote computer installation contacted by a telephone call. After telephone contact is made, the user sits at the terminal keyboard and "talks" to the computer by typing messages on the keyboard. The computer responds by flashing answers on the screen. Though this is a very good system, the researcher involved in initial research efforts using the SPSS is better off with batch mode.

The batch mode is simply a batch of computer cards developed as input by the researcher and given to the computer technicians to run off. A print out, which shows a one-time statistical analysis of the data, is received. No immediate interaction is possible, but the permanency of the deck of computer cards and the printout is valuable for research purposes. If instructed, the computer can "save" the program in its memory.

It is assumed, for purposes of discussion, that the researcher using the batch mode has developed a sample survey based on the principles set forth in chapter eight. Further, it is assumed that he or she knows some statistics or at least has read chapter nine. Also assumed is that the researcher has developed a questionaire such as that in Figure 10-1 and applied it to an appropriate sample of some defined population, say graduating seniors in the School of Business. Therefore, the researcher has developed some original data and is ready to process them with the help of the SPSS computer program.

FIGURE 10-1
SPSS COMPUTER RESEARCH ON BUSINESS
SCHOOL SENIORS' SURVEY ON ENERGY

1. ID _____

2. AGE ____

3. SEX (check one) ___MALE, ___FEMALE

4. INCOME (check one)

___$0-$9,999 ___$10,000-$19,999 ___20,000-$29,999 ___over $30,000

5. MARITAL STATUS (check one)

____Single   ____Married   ____Other

6. BIRTH ORDER ____

7. NUMBER OF SIBLINGS ____

8. EDUCATION (check one)
                        BA   MA
____ High School, ___BS, ___MS,

    Ph.D.
___Ed.D., ___Other

9. POLITICAL PARTY PREFERENCE (check one) ____Democratic,

____Republican, ____Independent, ____Other

10. MODE OF TRANSPORTATION to school or work (check one)

___Bus, ___Subway, ___Walk, ___Car, ___Other

11. At what percent level are you conserving energy? (check one)

___0%-25%, ___26%-50%, ___51%-75%, ___76%-100%

12. In your opinion, what will be the energy source in the future?
    (check one)

____Solar, ____Nuclear, ____Windmill, ____Fossil ____Other

Cards

In the batch mode the researcher's first job is to punch out the cards on the input device called the keypunch machine. This machine has an electric typewriter keyboard; its keys, when typed, cut holes in the blank cards stacked in the machine. When done in correct SPSS form, the keypunching results in a deck with an input that computer technicians can run off and thus create a printout of analysis for the researcher.

Without more ado, then, let us examine the character of the cards the researcher punches. There are three types of cards to be made:

1. JCL Cards or Job Control Language Cards

2. DD Cards or Data Definition Cards

3. TD Cards or Task Definition Cards

Let us examine each category in turn.

JCL cards   The JCL cards are indentification and security cards for the computer laboratory where the "job" is to be run. These cards vary from institution to institution depending on the regulations of that particular place. They also vary in number with each institution: College or universities, for instance, have only a few cards, while banks or insurance companies have as many as fifteen. Obviously, security problems involving money require more care and hence more cards. Typically, for university researchers, these JCL cards appear at the beginning and the end of the deck (FINISH). Typical types are the RUN NAME--which is anything the researcher calls his or her project (e.g., Technology Transfer, Solar Energy Study)--and the indentification or ID number, frequently the last six digits of the researcher's social security number. PASSWORD is another such JCL card (e.g., JWBT).

DD cards   The data definition or DD cards are control cards that describe the system file the researcher is creating, plus the quantitative data, he or she wishes to process. (SPSS refers to one's data as "raw data input.") The DD cards follow the JCL cards and begin with a FILE NAME card, which is simply a name a researcher assigns to this system file being created, as, for example, TEST FILE. The next DD card would be the DATA LIST card, which specifies those columns on the cards where the data are recorded. Thus, the ID number of each case would be in columns 1-4, age in 6-7, sex in 10, income in 11, marital status in 13, and so on. another DD card would be the MEDIUM card telling the computer your input is on cards, not disks or tapes. A N of CASES (or number of cases) card, a MISSING VALUES card, and VARIABLE LABELS card are other DD cards specifying various structures of the data for the computer.

TD cards   Lastly, there are the TD cards or task definition cards. In contrast to the DD cards, which define the structure and contents of the input data, the TD cards control or tell the computer what calculations to perform on the data. The READ INPUT DATA card is inserted before the cards with the data and at other required places. Following the data cards, TD cards such as STATISTICS tell the computer its task. The researcher uses this control card together with the subprogram card CONDESCRIPTIVE (descritive statistics for continuous data) to compute all or some of such famous statistical variables as mean, standard deviation, standard error, variance, minimum, maximum, and range. Another subprogram card FREQUENCIES tells the SPSS to make frequency counts for each variable in the study (age, sex, income, etc.). See Figure 10-2.

FIGURE 10-2
FREQUENCY DISTRIBUTION FOR AGES OF RESPONDENTS
MADE BY SPSS COMPUTER RUN

ENERGY SURVEY 2

FILE   TEST   (CREATION DATE = 07/01/81)   TEST RUN FOR SPSS

AGE

CATEGORY LABEL	CODE	ABSOLUTE FREQ	RELATIVE FREQ (PCT)	ADJUSTED FREQ (PCT)	CUM FREQ (PCT)
	18.	3	12.0	12.5	12.5
	19.	1	4.0	4.2	16.7
	20.	3	12.0	12.5	29.2
	21.	3	12.0	12.5	41.7
	22.	1	4.0	4.2	45.8
	23.	1	4.0	4.2	50.0
	24.	1	4.0	4.2	54.2
	28.	1	4.0	4.2	58.3
	29.	1	4.0	4.2	62.5
	31.	1	4.0	4.2	66.7
	32.	1	4.0	4.2	70.8
	35.	1	4.0	4.2	75.0
	37.	1	4.0	4.2	79.2
	38.	2	8.0	8.3	87.5
	40.	1	4.0	4.2	91.7
	49.	1	4.0	4.2	95.8
	50.	1	4.0	4.2	100.0
	99.	1	4.0	MISSING	100.0
	TOTAL	25	100.0	100.0	

MEAN	28.000	STD ERR	2.006	MEDIAN	23.500
MODE	18.000	STD DEV	9.829	VARIANCE	96.609
KURTOSIS	-.186	SKEWNESS	.994	RANGE	32.000
MINIMUM	18.000	MAXIMUM	50.000		

VALID CASES   24   MISSING CASES   1

Still another important TD card called CROSSTABS orders the performance of crosstabulation. Crosstabulation is a joint frequency distribution of several variables. Formally called "contingency table analysis," it is set up in matrix form. For example, we might suspect that the variables of age and income might be related. It might be hypothesized in a survey that older individuals tended to have more income. Crosstabulation then might show that the proportion of older people did in fact match with higher incomes. An explanation of crosstabs is given below (also see Figure 10-3). More complex CROSSTABS examples of three=way tables (showing relationship between A and B, while holding C constant) are provided in the SPSS Primer.[8]   Still another useful TD card is SCATTERGRAM, which tells SPSS to process a scatter diagram showing the relationship between two variables. Many more statistical procedures are available in SPSS and given appropriate card names.[9]

Card Sequencing, Punching, and Printouts   The cards in each deck must be arranged in a specific order: chiefly the JCL cards first and the DD and TD cards following. There may be some exceptions to this rule, such as the

JCL card FIN or FINISH coming at the end of the deck. There are also RECODE cards or data MODIFICATION cards for insertion in runs subsequent to the first. The control-card order for running with raw-input data is given in the SPSS Primer table.[10]

Initially punching the cards is a laborious procedure, which the researcher can pay to have done, but still the researcher must do some of the preparation. For all types of cards he or she must prepare the coding sheets from which the cards are punched. Further, the researcher should use the keypunch machine at least a little to get some feel for this portion of the work. In any case, he or she needs to specify which columns on the card are to be used for which type of information. For the control cards, SPSS reserves the first fifteen columns called control field for control words such as CROSSTABS. Columns 16-80 on the same control card are called specification field and embody the specification of what to do.

1	16
CROSSTABS	AGE WITH POLITICAL PARTY

For the researcher's data cards, he or she needs to establish a Code book, a paper specifying for what each column is being used. Obviously, it is important the researcher knows and remembers what he or she decided each column on his or her cards means. Thus, the researcher's decisions might look like this:

Research Code Book

Columns	Variables	Variable Description
1-4	ID	Four-digit number for each case
6-7	Age	99 stands for missing
9	Sex	1 Male 2 Female
11	Income	(1) 0-9,999, (2) 10,000-19,999; (3) 20,000-29,000; (4) Over 30,000; (5) Omission
etc.	etc.	etc.

Printouts

The output of the SPSS program and the researcher's data comes in the form of a computer printout. It will contain whatever statistical manipulation of the data was requested by the researcher. Thus, if SPSS was told to make a frequency distribution (TD card: FREQUENCIES) of the variable for age, the print out would give a table such as that shown in Figure 10-2. It will be noted that calculations for basic descriptive statistical measures suchs as mean, mode, and standard deviation (ordered by TD card: STATISTICS) are also made available in this table.

A third table in this chapter (Figure 10-3) shows a more complicated statistical analysis--a crosstabulation matrix of two variables, age and opinions on energy saving. This table in the printout, obtained by using the TD card: CROSSTABS, is a tabulation of peoples' ages and what they say is

FIGURE 10-3
CROSSTABULATION OF ENERGY SAVING OPINIONS
BY AGE MADE BY SPSS COMPUTER RUN

```
ENERGY SURVEY 2                                                      07/01/81        PAGE   11

FILE   TEST    (CREATION DATE = 07/01/81)    TEST RUN FOR SPSS

* * * * * * * * * * * * * * * * * *   C R O S S T A B U L A T I O N   O F   * * * * * * * * * * * * * * * * *
     ENERGYCS  CONSERVE ENERGY                                  BY  AGE
* * * * * * * * * * * * * * * * * * * * * * * * * * * * * * * * * * * * * * * * * * * * * * *  PAGE  1 OF  2

                        AGE
             COUNT  I
             ROW PCT I                                                                              ROW
             COL PCT I                                                                              TOTAL
             TOT PCT I    18.I    19.I    20.I    21.I    22.I    23.I    24.I    28.I    29.I    31.I
  ENERGYCS  --------I-------I-------I-------I-------I-------I-------I-------I-------I-------I-------I
                0.  I    1 I    0 I    0 I    0 I    0 I    0 I    0 I    0 I    0 I    0 I       1
                    I 100.0 I   .0 I   .0 I   .0 I   .0 I   .0 I   .0 I   .0 I   .0 I   .0 I     4.2
                    I  33.3 I   .0 I   .0 I   .0 I   .0 I   .0 I   .0 I   .0 I   .0 I   .0 I
                    I   4.2 I   .0 I   .0 I   .0 I   .0 I   .0 I   .0 I   .0 I   .0 I   .0 I
                    -I-------I-------I-------I-------I-------I-------I-------I-------I-------I-------I
                1.  I    0 I    0 I    1 I    1 I    0 I    0 I    0 I    0 I    1 I    1 I      10
       0-25         I   .0 I   .0 I 10.0 I 10.0 I   .0 I   .0 I   .0 I   .0 I 10.0 I 10.0 I     41.7
                    I   .0 I   .0 I 33.3 I 33.3 I   .0 I   .0 I   .0 I   .0 I 100.0 I 100.0 I
                    I   .0 I   .0 I  4.2 I  4.2 I   .0 I   .0 I   .0 I   .0 I  4.2 I  4.2 I
                    -I-------I-------I-------I-------I-------I-------I-------I-------I-------I-------I
                2.  I    2 I    1 I    1 I    1 I    1 I    1 I    1 I    0 I    0 I    0 I      10
       26-50        I 20.0 I 10.0 I 10.0 I 10.0 I 10.0 I 10.0 I 10.0 I   .0 I   .0 I   .0 I     41.7
                    I 66.7 I 100.0 I 33.3 I 33.3 I 100.0 I 100.0 I 100.0 I   .0 I   .0 I   .0 I
                    I  8.3 I  4.2 I  4.2 I  4.2 I  4.2 I  4.2 I  4.2 I   .0 I   .0 I   .0 I
                    -I-------I-------I-------I-------I-------I-------I-------I-------I-------I-------I
                3.  I    0 I    0 I    1 I    1 I    0 I    0 I    0 I    1 I    0 I    0 I       3
       51-75        I   .0 I   .0 I 33.3 I 33.3 I   .0 I   .0 I   .0 I 33.3 I   .0 I   .0 I     12.5
                    I   .0 I   .0 I 33.3 I 33.3 I   .0 I   .0 I   .0 I 100.0 I   .0 I   .0 I
                    I   .0 I   .0 I  4.2 I  4.2 I   .0 I   .0 I   .0 I  4.2 I   .0 I   .0 I
                    -I-------I-------I-------I-------I-------I-------I-------I-------I-------I-------I
             COLUMN     3      1      3      3      1      1      1      1      1      1       24
             TOTAL   12.5    4.2   12.5   12.5    4.2    4.2    4.2    4.2    4.2    4.2     100.0
(CONTINUED)
```

the amount of energy they save in percentages. In each cell of the table there are four unit values: First, there is the actual frequency count of persons who fell in that category; second, row percentages; third, column percentages; and fourth, a total response percentage. For example, let's say if we took the 20 year olds, the second box shows those who say they have made up to 25% saving energy. The first number says only one person falls in that category. This is 10% of the row, 33% of the column, and 4% of the total people in the sample. Row totals and column totals are also provided at the side and at the bottom of the table, both in absolute figures and percentages of the total. In this table, totals will not add up because the second page of the printout has not been reproduced here. Still more complicated statistical transformations such as scatter diagrams and multiple regression analysis could have been commanded on the input TD cards, and they would have been received as output in the printout.

Other Matters

Clearly, this skeletonized version of SPSS usage is extremely truncated. It is so because the researcher with some data to be processed must be encouraged to try this "do-it-yourself" computer system. No mention has been made here of the further runs beyond the first processing of data. Typically, researchers want to rework their data in subsequent reruns. SPSS provides specific techniques for data modification instructions. For example, one might want to combine several values of a variable into one. Thus, in the income variable it might be desirable to recode those cases in 0-9999 class with those in the 10,000-19,999 class. Recoding, transforming, and data modification have specific meanings in the SPSS system, which further work with the SPSS Primer will reveal.

Similarly, as SPSS tells us repeatedly, when a researcher generates a file and orders it retained (TD card: SAVE FILE), the data and the control system can be accessed in subsequent runs.   A GET FILE control card followed by the name of researcher's FILE enables the researcher to retrieve the file for further manipulation.   These and other fine points will follow naturally from a first simple effort.

In summary, this section began with the admonition to the researcher to plunge in and get experience.   It can only be iterated that a combination of a hands-on effort to secure a deck of cards for one's survey data and a purchase of a SPSS Primer for complementary and further study is the best prescription to gain researcher computer experience.   If one remembers that only a few years ago this opportunity for simple computer usage did not exist for a researcher, the time and money spent are very reasonable.

CHAPTER SUMMARY

It is incumbent on researchers to know something about computers and their use in research problems.   Emphatically, this does not mean they must become a computer technician or programmer.   Like using a telephone or driving a car, one does not need to know how to fix the machine to be successful in its use.

The best way to learn to use computers in research is the SPSS system. The researcher comes with his or her data to the SPSS, learns a little about creating a batch of cards based on this data, and with statistical calculations useful to his or her research project.   The big Catch 22 is the researcher must know some statistics.   Frequency distributions, crosstab relations, scatter diagrams, and regression analysis come with little effort on the computer.   But the researcher must know what these analyses are in order to use and interpret them.   Beyond statistical knowledge, the researcher must acquire some practice in using the SPSS system.   There is no substitute for hands=on experience with the batch process.   The researcher can acquire great insight by punching his or her cards (both control and data cards), arranging them correctly, and having them run off in a computer installation. The resulting printout yields quick results, which with hand tabulation would be impossible to obtain.   Further down the road, if the researcher's data has been "saved" in the memory of the computer, he or she may rerun and add-on data manipulation, making still greater data understanding possible.

DISCUSSION QUESTIONS

1. Go to the laboratory and identify some of the hardware mentioned in this chapter.   Are they what you expected?

2. Discuss the advantages and disadvantages of the batch mode as compared to the interactive or conversational mode.

3. Compare the JCL cards in two computer installations.   Why do they differ in number and nature?

4. Explain the meaning of a crosstabs matrix with two variables. Can we do more than two variables?   How?

5. Why does a researcher often need frequency distributions, measures of central tendency, and dispersion for each variable?

6. Who was Hollerith? Why did his ideas catch on so well?

7. Can the computer do scattergrams for any pair of variables? What limitations exist?

8. Is it possible that the computer gives the researcher too much information? Could the computer give misleading information? Explain.

NOTES

1.   Norman H. Nie, et. al., SPSS 2nd ed. (New York: McGraw-Hill, 1975); and the more introductory primer, William R. Klecka, et. al., SPSS Primer. (New York: McGraw-Hill, 1975)

2.   W.J. Dixon, ed., BMD--Biomedical Computer Programs (Berkeley, Univ. of California Press, 1971).

3.   Charles T. Clark and A.W. Hunt STATPAK: Computerized Statistical Analysis. 2nd ed. (Cincinnati: Southwestern, 1977). The authors say that although it may be used with any statistical textbook, it is specifically designed for use with Introduction to Business and Economic Statistics by Stockton and Clark. This textbook is recommended to researchers in the introduction of the previous chapter and cited in full there.

4.   Richard V. Andree, et. al., Computer Programming (Englewood Cliffs, N.J.: Prentice-Hall, 1973), p.3.

5.   Daniel L. McCracken, A Guide to FORTRAN IV Programming. 2nd ed. (New York: Wiley, 1972) is a widely used textbook.

6.   STAT/BASIC for system/3 Model 6 ITF... Program Reference Manual (White Plains, N.Y.: IBM, 1973).

7.   See SPSS, Primer, op.cit., chapters 4, 5, 7.

8.   ibid, p. 72

9.   These include regression and correlation analysis, analysis of variance, factor analysis, canonical correlation, and Guttman Scalogram analysis.

10. ibid, p. 54.

11
REPORTING THE RESEARCH

> Some people have the false idea that the written report is the study. Not at all. The report is merely the means by which a scholar informs his colleagues of the work he has done--his conclusions about the problem studied, his method of solving it, and the evidence he has been able to find in support of his hypothesis.

This quotation points out an important distinction between the research and the report. Frequently, they are confused by students and uninformed persons, but no one who works on a true research project ever again confuses them. In chapter four a three-fold division of the research process was set forth: (1) design and planning; (2) the actual research; and (3) the report of results. Each of these phases is distinct and should not be confused with another. The research is first planned and then carried out. The report phase tells us about the other two: What was planned, and what was done. Generally, it is easier than the first two, but is has its own rules and techniques, which will be described.

With the hard work of the first two phases finished, the researcher is ready with outline, notes, data, printout tables, and graphs, to write the results in acceptable, standard report form. Many people find this phase harder than they should because of psychological blocks, all types of interferences, and inability to concentrate. This chapter is designed to help the researcher overcome such handicaps by offering some guidelines to follow.

SPIRIT OF WRITING REPORTS

The first principle of writing is to make a rough draft. To accomplish this, the researcher should disappear into a quiet nook away from family, friends, daily problems, annoyances, and the myriad distractions of modern life. An impersonal library where you are not known is highly recommended. After such a place is found, sit down and write the rough draft. Writing was once defined as "the application of the seat of the pants to the seat of the chair"--a definition as true for the research report as for any other kind. Composing, as this draft effort is called, requires seclusion and concentration. However, report writing differs from other kinds of writing. The researcher is not telling a story, he or she is providing special information on a specific problem or key question he or she has developed. Indeed, the researcher is answering the question or describing the solution to the problem he or she has defined and formulated at the outset.

Moreover, this approach is different from that used in term papers, stories, and magazine and newspaper articles, or less exacting forms of communication. The researcher, it must be stressed, is a scientist. His or her report should present sound data and analysis in an objective tone or manner. The researcher is not persuading anyone of anything. Since this research has made him or her an authority on the subject, the researcher's report should be quite formal.

To this end, there is no room for racy, journalistic style. Written in good, plain English, the report should encourage the reader to feel the substance and method are of high quality. Personal opinions have little place in this kind of writing. The use of the first person "I" should not be employed except in the preface. A Nobel prize winner may break this rule, but it is expected that all other researchers conform sedulously to it in their reports. This formal tone does not mean the researcher must bore people who read the report. Indeed, he or she should try to arrange and present the facts, analyses, interpretations, and conclusions attractively. Heavy supportive tables, exhibits, interviews, and the like should be put in appendices with summary and referral sentences in the text of the report. All of this documentation should be reduced to the standard form of the report, typically typed on 8 1/2 by 11 paper.

A researcher should make an effort to summarize materials, leaving out anything extraneous or redundant. Most researchers collect far more material than they need. The test of inclusion is whether this material helps solve the problem being researched or answers the questions being posed. Material included that cannot meet the test is padding. It should be eliminated no matter how much it hurts to throw out data and information that took long hours to collect.

With these admonitory remarks the standard elements of the formal report are set forth in the next section.

FORMAT OF A RESEARCH REPORT

No universal standard can be followed in the write-up of research findings. Yet certain elements are found in all properly structured reports or papers, elements which are considered essential and are missed by the informed reader when not found. The following are typical items in a check list for the researcher:

1. Cover

2. Title Page

3. Preface or Foreword

4. Paged Table of Contents

5. List of Tables, Charts, Graphs, etc, (if any)

6. Abstract or Brief Summary

7. Introduction

8. Body of report broken into chapters or sections
(corresponding to the Table of Contents)

9. Conclusions and Recommendations

10. Appendices

11. Bibliography

Cover

All reports of research should be bound in a cover. It may be a simple transparent plastic enabling the reader to read the essential facts on the title page: title, author, date, and sponsor of the project. Alternatively, a more durable cover with the title=page facts typed on an affixed label is also appropriate. The cover is important in attracting the reader--the first step in marketing the product.

Title Page

The title page contains the title and subtitle (if any), the author's name, the date, and the person or organization sponsoring the research. Typing and spacing details are found in style manuals such as Kate Turabian's,[2] but graduate students working on theses and dissertations should check with their graduate dean's office for typing and form instructions. Basically, the rule is to keep the title page simple, attractive, while offering essential information to the reader.

Preface or Foreword

Technically, these terms differ: the preface is written by the researcher; the foreword, by someone else. The latter may praise the report; the former should not. In a loose way, they provide general information such as how or why the project was undertaken, the qualifications of the author, and acknowledgements. In a shorter report, the term "Prefatory Note" is a nice phrase for a paragraph or two of this same type of information. The preface should also not be confused with the introduction, which is an essential part of the main body of the report.

Paged Table of Contents

The reader requires a guide to what is in the report. The paged table of contents serves as a guide in two ways: as an outline of the structure of the ideas and as a paged index to some of the key subdivisions of the report. Selection of these readings in the report derives from the revised outline made in the earlier stages of the project, which may or may not be the same. The old outline should not be included with the table of contents, a mistake often committed by beginners in first research reports. Paging the table of contents correctly to the headings in the text is essential. It is very annoying to be informed in the table of contents that on page 12 "Finances" are treated, only to find no corresponding heading existing on that page. Even worse is an unpaged table of contents. Following the table of contents, should be a paged list of tables, charts, and graphs, which, like the table of contents helps the reader see the structure of the ideas contained in the body.

Abstract or Brief Summary

The abstract is a short statement, no more than 200 to 500 words, providing the busy reader with key points--the purpose, key question, hypothesis, research methods, findings, and recommendations. The abstract may be enough for many readers; or it may lure other readers to read the whole report.

Introduction

The previous materials are often called Front Matter, implying they are preliminary to the report itself. With the introduction we enter the main body of the report. It is essential for understanding what the report is all about. Typically, the introduction contains a statement of the problem and some background on the problem's nature and inportance, its scope and limitations. The key question and supporting questions, the hypothesis, the methods, and the data sources are other essentials of the introduction--many of these taken from the original research proposal. The introduction is also an organization of the report in a brief summary discussion--a quick preview of what the coming chapters contain. Sometimes an introduction offers a peak at the findings, but this peak should be discretionary and perhaps not even needed if there is an abstract. The introduction is an essential part of the report, and it should not be omitted or combined with the body of evidence found.

The Body of the Report

The chapters or sections of the report should cover the findings or evidence developed in covering the major problem or problems of the research. At this stage the researcher has his or her revised outline and notes that fit into that outline. As previously noted, these notes should be on cards with appropriate "slugs," which make it possible to group the cards with the same general content. When the cards are arranged in the subject order of the outline (revised!), they are studied and the first draft begins to emerge, section by section, chapter by chapter.

Each person has or develops his or her own way to compose. Some people work rapidly putting everything down in rough form. Others rework their sentences as they proceed. Some dictate into a tape recorder and transcribe the draft. Whichever way one works, the main goal is to put the first draft on paper. Though not the finished product, it is a milestone in that direction. After one has a draft, one can rework and reshape that draft. In professional work it is not unusual for a paper to go through as many as three or four drafts. For the beginning researcher a handwritten version, a first typed draft, and a second finished product is not unusual for good papers. A section on rewriting is provided in the next main section, offering some guidelines for reworking the first draft. When the final draft is completed, proofreading for typographical errors is essential. No matter how often one checks a draft, these annoying "typos" seem to creep in. At least, one should attempt to keep them to a minimum.

Summary and Conclusions

Depending on what the researcher wishes to say, this section may also be entitled "summary," "conclusions," or "conclusions and recommendations." This final section is important. It is the main impetus for the study--and the main reason why the reader is looking at the report. Basically, this final section should contain a selected overview of the work, summarizing the answers to the initial problems or questions being studied. Any qualifications or limitations to these answers should be stated carefully. For example, if a researcher has only a small sample, he or she should emphasize this point. The researcher should also note broad implications of the study and make recommendations based on the findings. Some people do not think that recommendations are permissable in a scientific report; however, in business research where strong applied emphasis prevails, recommendations are in order. However, for economic subjects, closer to pure science, one should be careful in exceeding the limits of presenting the evidence and the drawing conclusions therefrom.

REWRITING

After the completion of a first rough draft, it must be revised or reworked, though not immediately. It is wise to set the manuscript aside for a few days and then return to it. Most people are aware that if a writer examines his work later, he has more clarity and critical faculty of mind about it than when it was just composed. With a few days of vacation from his brainchild, the researcher gains detachment and is more perceptive in improving what was written. And improve he must. Like an artist who needs to refine the details of a painting or sculpture, the report writer must work to better the first draft. Nothing written comes out right the first time. Experienced writers may go through three or four drafts before they are satisfied.

What are the guidelines to revising a manuscript report into a better draft? First extraneous materials must be cut. Most researchers find this elimination hard; they reason that because they expended a vast amount of time and trouble in acquiring these research materials, they should be included. Not so. The test of inclusion of any material is its importance to the solution of the research problem and its communication to the reader of the report. Material that does not have a place in reporting the research project to the reader should be discarded.

Questioning what has been written and getting rid of extraneous material is a discipline forcing the author toward unity of the report. Unity, it will be recalled from one's English classes, is one important criterion in writing. It means that all the sentences in the paragraph should relate to one topic. The report itself should also have unity concentrated on the research project and its problem.

Another criterion of good English writing is coherence. Do the thoughts proceed in sequence? Are the parts of the report connected logically? Do the sentences and paragraphs contain transitional words or phrases such as "consequently," "futhermore," and "therefore" to make them hang together? If such coherence does not exist, rearrange sentences, paragraphs, even whole sections, and, if needed, add some connecting words.

Beyond these considerations, there are grammatical details to be checked, corrected, and polished: sentence structure, diction (the right word choice), spelling, punctuation, and matters of taste. It must be repeated that such first person expressions as "I think." and "I believe" are best deleted. There is no place for personal obtrusions in formal research reports.

Many points of detail and style cannot be summarized here, but consultation of a good composition manual will refresh the researcher's mind on many such matters.[3] Also, asking a colleague or friend to read over the revised manuscript may yield many helpful corrections or suggestions.

OTHER TYPES OF REPORTING

In the busy life of business, government, or even academic agencies, other less formal reports are used. These include memoranda, letters, progress reports, interim reports, and oral briefings. Memoranda and letters are used for quick summaries of findings, often an interim or progress report on what has been discovered thus far in the research effort. Also, they may be used when the subject is inherently simple or limited. For example, any business or government supervisor may need data on any conceivable topic and some interpretation immediately. Say the supervisor wants data on the Consumer Price Index (CPI) over the last ten years. It is relatively easy to find this information in the Statistical Abstract of the U.S., xerox a copy, and send it to the supervisor with a covering memorandum. This memorandum should make some analysis, for example, that the rate of growth of inflation intensified in the 1979-80 period but had been held down after the 1974-75 recession for some years. A forecast by the daring researcher for the future growth rate of the CPI might also be appropriate if he knows the boss will not hold him responsible if he is wrong.

Oral Briefing

The oral report or briefing differs significantly from the written formal report. In the first place, it may be made to different types of audiences--a single individual, a group of peer group researchers, a group of technical or executive people, or to the public (TV audience perhaps) who want a popularized version. Therefore, the audience is a first consideration. Obviously, an oral report to the public must be more simplified and truncated than to one's peers or knowledgeable executives.

Yet by their nature, all oral reports are simplified and condensed as compared to a written report. Time is the big factor. Whether conversations or speeches, we humans are limited by our speaking capability. In this busy twentieth century a speech of an hour is a rarity. Even a half=hour may be too much to retain the audience's attention span. Probably 10 to 15 minutes is all people are willing to listen. If another 5 to 10 minutes is allowed for questions and discussion, the whole performance time span may be 15 to 25 minutes. In fact, the audience chairperson may impose a time constraint.

With this constraint in mind, the reporting researcher must plan his or her time well to be effective. He or she needs careful forethought and preparation. Fortunately, there is an important tool to use in preparing a briefing: the visual aids available to almost any organization. These consist of such tools as the overhead projector--transparency system, flip charts, outlines in multiple copies, and the humble blackboard. Slides and projectors, motion pictures, and physical models are a possibility; but usually they take too long or are too expensive for a one-time report.

The overhead projector-transparency screen system provides a good way to summarize and condense materials. A well=prepared statement of the project, its title, background, key question, hypothesis, and method--all drawn form the proposal--can be flashed on the screen with the first transparency. Another transparency can detail some outstanding bibliographical sources, while a third may be the questionaire used in the survey. A fourth may summarize findings and a fifth may be used for analysis and conclusions. Flip charts give the same sort of visual assistance, but take more time to prepare and are not as flexible. Tabular material and computer print out results such as scatter diagrams, crosstabs, and regression analyses take time to copy and require some artistic ability. Blackboards and other briefing materials such as handouts have obvious limitations but can be pressed into service if there is no time to prepare carefully. Some combination of the above types is also possible.

Some Rules on Presentations

1. First do not read your materials. Nothing bores people faster than listening to a reader droning on.

2. Use three-by-five cards to outline your ideas and sequence; then practice them to memorize your materials as you would flash cards in learning a foreign language. You may cross reference your cards to your notes in case your memory slips during the performance.

3. Organize the material according to some plan. What is the problem? What key question are you asking? What supporting questions were framed? What are your answers? What is the evidence found in the project?

4. Practice briefing with several "dry runs" until you feel confident you know and can handle it. Check the transparencies and the machine to make sure they are working correctly. Practice rehearsals alone or before friends.

5. Eliminate extraneous materials that do not appear relevant. Fit everything to the alloted time span. Including a little joke to set the audience and you at ease is a good idea.

6. Wear nice clothing when making your presentation. Do not slouch or sit on the desk or other furniture. Stand up for your delivery. You hold your audience by standing when talking. You also do well by commanding the attention of your audience and maintaining eye contact.

7. Make a good show out of it. Use a pointer with your transparencies. Modulate your voice, emphasizing the important points. Smile a lot and try to develop a style. Remember in this briefing, the talents of an actor are required. Yet, you must act gracefully and not "ham" it up.

8. Get to the scene ahead of time. Check your equipment, survey the layout of the room, and get some feeling for the coming situation. Try to anticipate the audience--where they will sit, how they may react, and the questions they will ask.

9. Leave some time for questions and discussions.

10. At the end, return your visual aid equipment to where you borrowed it.

CHAPTER SUMMARY

In reporting research it is imperative not to confuse the research itself with the report of that research. Though reporting is usually in the form of a written report, it may also take other forms like oral briefings, memoranda, or letters. The written report is a formal document and should not be marred by personal, journalistic, or slangy English. Style manuals should be followed carefully in the development of written reports. The oral briefing must also be carefully cultivated as a stylized method of reporting essentials.

DISCUSSION QUESTIONS

1. What visual aids are available to a research reporter? Evaluate the advantages and disadvantages of each.

2. What style manuals are available other than those mentioned in the text? Find these manuals and discuss their usage.

3. Tyrus Hillway is quoted at the beginning of this chapter. What is the point of quotation? Why quote this scholar or for that matter, anybody?

4. Is the report content rigidly defined or may variations be permitted? Explain.

5. What is the difference between the table of contents and the outline? Why is one paged to the text and the other not?

6. How should interviews and survey questionaires be handled? In the text? In the appendices? In a separate cover? Discuss.

7. What is the relationship of the research proposal and the final report? Should the first be included with the second? Defend your answer.

NOTES

1. Tyrus Hillway, Introduction to Research. (Boston: Houghton Mifflin company, 1956), p.253.

2. Kate L. Turabian, A Manual for Writers of Termpapers, Theses, and Dissertations, 4th ed. (Chicago: Univ. of Chicago Press, 1973); William G. Campbell and Stephen V. Ballou, Form and Style, 5th ed. (Boston: Houghton

Mifflin, 1978); <u>MLA Handbook for Writers of Research Papers, Theses, and Dissertations</u> (New York: Modern Language Association, 1977).

3.   There are many good books on the English language: L. Elsbree and F. Bracher, <u>Heath's College Handbook of Composition,</u> 8th ed. (Lexington, Mass.: Heath, 1972); J.C. Hodges and M.E. Whitten, <u>Harbrace College Handbook,</u> 7th ed. (New York: Harcourt Brace Jovanovich, 1972); Glenn Leggett, et. al., <u>Prentice Hall Handbook for Writers</u>, 6th ed. (Englewood Cliffs, N.J.: Prentice-Hall, 1974); R.L. Shurter, et. al. <u>Business Research and Report Writing</u> (New York: McGraw-Hill, 1965).

APPENDIX A
SAMPLE RESEARCH PROPOSAL

Civilian Uses of Military Training and Service

A Proposal Submitted to the
Air Force Office of Scientific Research
Arlington, Virginia 22209

A Study Proposal Submitted by
    Operations and Policy Research, Inc.

June 13, 1968

Cornelius W. Vahle, Jr.
Vice President for Administration
Operations and Policy Research, Inc.

TABLE OF CONTENTS

A

I. STARTING DATE AND TIME PERIOD

The proposal assumes that the project could be initiated on November 1, 1968, and would require two years to complete. A final report would be submitted by October 31, 1970.

II. DESCRIPTION OF PROPOSED BASIC RESEARCH

A. Abstract

The purpose of the study is to develop an input-ouput relationship between military training and later civilian utilization of this training. It will investigate samples of retired and resigned military personnel and estimates of the contribution that military training and skills have made to income capability in civilian life. The longrun objective is to develop a method that continues estimating the value of military inputs in the U.S. civilian economy. In the short run, the aim is to test the hypothesis that modern military training and service has value that transfers to civilian life. To this end, the crucial questions to be answered in the research seem to center on such nodes as:

1. What is the value of military training in a modern economy like the United States? How significant is this contribution?

2. By what methods and procedures can it be systematically estimated?

3. How can a data bank for retrieval of this information and estimated value be established for use by military and civilian consumers?

4. Are there ways for improving the successful transfer and use of militarily acquired skills and experience by the civilian economy?

5. What implications are there for a cost-benefit analysis of expenditures on military training?

Other relevant questions no doubt may develop as the research proceeds; and, if they suggest feasible and productive, closely related lines of investigation, they will be incorporated. However the core of the project would center on the ideas expressed above.

B. Proposal

1. Background. The idea that military training and service has utility in civilian life and work has long glimmered in thought and conversation. Louis Mumford's classic work, <u>Technics and Civlization</u>, for example, has shown

B

how the discipline of the factory systems is a byproduct of the discipline of the evolving military system. Spillover of the fruits of military research and development has been noted and described for the domestic economy.[1] In related research the author has shown many subtle and important influences of U.S. military on less developed economics.[2]

But neither the author nor others have attempted to pinpoint the carryover of military training in the domestic civilian economy and identify its contribution with some degree of specificity. Such an attempt would be of seminal importance in opening a new vista on training activities undertaken by military forces. It is to this vision of civilian use of military training that this proposal is addressed.

2. <u>Study Objective</u>. The central idea is to investigate appropriate samples of retired and resigned military personnel and estimates the contribution that military training and skills have made to their income capability in civilian life. The long-run objective is to develop a method that continues estimating the value of military inputs in the US civil economy. In the short run, the aim is to test the hypothesis that modern military training and service has value that transfers to civlian life and that this value can be estimated. The study will use the Air Force retired and resigned personnel as the base of the samples to be investigated. Other military services might have been used, but confining investigation to the Air Force, at least at the outset, maintains manageability and has more focus.

The initial phase of the work will consist of interviewing knowledgeable Air Force officers, civilian personnel managers, manpower specialists, and others to develop a line on which military specialities carry over into civilian life in the greatest numbers. After some promising ideas are selected a carefully stratified set of samples will be constructed for examination. People will be selected at random in some cases, and in others, with a regard to such obvious factors as age, race and length of service.

A second and somehwhat later phase will design an information form according to military inputs and civilian outputs or outcomes. Careful design of this kind of form, the information of which can be translated to computer cards and tapes, will require many consultations and ideas derived from the initial phase; the general idea of a sample coding, however, is suggested as Appendix A. As can be seen, the program will assemble data on an individual, first from his military "inputs" and second from his civilian "outputs". In a still later and third phase, the objective will be to correlate the inputs with the outputs and develop some type of formula that might show functional relationships between military training and after-service civilian life.

Naturally, other more qualitative approaches will be attempted in addition to the derivation of hard core quantitative relationships and functions. Profiles on resignees and retirees will be developed to provide a model method of collecting such information as well to begin to provide a data bank of information of this kind. Such files might prove to be valuable

C

models for larger operational activity along these lines. Moreover, working closely with the data will no doubt suggest ancillary lines of retrieval, segregation, coding, and clarification of this type of information. These qualitative insights will almost certainly provide a rich harvest to accompany the quantitative analysis.

In summary, the hypothesis to be examined is that military training has some measurable impact on the civilian economy. To this end the crucial questions to be answered in the research seem to center on such modes as:

a) What is the value of military training in a modern economy like the US? How significant is this contribution?

b) By what methods and procedures can it be systematically estimated?

c) How can a data bank for retrieval of this information and estimated value be established for use by military and civilian consumers?

d) Are there ways for improving the successful transfer and use of militarily acquired skills and experience by the civilian economy?

e) What implications are there for cost-benefit analysis of expenditures on military training.

Other relevant questions no doubt may develop as the research proceeds; and if they suggest feasible and productive, closely related lines of investigation, they will be incorporated. However, the core of the project will center on the ideas previously expressed.

3. Expected Results. The objective of pursuing this line of investigation will be to present some definitive data showing that military training can transfer to civilian. The resulting monograph and/or papers will show what has long been suspected but never estimated or measured--namely, the beneficial economic results of military training flowing into the civilian economy.

Beyond this, a methodology will be developed regarding retrieval, recording, estimation, and evaluation of these civilian yields of military inputs. Foundation for further work along these pioneering lines will be laid down and strategic hypotheses developed, which will open new investigations on the creative role of military training and service.

In relation to the present state of knowledge, little work in this field can be cited. The investigater's researches in transfer of technology abroad have included some analysis of a sample of 200 Japanese airmen. Other data are found in his monograph, Military Transfer of Technology. But the systematic evaluation of military inputs suggested here has not been tried.

D

There is a theoretical literature on the contributions of education, cited in Appendix B, but this a priori reasoning has not been supported by the type of empirical work suggested in this project. In any case, research has not been oriented toward military activities in the training and education field. Literature from fields other than economics is, of course, available, but the emphasis has not been on the central issue: estimating the value of military training.

III. PERSONNEL

The principal investigator will be Daniel L. Spencer, Professor of Economics and Chairperson, Department of Economics, Howard University. Professor Spencer has long been interested in problems of civilian use of military activity. His previous research on foreign impacts of military forces has provided broad experience in this field of investigation. A list of his publications (Appendix C), which is attached, indicates his acquaintance with this field. A personal history summary (Appendix D) is also attached.

Professor Spencer plans to devote two summers to the project as well as approximately one day per week during the academic year. He will assume full responsibility for supervising the work of other personnel.

The proposal contemplates the employment of a research associate, Alexander Woroniak, Assistant Professor of Economics, The Catholic University of America, who will be responsible for conducting the surveys and for undertaking some of the basic research. He will devote one-fourth of his time to the project.

Also included in the proposal are provisions for the use of consultants and research assistants on an hourly basis. Funds for typing services are included under publication costs.

IV. CAPABILITIES AND ACCOMPLISHMENTS

Operations and Policy Research, Inc., was founded in 1955 as a nonprofit social science research and educational institution. It was created to conduct and sponsor interdisciplinary research and to encourage its application to public policy.

Since 1955 OPR has developed and maintained a varied program of public policy research, opinion surveys, educational activities, and university services. In preparing policy studies OPR draws not only upon its in-house staff but also upon the skills of over 200 associates from various academic disciplines. Some recent studies include an analysis of cabinet-level Marine Science, Engineering and Resources, a study for the Department of State on the views and reactions of foreign studies in this country, and a survey for the National Coal Policy Conference on the impact of the coal industry on the national economy.

During the past decade associates from the various academic disciplines

E

have provided an expert advisory service to the United States Information Agency. Over 200 scholars and specialists in the social sciences and on foreign areas have assessed and edited manuscripts and reviewed and condensed books.

OPR conducts a broad continuing program of research on all phases of elections both in the United States and in Latin America. This program includes investigation of voter behavior and studies of the political and legal contexts of elections. Studies of American elections include a continuing survey of political attitudes, a comprehensive analysis of parties and presidential elections, and special reports on state and local contests. Work on the election systems of Latin America led to the publication of a series of election factbooks and to the production of numerous monographs on specific election systems.

OPR also publishes descriptive and theoretical studies to promote international understanding of human problems in the developing world. It seeks to promote better understanding of the changing cultures of ethnic groups throughout the world--understanding of the ways these people cope with new economic, social, political, religious, and technological stiuations. It publishes resource guides, field guides, essays, monographs, and translations in nontechnical language, and serves students, planners, and technicians who may benefit from the insights of specialists.

V. COST ESTIMATE

Salary costs		Annual
Principal Investigator (based on a nine month academic salary of $18,000)		
(1) 3 months during summer	$6,000	
(2) 1 day per week for 39 weeks	3,578	$ 9,578
Research Associate (¼ time, based on a nine-month academic salary of $10,000)		2,500
Research Assistants		3,000
Wage Assistants ($3.00 per hour)		3,000
Secretary (during summer -- 12 weeks @ $100)		1,200
Employee Benefits		875
		$20,153

F

Travel

Transportation to installations in Washington area $ 250

Trips to selected installations outside Washington area

(1) Air fare   380
(2) Per diem (20 days at $16 per day)   320
                                                          $ 950

Publication

Typing Services ($3.50 per hour -- 8 hours per week
for 39 weeks) $ 1,092

Reproduction (mimeo, xerox, etc.)   100

Supplies and materials   175
                                                          $ 1,367

Consultants

8 @ $50 per day $ 400

Communications

Telephone (at rate of $15 per month for
3 motnhs for regular service) $ 45

Long distance calls   55

Postage   50
                                                          $ 150

Other direct costs

Computer rental -- IBM 1620 (40 hours
@ $70 per hour)   2,800

Office Space Rental ($100 per month for
3 months)   300
                                                          $ 3,100

Fee (15% of direct costs)   2,800

Total (one year) $28,920

Two-year estimate $57,840

APPENDIX B
HOW TO FIND BUSINESS AND ECONOMICS INFORMATION SOURCES IN THE LIBRARY OF CONGRESS

GENERAL READING ROOMS DIVISION
REVISED FEBRUARY 1980

This guide is a selective list of basic sources of information in the field of business and economics. Items included in the list contain both national and international data. Most of the sources are available in the Main Reading Room Reference Collection with the exception of some periodical titles which are housed in the Newspaper and Current Periodical Reading Room, Room 1026 in the Thomas Jefferson Building.

Section I of the guide includes general sources of information and Section II arranges sources according to subject. Section III functions as a partial index to the Guide and also cites sources answering specific questions. If you need any assistance in your research, please consult a reference librarian.

I would like to express special appreciation to Margaret Clark of the George Washington University Library whose "Sources of Financial Information" forms the basis for this guide.

Alan Solomon
Reference Librarian

Outline of Contents:

I. GENERAL INFORMATION SOURCES

    A. Bibliographies and Guides

    B. Dictionaires, Encylopedias, and Handbooks

    C. Indexing and Abstracting Services

    D. Statistical Information Sources
        1. Guides
        2. Sources

    E. Business and Financial Periodicals

II. SOURCES OF INFORMATION BY SUBJECT

    A. Industries, Corporations, and Companies
        1. National
        2. International

    B. Stocks

    C. Bonds

    D. Banks and Banking

    E. Trade and Commodities

    F. Government Finance

III. SOURCES FOR SPECIFIC INFORMATION

I. GENERAL INFORMATION SOURCES

A. Bibliographies and Guides

The following bibliographies and guides identify sources where
you can find business and financial information.

Brealey, Richard A. A bibliography for finance and investment.
Cambridge, Mass., MIT Press, 1973. (Z7164.F5B77 MRR Alc. 3)

Brownstone, David M. Where to find business information:
A worldwide guide for everyone who needs the answers to
business questions. New York, Wiley, 1979. (HF53353.B715
MRR Ref Desk Alc.4)

Cambridge Information and Research Services Ltd. Sources
of European economic information. Farnborough, Eng., Gower
Press, 1977. (Z7165.E8C34 1977 MRR Alc. 3)

   This source describes foreign statistical data, economic surveys,
   bank letters, etc.

Daniells, Lorna M. Business information sources. Berkeley,
University of California Press, 1976. (Z7164.C81D16 MRR Ref
Desk Alc.5)

Diretory of business and financial services. 7th ed. New
York, Special Libraries Association, 1976. (HG5353.D57 1976
MRR Ref Desk Alc.3)

   A directory which describes business, economic, and financial
   services that are periodcially published.

Rock, James M. Money, banking, and macroeconomics. Detroit,
Gale Research Corp., 1977. (Z7164.F5R63 MRR Alc 3)

Smith, George M. Worldwide business publications directory.
New York, Simon and Schuster, 1971. (HG5353.C8S55 MRR Ref Desk
Alc.4)

Wasserman, Paul. Encyclopedia of business information sources.
3rd ed. Detroit, Gale Research Corp., 1976. (HG5353/E9 MRR Ref
Desk alc. 4)

Woy, James B. Investment information: a detailed guide to
selected sources. Detroit, Gale Research Corp., 1970.
(Z7164.F5W93 MRR Alc. 3)

B.   Dictionaries, Encyclopedias, and Handbooks

The works listed below provide definitions and explanations of
financial terms and methods as well as short articles on a variety
of business and financial subjects.

Bannock, Graham. Penguin dictionary of economics. London,
Penguin Books Ltd., 1977. (HB61.B33 1978 MRR Alc. 3)

Davids, Lewis E. Dictionary of banking and finance. Totowa,
N.J., Littlefield, Adams, 1978. (Hg151.D365 MRR Alc. 3)

Dow Jones-Irwin. Dow Jones-Irwin business almanac. 1977-
Annual. (HF5003.D68a MRR Alc. 3 Lastest ed. only)

  Gives a wide range of information on business, finance, and
  economics including ratios, GNP, income, price data, etc.

Dun and Bradstreet's guide to your investments. 19th ed.
1974/75-date. Annual. (HG4905.Y6 MRR Alc. 3 Latest ed. only)

Economics: encyclopedia. 1973/74-date. Guilford, Conn.,
Dushkin Pub. Group. Annual. (HB61.E26 MRR Ref Desk Alc. 3
Latest ed. only)

European financial almanac. 1974/75-date. Biennial. (HG70.
E9 MRR Alc. 3 Latest ed. only)

  Covers markets, economic conditions by country,
  organizations, and key personnel of the European financial
  field.

Goodman, Steven E. Financial market place; a directory of
major corporations, institutions, services and publications.
New York, Bowker, 1972. (HG65.G62 MRR Ref Desk Alc. 4)

Herbst, Robert. Dictionary of commercial, financial, and
legal terms. 2nd ed. Zug, Translegal, 1966-date. (HB61.
H462 MRR Alc. 3)

  Provides excellent explanations of the principles of and
  procedures for successful investment management

McGraw-Hill dictionary of modern economics: a handbook of terms and organizations. New York, McGraw-Hill, 1973. (HB61.M16 1973 MRR Ref Desk Alc. 4)

Moore, Norman D. Dictionary of business finance and investment. Dayton, Ohio, Investor's Systems, Inc., 1975. (HF1001.M76 MRR Alc. 3)

Nemmers, Erwin. Dictionary of economics and business. 3rd ed. Totowa, N.J., Littlefield, Adams, 1974. (HB61.N45 1974 MRR Alc. 3)

Rosenberg, Jerry M. Dictionary of business and management. New York, Wiley, 1978. (HF1002.R68 MRR Alc. 3)

U.S. Dept. of Commerce. Office of the Assistant Secretary for Economic Affairs. Dictionary of economic and statistical terms. Washington, 1975. (HB61.U55 MRR Alc. 3)

C. Indexing and Abstracting Services

In many cases, the latest and best information in the fields of business and finance can be found in journals and newspapers. The following indexing and abstracting services are your main sources for locating this information. Most of these services are arranged alphabetically by subject. Please read the explanatory section at the beginning of each volume for information about contents and access and for a listing of journals indexed.

Business periodicals index. v. 1- . Jan. 1958-date. Monthly with annual cumulations. (Z7164.C81B983 MRR Circ.)

Conference Board. Cumulative index. Annual. (Z7164.E2N28 MRR Alc. 3)

F. & S. index international: industries, countries, companies. 1st- ed.; 1968- . Monthly with quarterly and annual cumulations. (Z7164.C81F3 MRR Alc. 3)

F. & S. index of corporations and industries. 1st- ; 1967- . Weekly with monthly, quarterly, semiannual, and annual cumulations. (Z7165.U5F23 MRR Circ.)

Index of economic articles in journals and collective volumes. v. 8- ; 1966- . Annual (Z7164.E2;4812 MRR Alc. 3)

International bibliography of economics. v. 1- ; 1952- . Annual. (Z7164.E2I58 MRR Alc. 3)

Journal of economic literature. v. 1- ; 1963- . Quarterly.
(HB1.J6 MRR Alc. 3)

New York Times (indexes) The New York Times index. v. 1- ;
Jan./Mar. 1913- . Semimonthly with annual cumulations.
(AI21.N44 MRR Alc. 3)

Public Affairs Information Services. Bulletin. 1st- ed.;
1915- . Weekly with quarterly and annual cumulations.
(Z7163.P9 MRR Circ.)

Selectively indexes journals, books, government publications,
and reports of public and private agencies.

Wall Street Journal. Index. 1958- . Monthly with annual
cumulations. (HG1.W6 MRR Alc. 3)

D. Statistical Information Sources

1. Guides

American statistics index. 1973- . Monthly with annual
cumulations. (Z7554,U5A46 MRR Alc. 3)

This index is designed to locate statistics published by
all government agencies, congressional committees, and
statistics-producing programs. Arranged by subject and
name, by category, and by title and report number, the
index gives source citation and abstract of the publication
Microfiche copies of almost every report are available
in the Microform Reading Room.

Balachandran, M. A guide to trade and securities statistics.
Ann Arbor, Mich., Pierian Press, 1977. (Z7165.U5B338 MRR Ref
Desk Alc. 5)

Provides a subject analysis of 30 of the most used serials
in the areas of trade and securities.

Harvey, Joan M. Statisitcs Africa: sources for market research.
Beckenham, Eng., CBD Research Ltd., 1970. (Z7554.A34H37 MRR
Alc. 3)

_____. Statistics Asia and Australasia: sources for
market research. Beckenham, Eng., CBD Research Ltd., 1974.
(HA37. A775H37 MRR Alc. 2)

_____. Statistics Europe: sources for social, economic, and market research. 3rd ed. Beckenham, Eng., CBD Research Ltd., 1976 (Z7554.E8H35 1976 MRR Ref Desk Alc. 5)

Pieper, Frank C. Subject index to sources of comparative international statistics. Beckenham, Eng., CBD Research Ltd., 1978 (Z7551.P54 MRR Alc.)

Statistics sources: a subject guide to data on industrial, business, social, educational, financial, and other topics for the United States and internationally. 5th ed. Detroit, Gale Research Corp., 1977. (Z7551.S84 1977 MRR Ref Desk Alc. 5)

2. Sources

Business statistics. 1951- . Biennial. (HC101.A13122 MRR Alc. 3 Latest ed. only)

Updated monthly by the Survey of current business. (HC101. A1312 Recent issues in Newspaper and Current Periodical RR)

Commodity year book. 1st- ed.; 1939- . Annual. (HA1107.E87 MRR Alc. 3 Latest ed. only)

European marketing data and statistics. v. 1- ; 1962- . Annual. (HA1107.E87 MRR Alc. 3 Latest ed. only)

   Statistics for European countries cover standard of living, basic economic indicators, the consumer, education, mass media, communications, industrial consumption, etc.

International Labour Office. Year book of labour statistics. 1st- ed.; 1953/36- . Annual. (HD4826.I63 MRR Alc. 3 Latest ed. only)

International marketing data and statistics. 1st ed.; 1975/76- . Annual. (HA42.I56 MRR Alc. 2 Latest ed. only)

   Similar to European marketing data and statistics with statistics for 43 key countries outside Europe.

International Monetary Fund. Balance of payments yearbook. 1946/47- Annual. (HF1014.15 MRR Alc. 3 Latest ed. only)

Mitchell, Brian R. European historical stistics, 1750-1970. New York, Columbia University Press, 1975. (HA1107.M 1975 MRR Ref Desk Alc. 4)

Organization for Economic Cooperation and Development. Industrial statistics, 1900-1962. Paris, 1964. (HC240.A106916 MRR Alc. 3)

_____. National accounts statistics. Annual. (HC79,1507a
MRR Alc. 3 Latest ed. only)

This sources gives 10-year statistics for national account
aggregates by country, with separate tables covering rates
of change for selected aggregates.

Robert Morris Associates. Statement studies. 1979- . Annual.
(HF681.B2R6 MRR Alc. 3 Latest ed. only)

Provides financial and operating ratios for about 300 lines
of business. Balance sheet and profit-and-loss composites
as well as selected ratios are arranged by company size
groups.

Troy, Leo. Almanac of business and industrial financial ratios.
Englewood Cliffs, NJ, Prentice-Hall, 1978. (HF5681.R25T7 MRR Alc.
3)

United Nations. Centre for Development Planning, Projections,
and Policies. World economic survey. 1957- . Annual. (JX1977.
A2 sub. ser. MRR Ref Desk Alc. 4 Latest ed. only)

Summary statistics for member nations on world production,
trade, balance of payments, international reserves, consumer
prices, money supply, etc.

_____. Statistical office. Statistical yearbook. 1st-
issue; 1948- . Annual (HA12.5.U63 MRR Ref Desk Alc. 4 Latest ed.
only)

_____. Yearbook of international trade statistics. 1st
issue; 1950- . Annual. (HF91.U473 MRR Ref Desk Alc. 4 Latest
ed. only)

_____. Yearbook of national accounts statistics. 1957-
Annual. (HC79.I5U53 MRR Ref Desk Alc. 4 Latest ed. only)

Contains detailed statistics for 121 nations and regions
including gross domestic product and expenditures, national
income and national disposable income, capital transactions
of the nation, etc.

US Bureau of Labor Statistics. Handbook of labor statistics.
1924/26- . Annual. (HD8064.A3 MRR Ref Desk Alc. 4 Latest ed
only)

_____. Historical statistics of the United States, colonial
times to 1970. Washington, US Dept. of Commerce, Bureau of the
Census, 1975. (HA202.B87 1975 MRR Ref Desk Alc. 4)

_____. Statistical abstract of the United States. 1st ed.-
1878-   . Annual. (HA202 MRR Ref Desk Alc. 4 Latest ed. only)

_____. County business patterns.   1946-   . (HC101.A184
MRR Alc. 3 Latest ed. only)

US Dept of Agriculture. Agricultural statistics.   1936-   .Annual.
(HD1751.A43 MRR Ref Desk Alc. 4 latest ed. only)

Yearbook of industrial statistics. 1974-   . Annual. (HC59.Y4 MRR
Alc. 3 Latest ed. only)

Note on state and foreign country statistical abstracts;   The Main
Reading Room reference collection contains statistical abstracts for
many states and foreign countries. Call numbers for statistical
abstracts can be found by consulting the Main Reading Room
Reference Subject Catalog under the heading, '"Name of state or
country'-- Statistics." Most statistical abstracts in the Main
Reading Room are shelved between class numbers HA230 and HA3000.

E.   Business and Financial Periodicals

Listed below are some of the key periodicals in the fields of
business and finance. Current issues of these periodicals, unless
otherwise indicated, are located in the Newspaper and Current
Periodical Reading Room. Back issues, usually those over a year
old, are bound and sent to the stacks under their respective call
numbers.

American banker. 1894-   . Five issues per week. (HG1501.A5)

>   The daily banking journal covers news about bank
>   developments, pending legislation, monetary fairs,
>   bank stock quotations, etc. Various issues list
>   largest banks, largest savings and loan associations,
>   and largest finance companies.

Barron's national business and financial weekly. v.1-   ; May 9,
1921- . Weekly v. 1- ; May 9, 1921-   . Weekly. (HG1.B3)

>   Includes articles on prospects for industries and companies,
>   on investment companies, and on other business and financial
>   topics. Carries weekly stock and bond prices for the NYSE,
>   AMEX, OTC, Chicago Board Options Exchange, and for
>   mutual funds. Foreign exchange rates, market indicators,
>   Dow-Jones averages, etc. are also included.

Business week. No. 1- ; Sept. 7, 1929-   . Weekly. (HF5001.B89)

Articles on all aspects of business. Select issues include:
"Survey of Corporate Performance," "Annual Survey of
International Corporate Performance," and "Annual Survey of
Bank Performance".

Commercial and financial chronicle. v.1- ; 1865. Weekly.
(HG1.C7)

Each issue gives brief notes on selected individual companies
and stock quotations for all exachanges. Monthly range of
prices on the NYSE for the previous year appears in a late
January issue.

Conference Board. Statistical bulletin. v.4- ; Mar. 1971- .
Monthly. (HC101.C62a)

Includes short-range forecasts for leading economic and
business indicators.

Dun's review. v.1- ; Aug. 1893- . Monthly. (HF1.D8)

An important source for information on business failures,
operating ratios, and indexes on retail trade. Issues for
Sept.-Nov. contain ratios.

Forbes magazine. 1918- . Semimontly. (HF5001.F6)

Analyzes individual companies, industries, and the overall
economy. The "Annual Report on American Industry" appears
in the first January issue, while special issues for banking
and mutual funds appear on July 1 and Aug. 15 respectively.

Fortune. v. 1- ; Feb. 1930- . Monthly. (HF5001.F7 Current
May issue kept at MRR Ref Desk)

A business roundup section appears monthly. Alist of 500
leading US companies appears in the May issue and the top
300 international companies appear in the August issue.

Harvard business review. v.1- ; Oct. 1922- . Bimonthly.
(HF5001.H3)

International currency review. Feb. 1969- . Bimonthly.
(HG3881.I5756)

Every issue includes currency reviews of the major currencies.

International Monetary Fund. International financial statistics. v.1- ;
1948- . Monthly (HG3881.I626 MRR Ref Desk Alc. 4 Latest ed. only)

General and individual statistics on exchange rates, international liquidity, interest, prices, production, international transactions, government finance, etc.

Journal of finance. v.1- ; Jan. 5, 1907- . (HG5071.A1J7)

Covers all phases of finance. Includes a good book review section and lists abstracts of dissertations.

New York Times (Newspaper) Paper issues replaced by microfilm as available. Copies of the New York Times (indexes) can be found in MRR Alc. and in the Newspaper and Current Periodical Reading Room (AI21.N44)

US Board of Governors of the Federal Reserve System. Federal reserve bulletin. v. 1- ; May 1, 1915- . Monthly. (HG2401.A5)

Includes statistics on US banking and monetary conditions as well as statistics on construction, employment, prices, national income, and international affairs.

US Bureau of Foreign and Domestic Commerce. Office of Business Economics. Survey of current business. v.1- ; Aug. 1, 1921- . Monthly. (HC101.A13)

Summary of business and financial situation and forecast with statistics on commodity prices, domestic and foreign trade, labor force, employment and earnings, and all major industries. Annual statistics are published in the February issue.

US Bureau of Labor Statistics. Montly labor review. v.1- ; July 1915- . Monthly. (HD8051.A78)

Provides current statistics on employment, unemployment, hours, earnings, consumer and wholesale prices, productivity, and labor-management data.

Wall Street Journal (newspaper) Paper issues replaced by microfilm as available. Copies of the Wall Street Journal (indexes) can be found in MRR Alc. and in the Newspaper and Current Periodical Reading Room (HG1.W26).

II. SOURCES OF INFORMATION BY SUBJECT

A. Industries, Corporations, and Companies

The following titles provide a variety of information about industries and companies, including histories, directors, financial statements, and future trends of stocks and bonds. The sources are divided into two sections, National and International.

1. National

Angel, Juvenal L. Directory of inter-corporate ownership. New York, Simon and Schuster, 1974. (HG4057.AI56 MRR Alc. 3)

    Lists American companies and their subsidiaries.

Best's insurance reports, life-health. 1st- ed; 1906/7- . Annual. (HG8943.B3 MRR Alc. 3 Latest ed. only)

Best's insurance resports, property-casualty. 77th- ed.; 1979- . Annual. (HG9655.B5 MRR Alc. 3 Latest ed. only)

Directory of American firms operating in foreign countries. New York, Simon and Schuster, 1969- . (HG4538.AID5 MRR REf Desk Alc. 4 Latest ed. only)

Directory of corporate affiliations. Skokie, Ill., National Register Pub. Co. Annual. (HG4057.A219 MRR Alc. 3 Latest ed. only)

    Lists about 3,000 American parent companies with their divisions, subsidiaries, and affiliates.

Dun and Bradstreet, Inc. Dun's reference book of corporate management. 1st- ed.; 1967- . Annual. (HD2745.D85 MRR Ref Desk Alc. 4 Latest ed. only)

    Biographical information about leading US executives, arranged by name of company with an index by executive's name of company with an index by executive's name.

_____. Middle market directory. (v. 2 of the Million Dollar direcotry). Annual. (HD102.D8 MRR Ref Desk Alc. 4 Latest ed. only)

    Brief information about companies with net worthy of $500,000 to $1,000,000 arranged in alphabetical, geographical, and product sections and including an index by SIC numbers.

_____. Million dollar directory. (v.1 of the Million dollar directory. Annual. (HC102.D8 MRR Ref Desk Alc. 4 Lates ed. only)

    Same arrangement as the preceding entry for companies with a net worth of at least $1,000,000.

_____. Reference book. v.1- ; 1859- . Bimonthly.
(HF5573.D7 MRR Alc. 3 Latest ed. only)

Provides a detailed geographical list of US and Canadian
business firms of all types, giving for each the SIC number,
an abbreviation for line of business, a code for estimated
financial stranegth and for credit appraisal.

Moody's Investor's Service, New York
The following manuals cover US., Canadian, and other foreign
firms listed on US excahnges. Information on the firms
includes a brief corporate history, a list of subsidiaries,
plants and properties, products, officers and directors,
comparative income statements, balance sheets, selected
financial ratios, etc. Center blue sheets contain a
cumulative annual index and useful statistics.

Moody's industrial manual. 1954-   . Annual with supplements.
(HG4961.M67 MRR Ref Desk Alc. 4 Latest ed. only)

Contains data on major manufacturing, mining, and retail industries.

Moody's OTC industrial manual. 1976- . Annual with supplements.
(HG4961.M7237 MRR Ref Desk Alc. 4 Latest ed only)

Moody's public utility manual. 1954- . Annual with supplements.
(HG4961.M7245 Alc. 3 Latest ed. only)

Moody's transporation manual: railroads, airlines, shipping, traction,
bus and truck lines. 1954- . Annual with supplements. (HG4971.
M74 MRR Alc.3 Latest ed. only)

Standard and Poor's Corporation. Standard and Poor's industry
surveys. Jan 3, 1973-   . Quararterly. (HG106.6.S7663 MRR Alc.
3 Latest ed. only)

Covers approximately 36 major domestic industries giving
financial comparisons for leading industries in each group.

_____. Standard and Poor's register of corporations, directors

and executives . 3 v. 1928-   . Annual (HG106.6.S74 MRR Ref
Desk   Alc. 4 Latest ed. only)

Vol.1 lists alphabetically over 36,000 US and Canadian
companies giving for each officers, product line or service,
SIC number, approximate sales, and number of employees.
Vol. 2 lists executies and diretors. Vol. 3 contains indexes
of the companies by SIC number and by location.

_____. Standard corporation records Dec. 1940- .
Looseleaf with bimonthly supplements. (HG4501.S76635 MRR Alc.
3 Latest ed. only)

Contains information about companies with listed and unlisted
securities including product lines, subsidiaries, stock data,
earnings and finances, balance sheets, and a brief annual report.

Thomas register of American manufactures and Thomas register
catalog file. 1st ed.; 1905/06- . Annual. (T12.T6 MRR Alc.
7 Latest ed. only)

Vol. 1-6 arranged alphabetically by product, listing manufacturers
under each. Vol. 7 gives brief information about companies and vol.
8 is an index to products, services, and brand names. Vol. 9-11
contain alphabetically arranged catalogs of selected companies.

US Bureau of the Census. Annual survey of manufactures.
1949/50- . Annual. (HD9724.A211 MRR Alc. 3 Latest ed. only)

> Gives statistics for broad industry groups and for
> products.

US Office of Management and Budget. Statistical Policy Division.
Standard industrial classification manual. Washington, US
Govt. Print. off., 1972 (HF1042.A55 1972 MRR Ref Desk Alc. 4)

U.S. Industrial outlook. 1969- . Annual. (HC106.6.A23 MRR Alc.
3 Latest ed. only)

> Provides information on recent trends and an outlook in
> over 200 individual industries. Short narratives with
> statistics give discussions of supply and demand changes,
> domestic and overseas market developmens, price changes,
> employment trends, and capital investment.

Value line investment survey. 3 v. Weekly. (Newspaper and Current
Periodical RR)

> The weekly issues include 3 parts: Summary and Index,
> Selection and Opinion, and Ratings and Reports. The
> service analyzes about 1,500 stocks in about 76 major
> industry groups. The statistics and text are updated on
> a rotating basis thus giving revised quarterly information
> on each company included. Also provides editorial opinions
> on political and economic conditions affecting the market.
> Includes special situation reports on favorable and
> unfavorable stocks and companies, and sets of a model
> investor's portfolio.

Who owns whom. North American ed. Annual. (HG4538.W423 MRR Alc. 3 Latest ed. only)

Note on annual reports of companies: Microfiche copies of annual reports of many companies on the New York and American Stock Exchanges are housed in the Microform Reading Room.

2. International

Angel, Juvenal L. Directory of foreign firms operating in the United States. 4th ed. New York, World Trade Academy Press, 1978. (HG4057.A155 1978 MRR Ref Desk Alc. 4)

Bottin. Bottin international; international business register. 1947- . Annual. (HF54.F8B6 MRR Alc. 3 Latest ed. only)

Dun and Bradstreet, Inc. International market guide; Continental Europe. 1961- . Annual (HC240.D8 MRR Alc. 3 Latest ed. only)

> Lists firms by geographical location and gives for each a trade classification code as well as financial strength and composite credit appraisal.

_____ . International market guide; Latin American. v.1- .1938- . Semiannual. (HF54.F8B6 MRR Alc. 3 Latest ed. only)

> Gives same information as previous citation.

_____ . Principal international businesses. 1974- . (HF54.U5P74 MRR Alc. 3 Latest ed. only)

Provides information on 50,000 leading companies in 136 coutries. Arranged in 4 sections; by company, by product classification, by geographic location, and by SIC numbers.

Europe's 5000 largest companies. 1975. Annual. (HD2356.E9E93 MRR Alc. 3 Latest ed. only)

Ranks Europe's largest industrials by sales and number of employees and includes information on assets, equity capital, profit, exports, etc.

Jane's major companies of Europe. 1st- ed.; 1965- . Annual. (HG5421.J35 MRR Alc. 3 Latest ed. only)

Provides information about the major companies of Western Europe. Arranged by subject with indexes by country, company, and industry.

Kelley's manufacturers and merchants directory, including industrial services. 82d- ed.; 1968/69 . Annual. (HF54.G7K4 MRR Alc. 3 Latest ed. only)

Who Owns whom. Australasia and Far East. 1972- . Annual. (HD2927.W48 MRR Alc. 3 Latest ed. only)

Who owns whom. Continental ed. 1st- ed.; 1961/62- . Annual. (HG4132.Z5W5 MRR Alc. 3 Latest ed. only)

B. Stocks

The works listed below provide investment and securities information about stocks and stock exchanges, both domestic and foreign, giving such information a statements, price ranges, ratios, and recommendations for buying, selling, or holding.

Financial stock guide service. Annual. (HG4512.R4 MRR Alc.3 Latest ed. only)

> The first section, the Directory of Active stocks, deals with currently traded issues, both listed and unlisted, domestic and foreign, and their recent changes. The second section, the Directory of Obsolete Securities, covers name changes, mergers, dissolutions, liquidation, reorganizations, bankruptcy, charter cancellations, etc. For each change it gives the manner in which identity was lost, the year, and new name if any.

International stock and commodity exchange directory. Canaan, NH, Phoenix Publ, 1974. (HG4512.157 MRR Alc. 3)

> Gives profile data on exchanges around the world, arranged by country and including such information as history, regulatory laws, officers, etc.

Investment companies. New York, A. Wiesenberger. Annual. (HG4530.15 MRR Alc. 3 Latest ed. only)

> Provides information on all leading mutual funds and other types of investment companies.

Kent, C.H. European stock exchange handbook. Park Ridge, NJ, Noyes Data Corp., 1973. (HG4551.K45 MRR Alc. 3)

Moody's handbook fo common stocks. 1965, 3d quarterly- ed. Quarterly. (HG4501.M59 MRR Alc. 3 Latest ed. only)

Financial statements, price ranges, and ratios for about 800 widely held stocks.

Standard and Poor's Corporation. Daily stock price record: American Stock Exchange. Quarterly. (HG4915.S66 MRR Alc. 3)

_____. Daily stock price record: New York Stock Exchange. Quarterly. (HG4915.S664 MRR Alc. 3)

_____. Daily stock price record: over-the-counter. Quarterly. (HG4915.S665 MRR Alc. 3)

_____. Dividend record. Looseleaf, weekly with quarterly and annual cumulations. (HG4908.S8 MRR Alc. 3 Latest ed. only)

Covers declarations and payments of cash and stock dividends, stock splits, and right offerings.

_____. Security owner's stock guide. Monthly. (HG4915.S67 Recent issues in Newspaper and Current Periodical RR)

Gives ratios, stock price ranges, dividends, annual earnings, etc. for about 4,200 common and preferred stocks and selected mutual funds. Includes a Stock Guide issue of year-end prices.

_____. Standard and Poor's international stock report. Monthly. (HG4501.S7665a Recent issues in Newspaper and Current Periodical RR)

Current and background information on over 70 foreign stocks excluding Canadian stocks. Also includes a commentary on economic developments in various countries, appraisal of foreign securities markets, and charts of market actions in the U.S., Japan, and five European countires.

_____. Standard and Poor's stock market encyclopedia. 1977- . Annual. (HG4921.S68 MRR Ref Desk Alc. 4 Latest ed. only)

_____. Standard and Poor's stock reports: American Stock Exchange. Feb. 1973- . Quarterly. (HG4905.S443 MRR Alc. 3 Latest ed. only)

_____. Standard and Poor's stock reports: New York Stock Exchange. Jan. 1973- . Quarterly. (HG4905.S433 MRR Alc. 3 Latest ed. only)

_____. Standard and Poor's stock reports: over-the-counter. Mar. 1973- . Quarterly. (HG4905.S433 MRR Alc. 3 Latest ed. only)

_____. Standard and Poor's stock summary. 1973- . Monthly. (HG4921.S69 Recent issues in Newspaper and Current Periodical RR)

> Statistical data on over 1,900 common stock, including all traded on the NYSE, and a selection ASE, OTC, and regional exchange stocks.

Value line investment survey. 3 v. Weekly. (Newspaper and Current Periodical RR)

C. Bonds

Moody's bond record. 1931- . Semimonthly. (HG4905.M78 Recent issues in Newspaper and Current Periodical RR)

Moody's bond survey. v. 28- ; Jan. 6, 1936- . Weekly. (HG4905.M785 MRR Alc. 3)

> Gives trends and prospects for the market and for individual bonds, with recommendations for purchase or sale. Convertible bond coverage is included in the third issue each month.

Moody's municipal and government manual. 1955- . Annual with supplements. (HG4931.M58 MRR Alc. 3 Latest ed. only)

D. Banks and Banking

American bank directory. Semiannual. (HG2441.A56 MRR Alc. 3 Latest ed. only)

> Provides full information on the principal of banks of the United States.

Banker's almanac and yearbook. 1976/77- . Annual. (HG2984. B3 MRR Alc. 3 Latest ed. only)

> A Listing of British and international banks, giving officers, correspondents, balance sheet statistics, etc. Also includes a geographic listing of banks without details.

Business international money report. 1975- . Weekly. (HG1.
B96a Recent issues in Newspaper and Current Periodical RR)

    Weekly report about the international money situation,
including exchange rates for major countries and
comments on current money topics. Includes quarterly
index.

Moody's bank and finance manual. 1941- . Annual with
supplements. (HG4961.M65 MRR Alc. 3 Latest ed. only)

    Basic financal information covers not only U.S. and
some foreign banks and trust companies; but also
insurance, investment, and finance companies, U.S.
real estate companies, real investment trusts, and
saving and loan associations. Center blue pages
include a 10-year price range of stocks and bonds
as well as lists of the largest banks, mutual
savings banks, and savings and loan associations.

Munn, Glen G. Glen G. Munn's encyclopedia of banking and
finance. Boston, Bankers Pub. C., 1973. (HG151.M8 MRR
Alc. 3)

Polk's world bank directory: international section. 1970- .
Annual. (HG1536.P633 MRR Alc. 3 Latest ed. only)

    Information about banks around the world. Includes
a list of U.S. banks offering international banking
services.

Polk's world bank directory: North American section. 15th-
ed.; sept. 1971- . Semiannual. (HG1536. P635 MRR Alc. 4
Latest ed. only)

    Gives information about all banks and branches in
the U.S. and its possessions. Arranged by state
and city. Federal banks included.

Rand McNally international banker's directory. Semiannual.
(HG2441.R3 MRR Ref desk alc. 4 Latest ed. only)

E. Trade and Commodities

    Business International Corporation, New York.
Business International Corporation publishes the following
titles which cover business and financial information on
the areas indicated.

Business Asia. Weekly. (Newspaper and Current Periodical RR)

Business Eastern Europe. Weekly. (Newspaper and Current Periodical RR)

Businss Europe. Weekly. (Newspaper and Current Periodical RR)

Business international. Weekly. (Newspaper and Current Periodical RR)

> Covers worldwide business operations, providing current news about companies; recent developments in laws and practices relating to taxes, licensing, capital sources, politics, profitability; trends and news about specific countries; and checklists and statistical tables.

Business Latin America. Weekly. (HF6.B95 Recent issues in Newspaper and Current Periodical RR)

Commodity yearbook. 1st- ed.; 1939- . Annual. (HF1041. C56 MRR Alc. 3 Latest ed. only)

Croner, Ulrich. Reference book for world traders. Queens Village, N.Y., Croner Publications, 1961- . (HF1010.C66 MRR Alc. 3 Latest ed. only)

> Provides continuously updated information on the import and export trade of all foreign countries. Contains conversion tables, currency rates, freight and postal rates, etc.

Foreign trade market place. Detroit, Gale Research Co., 1977. (HF1010.F67 MRR Alc. 3)

> Gives information on conditions of trade plus a directory of organizations and services connected with trade.

Food and Agriculture Organization of the United Nations. Trade yearbook. v. 12- . Annual. (HD9000.4.F58 MRR Alc. 3 Latest ed. only)

> Contains inforamtion on the export and import of food and agriculture commodities.

International trade reporter's U.S. export weekly. no.1- ; Apr.9, 1974- . Weekly. (HF.I66 Recent issues in Newspaper and Current Periodical RR)

Mineral yearbook. 1932/33- . Annual. (TN23.U612 MRR
Alc. 7 Latest ed. only)

> Contains information and statistics on the mineral
> industry by states, more than 130 foreign countries,
> and by mineral commodities

United Nations. Statistical Office. Yearbook of international
trade statistics. 1st- ed.; 1950- . Annual. (HF91.U473
MRR Ref Desk Alc. 4 Latest ed. only)

U.S. Bureau of the Census. U.S. exports: commodity groupings
by world area. FT 450. (HF105.C13752 MRR Alc. 3 Latest ed.
only)

_____ . U.S. exports: Domestic merchandise SIC-based
products by world area. FT 610. (HF105.C137166 MRR Alc. 3
Latest ed. only)

_____ . U.S. exports: world area by commodity groupings.
FT 455. (HF105.B73d MRR Alc. 3 Latest ed. only)

_____ . U.S. general imports: commodity groupings
by world area. FT 150. (HF105.C137182 MRR Alc. 3 Latest ed.
only.

_____ . U.S. general imports: world area by commodity
groupings. FT 155. (HF105.C137172 MRR Alc. 3 Latest ed. only)

_____ . U.S. imports for consumption and general imports:
TSUSA commodity by country of origin. FT 246. (HF105.B731
MRR Alc. 3 Latest ed. only)

Wasserman, Paul. Commodity prices: a source book and index
providing references to wholesale and retail quotations for
more than 5,000 agricultural, commercial, industrial and
consumer products. Detroit, Gale Research Corp., 1974.
(Z1764.P94W33 MRR Alc. 3)

F. Government Finance

Moody's municipal and government manual. 1955- . Annual with
supplements. (HG4931.M58 MRR Alc. 3 Latest ed. only)

> Provides information on federal, state and municipal
> finances and obligations, usually including assessed
> value, tax rates, tax collections, schedule of bonded
> debt, bond rating, etc.

Tax Foundation, New York. Facts and figures on government finance. 1941- . Annual. (HJ257.T25 MRR Ref Desk Alc. 4 Latest ed. only)

Provides statistics on the fiscal activities of federal, state, and local governments as well as selected basic economic statistics.

U.S. Bureau of the Census. City government finances. 1964/65- . (HJ9011.A4b MRR Alc. 3 Latest ed. only)

_____. County government finances. 1972/73- . (HJ9011.A4c MRR Alc. 3 Latest ed. only)

_____. Local government finances in selected metropolitan areas and large counties. 1964/65- . (HJ9011.A4a MRR Alc. 3 Latest ed. only)

_____. State government finances. 1958- . (HJ275.57 MRR Alc. 3 Latest ed. only)

U.S. Office of Management and Budget. The budget of the United States Government. 1971/72- . Annual. (HJ2051. A59 MRR Ref Desk Alc. 4 Latest ed. only)

_____. Appendix. 1971/72- . Annual. (HJ2051. A59 Suppl. MRR Ref Desk Alc. 4 Latest ed. only)

_____. Special analysis, budget of the United States Government. 1971/72- . Annual. (HJ2051.U52a MRR Ref Desk Alc. 4 Latest ed. only)

_____. The U.S. budget in brief. 1971/72- . Annual. (HJ2051.A5974 MRR Ref Desk Alc. 4 Latest ed. only)

U.S. President. The economic report of the President to the Congress. Jan. 1974- . Annual. (HC106.5.A272 MRR Alc. 3 Latest ed. only)

III. SOURCES FOR SPECIFIC INFORMATION

Balance of payments:

Balance of payments yearbook. (HF1014.15 MRR Alc. 3 Latest ed. only)

Federal Reserve bulletin. (HG2401.A5 Recent issues in
Newspaper and Current Periodical RR)

Survey of current business. (HC101.A13 Recent issues in
Newspaper and Current Periodical RR)

Bond yields and ratings:

Moody's bond record. (HG4905.M78 Recent issues in Newspaper
and Current Periodical RR)

Moody's bond survey. (HG4905.M785 MRR Alc. 3)

Moody's municipal and government manual. (HG4931.M58 MRR
Alc. 3 Latest ed. only)

Business failures:

Dun's review. (HF1.D8 Recent issues in Newspaper and Current
Periodical RR)

September-November issues.

Survey of current business. (HC101.A13 Recent issues in
Newspaper and Current Periodical RR)

Business trends and forecast:

Conference Board record. (HC101.C64 Recent issues in Newspaper
and Current Periodical RR)

Financial world. (HG4501.F5 Recent issues in Newspaper and
Current Periodical RR)

New York times (Newspaper) (Newspaper and Current Periodical
RR)

Sunday edition gives brief factual report.

Value line investment survey. (Newspaper and Current
Periodical RR)

Forecast in the "Fortnightly Commentaries."

Commodity prices:

Commodity yearbook. (HC1041.C56 MRR Alc. 3 Latest ed. only)

Federal Reserve bulletin. (HG2401.A5 Recent issues in
Newspaper and Current Periodical RR)

Monthly labor review. (HD8051.A78 Recent issues in Newspaper
and Current Periodical RR)

New York times (Newspaper) (Newspaper and Current Periodical RR)

Saturday issue gives summary of commodity prices
for the preceding week.

Wasserman, Paul. Commodity prices. (Z7164.P94W33 MRR Alc. 3)

Lists price sources by commodity.

Consumer credit:

Dun's review. (HF1.D8 Recent issues in Newspaper and Current
Periodical RR)

Federal Reserve bulletin. (HG2401.A5 Recent issues in Newspaper
and Current Periodical RR)

Consumer income:

Federal Reserve bulletin. (HG2401.A5 Recent issues in Newspaper
and Current Periodical RR)

Monthly labor review. (HD8051.A78 Recent issues in Newspaper
and Current Periodical RR)

U.S. Bureau of the Census. Current population reports:
consumer income. Series P-60. (HC110.15 Recent issues in
Newspaper and Current Periodical RR)

United Nations. Statistical Office. Statistical yearbook.
(HA12.5.U63 MRR Ref Desk Alc. 4 Latest ed. only)

Corporate profit:

Moody's industrial manual. (HG4961.M67 MRR Ref Desk Alc. 4
Latest ed. only)

Value line investment survey. (Newspaper and Current Periodical RR)

Survey of current business. (HC101.A13 Recent issues in
Newspaper and Current Periodical RR)

July issue.

Currency rates:

Business international money report. (HG1.B96a Recent issues in Newspaper and Current Periodical RR)

Daily newspapers. (Newspaper and Current Periodical RR)

Federal Reserve bulletin. (HG2401.A5 Recent issues in Newspaper and Current Periodical RR)

International currency review. (HG3881.I5756 Recent issues in Newspaper and Periodical RR)

International financial statistics. (HG3881.I626 MRR Ref Desk Latest ed. only)

New York times (newspaper). (Newspaper and Current Periodical RR)
   Tuesday issue lists foreign exchange rates.

Dow-Jones averages:

Wall Street journal (newspaper). (Newspaper and Current Periodical RR)
   Monday edition.

Export and import:

See Section II E. of this guide.

International stock and commodity exchange directory. (HG4512.I57 MRR Alc. 3)

U.S. Bureau of the Census. Highlights of U.S. export and import trade. (HF105.C1332 Recent issues in Newspaper and Current Periodical RR)

Gross National Product:

Europe yearbook. (JN1.E85 MRR Ref Desk Alc. 4 Latest ed. only)

Federal Reserve bulletin. (HG2401.A5 Recent issues in Newspaper and Current Periodical RR)

Statistical abstract of the United States. (HA202 MRR Ref Desk Alc. 4 Lastest ed. only)

Survey of current business. (HC101.A13 Recent issues in Newspaper and Current Periodical RR)

United Nations. Statistical Office. Statistical yearbook. (HA12.5.U63 MRR Ref Desk Alc. 4 Latest ed. only)

Industrial production index:

Federal Reserve bulletin. (HG2401.A5 Recent issues in Newspaper and Current Periodical RR)

Investments overseas:

See Section II E. under Business International Corporation, New York.

European financial marketplace. (HG70.E9 MRR Alc. 3 Latest ed. only)

European marketing data and statistics. (HA1107.E87 MRR Alc. 3)

International marketing data and statistics. (HA42.I56 MRR Alc. 3)

Statistics Africa. (Z7554.A34H37 MRR Alc. 3)

Statistics Asia and Australasia. (HA37.A775H37 MRR Alc. 2)

Statistics Europe. (Z7554.E8H35 MRR Ref Desk Alc. 4)

International companies:

Bottin international. (HF54.F8B6 MRR Alc. 3 Latest ed. only)

Dun and Bradstreet, Inc. Principal international businesses. (HF54.U5P74 MRR Alc. 3 Latest ed. only)

Fortune. (HF5001.F7 Recent issues in Newspaper and Current Periodical RR)

August issue lists 300 largest companies.

Ratios:

Almanac of business and industrial financial ratios. (HF8681.R25T68 1978 MRR Alc. 3)

Dow-Jones-Irwin business almanac. (HF5003.D68a MRR Alc. 3 Latest ed. only)

Dun's review. (HF1.D8 Recent issues in Newspaper and Current Periodical RR)

    September and November issues.

Robert Morris Associates. Statement studies. (HF681.B2R6 MRR Alc. 3 Latest ed. only)

Subsidiaries and affiliates:

Directory of corporate affiliations. (HG4057.A219 MRR alc. 3 Latest ed. only)

Directory of inter-corporate ownership. (HG4057.A156 MRR Alc. 3)

Moody's industrial manual. (HG4961.M67 MRR Ref Desk Alc. 4 Latest ed. only.

Who owns whom: Australasia and Far East. (HD2927.W48 MRR Alc. 3 Latest ed. only)

Who own whom. Continental edition. (HG4132.Z5W5 MRR Alc. 3 Latest ed. only)

Who owns whom. North American edition. (HG4538.W423 MRR Alc. 3 Latest ed. only)

Wholesale price index:

Federal Reserve bulletin. (HG4538.W423 MRR Alc. 3 Latest ed. only)

Statistical abstract of the United States. (HA202 MRR Ref Desk Alc. 4 Latest ed. only)

APPENDIX C
SAMPLE COVER LETTER
AND MAILED QUESTIONNAIRE

RESEARCH FOR INDUSTRY associates
Commercial and Industrial Surveys
137 West 48th Street, New York,NY10020

August 11,1980

Dear Sir:

This is the survey I recently wrote to you about.

One of our clients is very interested in knowing how well it
is known and thought of among leaders of the business community.

We'd appreciate your taking just a few minutes out of your
busy schedule to answer the questions appearing in this folder.
Your answers to these questions are most important, since we
are surveying only a sample of the business community, and
your response will therefore be representative of many of your
colleagues.

Responses to this study are totally anonymous. There is no
way that either we or our clients can identify the names of
the people who answer this questionnaire.

We have supplied you with a postage-paid return envelope for
forwarding your response to us.

Thankyou for your help.

Sincerely,

Robert LeGoff
Director of Research

1.   Are you familiar with the name "Eaton"?

Yes ( )   No ( )*

* (If "No", please skip to question 7. Return the
  questionnaire even if you do not recognize the name.)

2.   Please check any of the following product areas you would
     associate with the name "Eaton".

Advanced Electronics	( )	Fluid Power Products	( )
Automated Systems	( )	Forestry Equipment	( )
Automotive Products	( )	Materials Handling	( )
Control Products	( )	Molded Products	( )
Electrical/Electronic Control	( )	Power Transmission Systems	( )
Engineered Fasteners	( )	Semiconductor Equipment	( )
Engineered Polymer Products	( )	Truck Components	( )

All of the above ( )

3.   Are you now a user, or could you be a user of any of the
     products listed above?

Yes ( )   No ( )

4.   Please check only one answer for each statement to indicate
     your impression of "Eaton".

	Excellent	Good	Average	Fair	Poor
As a company to do business with:	( )	( )	( )	( )	( )
As investment potential:	( )	( )	( )	( )	( )
For a new product development:	( )	( )	( )	( )	( )
As a financially strong company:	( )	( )	( )	( )	( )

5.   Have you recently seen or heard any advertising for "Eaton"?

Yes ( )   No ( )

6.   If "Yes", what was the theme behind the advertising?

_____

_____

_____

7. Please check the category which best describes the activity
    of your company or organization. (PLEASE CHECK ONLY ONE.)

    Aerospace/Aircraft   ( )   Government   ( )
    Automotive   ( )   Agriculture   ( )
    Chemicals/Petroleum   ( )   Manufacturing   ( )
    Computer and EDP Services   ( )   Medicine/Clinical   ( )
    Education   ( )   Transportation/Communications ( )
    Electronics   ( )   Other (PLEASE SPECIFY)   ( )
    Wholesale/Retail
      Distributors   ( )   _____

8a. What is your exact title?

    _____

b. Please check the one category which best describes the function
    you perform within your company. (PLEASE CHECK ONLY ONE.)

    ( ) Accounting or Finance   ( ) Purchasing
    ( ) Advertising or Sales Promotion ( ) Sales Management
    ( ) Engineering   ( ) Technician
    ( ) Maintenance   ( ) Salesman
    ( ) Office Management   ( ) Professor/Instructor
    ( ) Personnel   ( ) Other (PLEASE SPECIFY)
    ( ) Production Operations
    ( ) Planning   _____

                    THANK YOU FOR YOUR COOPERATION!

BIBLIOGRAPHY
ON METHODS OF RESEARCH

This list is not a bibliography like conventional ones cited in the text or consulted in its development. Rather, it is a collection of books that serious students of research may consult to pursue their objectives further or explore methodological subjects covered lightly or not at all in this guidebook. To that end, the first section provides some selected bibliographies. The second section is a melange of general and philosophical works on research and scientific method, the authors drawn from varying scientific disciplines. The third section consists of selected books on economic and business research. And the last section provides a few well-known manuals of style and form. With a few exceptions this bibliography does not cover the same ground as the Library of Congress bibliography, reproduced in Appendix B. The latter is concerned with the reference tools of research on how to find information sources, whereas this list covers books on research methods or studies illustrating types of methodological approaches in scientific research, drawn from various disciplines.

I. BIBLIOGRAPHIES

Belson, William A., and Beryl-Anne Thompson. Bibliography on Methods of Social and Business Research. New York: Wiley, 1973.

Bibliographic Guide to Business and Economics. Boston: G.K. Hall, 1975-date.

Daniel, Wayne W. The Lost Letter Technique: An Annotated Bibliography. Monticello, Ill: Vance Bibliographies, 1980.

Gale Research Company. Management Information Guide Series. Detroit: Gale, 1970-date. 36v.
    Includes book bibliographies on such subjects as transportation, insurance, business trends and forecasting, government regulation of business, systems and procedures including office management, international business and foreign trade, computers and data processing, commercial law, accounting, investment, ethics in business conduct, public

relations, business history. Each book is individually
authored. Full list available from Gale Research
Company.

Gale Research Company. Economics Information Guide Series. Detroit:
Gale, 1972-date. 20v.
Includes book bibliographies on such subjects as
American economic history, economic development,
economic education, East Asian economies, economic
history of Canada, economics of education, economics
of minorities, health and medical economics, history
of economic analysis, international trade, labor
economics, mathematical economics and operations
research, money, banking, and macroeconomics; public
policy; regional economics; Russian economic history
Soviet-type economic systems; statistics and
econometrics; transportation economics; urban
economics. Complete list with exact titles and
authors available from Gale Research Company.

McFarland, Dalton E. Research Methods in the Behavioral Sciences:
A Selected Bibliography, revised and updated. Monticello,
Ill.: Vance Bibliographies, 1979, 27 pp.

Pareek, Udai N. A Guide to Literature of Research Methodology in
Behavioral Sciences. Delhi, India: Sterling Publishers, 1966,
64 pp.

Potter, Dale R. (and others). Questionaires for Research: an Annotated
Bibliography on Design, Construction and Use. Portland, Ore.:
Pacific Northwest Forest and Range Experiment Station, 1972.

II. SELECTIONS ON RESEARCH AND SCIENTIFIC METHOD FROM VARIOUS DISCIPLINES

Ackoff, Russell L. Scientific Method, Optimizing Applied Research
Decisions. New York: Wiley, 1962.

Barzun, Jacques, and Henry F. Graff. The Modern Researcher. 3rd ed.
New York: Harcourt Brace Jovanovich, 1977.

Beveridge, William I.B. The Art of Scientific Investigation. 2nd ed.
Melbourne: Heinemann, 1953.

Blalock, Hubert M. ed. Measurement in the Social Sciences: Theories
and Strategies. Chicago: Aldine, 1974.

Bronowski, Jacob. Common Sense of Science. Cambridge, Mass: Harvard
Univ. Press, 1963

Bunge, Mario A. Method, Model and Matter. Dordrect and Boston:
Reidal, 1973

Freedman, Paul. The Principles of Scientific Research. Washington, D.C.: Public Affairs Press, 1950

Kerlinger, Fred N. Foundations of Behavorial Research. 2nd ed. New York: Holt, Rinehart and Winston, 1973.

Kuhn, Thomas S. The Structure of Scientific Revolutions. Chicago: Univ. of Chicago Press, 1962.

Latsis, Spiro J., ed. Method and Appraisal in Economics. London: Cambridge Univ. Press, 1976

Payne, Stanley L. The Art of Asking Questions. Princeton: Princeton Univ. Press, 1951.

Tullock, Gordon. The Organization of Enquiry. Durham: Duke Univ. Press, 1966.

III. SELECTED BIBLIOGRAPHY OF ECONOMICS AND BUSINESS RESEARCH BOOKS

Ahmed, S. Basheer. Quantitative Methods for Business. Columbus: Grid, 1974.

Andreano, Ralph L., Evan I. Faber, and Sabron Reynolds. The Student Economists Handbook: A Guide to Sources. Cambridge, Mass: Schenkman, 1967.

Berenson, Conrad, and Raymond Colton. Research and Report Writing for Business and Economics. New York: Random House, 1971.

Clover, Vernon T. Business Research, Basic Principles and Techniques. Lubbock, Tex.: Rodgers Lithograph, Inc., 1959.

Clover, Vernon T. and Howard L. Balsley. Business Research Methods. Columbus, Ohio: Grid Inc., 1974.

Emory C. William. Business Research Methods. Homewood, Ill.: Irwin, 1976.

Ferber, Robert, and P.J. Verdoorn. Reserch Methods in Economics and Business. New York: MacMillan, 1962.

Glover, John G. Business Operational Research and Reports. New York: American Book Company, 1949.

Hellpie, Charles E., and others. Research Guide in Economics. Morristown, N.J.: General Learning Press, 1974.

Murdick, Robert G. Business Research: Concept and Practice. Scranton: International Textbook, 1969.

Nemmers, Erwin E., and John H. Myers. Business Research Text and Cases. New York: McGraw-Hill, 1966.

Rigby, Paul H. Conceptual Foundation of Business Research. New York: Wiley, 1965.

_____. Models in Business Analysis. Columbus, Ohio: Merrill, 1969.

Rummel, J. Francis, and Wesley C. Ballaine. Research Methodology in Business. New York: Harper and Row, 1963.

Sterling, Robert R., ed. Research Methodology in Accounting. Papers from Accounting Colloquium II. Lawrence, Kans.: Scholars Book Company, 1972.

Tull, Donald S., and Del I. Hawkins. Marketing Research. New York: McMillan, 1976.

Wasson, Chester R. The Strategy of Marketing Research. New York: Appleton-Century-Crofts, 1964.

Waugh, Fredrick W. Graphic Analysis in Economic Research. Washington, D.C.: Government Printing Office, 1955, U.S. Department of Agriculture Handbook. No. 84.

IV. STYLE AND REPORT WRITING MANNUALS

Allen, George R. The Graduate Students' Guide to Theses and Dissertations. A Practical Mannual for Writing and Research. San Francisco: Jossey-Bass, 1973.

Campbell, William G., and Stephen V. Ballou. Form and Style: Theses, Reports, Termpapers. Boston: Houghton Mifflin, 1978.

Modern Language Association of America. MLA Handbook for Writers of Research Papers, Theses, and Dissertations. New York: MLA, 1977.

Strunk, William, Jr. The Elements of Style. 3rd ed. New York: MacMillan, 1979. With revisions, an introduction, and a chapter on writing by E.B. White.

Turabian, Kate L. A Mannual for Writers of Term Papers, Theses, and Dissertations. 4th ed. Chicago: Univ. of Chicago Press, 1973.

University of Chicago Press. A Manual of Style. 12th ed. rev. Chicago: 1969.

AUTHOR INDEX